THE URBAN FIELD

URBAN WORLDS

Urban areas are dynamic spaces where people come together in close proximity to live, work, learn and be entertained. They are also places of great contrast, extremes and inequalities. At a time of enormous global pressures, not least the vulnerability of urban areas and their populations to the effects of climate change, the Urban Worlds series interrogates the challenges – from governance and planning to consumption and sustainability – facing urban areas today and examines how the drivers of urbanization continue to shift and change.

Published

The Cultural Infrastructure of Cities
Edited by Alison L. Bain and Julie A. Podmore

Insurgent Planning Practice
Edited by Roberto Rocco and Gabriel Silvestre

The Urban Field: Capital and Governmentality in the Age of Techno-Monopoly
Sami Moisio and Ugo Rossi

THE URBAN FIELD

Capital and Governmentality in the Age of Techno-Monopoly

SAMI MOISIO AND UGO ROSSI

© Sami Moisio and Ugo Rossi 2024

This book is copyright under the Berne Convention.
No reproduction without permission.
All rights reserved.

First published in 2024 by Agenda Publishing

Agenda Publishing Limited
PO Box 185
Newcastle upon Tyne
NE20 2DH
www.agendapub.com

ISBN 978-1-78821-450-6 (hardcover)
ISBN 978-1-78821-451-3 (paperback)

British Library Cataloguing-in-Publication Data
A catalogue record for this book is available from the British Library

Typeset by Newgen Publishing UK
Printed and bound in the UK by CPI Group (UK) Ltd, Croydon, CR0 4YY

CONTENTS

Acknowledgements	vii
Introduction: neo-feudalism or new monopoly capital?	1
Part I – Macro-political economy of the urban field	9
1 The rise of the corporatized state	11
2 The urban field and the strategic urbanization of the state	33
Part II – Micro-political economy of the urban field	55
3 Labour	57
4 Human capital	79
5 Startups	103
6 Forms of life	129
Coda: the value of the urban field	151
References	159
Index	177

ACKNOWLEDGEMENTS

We would like to thank the friends and colleagues who read previous versions of this text and whose comments helped us improve our manuscript: Arnab Bhattacharya, Filippo Celata, Borys Cieslak, Anna Fava, Olivier Godechot, Martina Locorotondo, the late Toni Negri, Francesco Nurra, Andrea Pollio, Carlo Vercellone.

Writing this book has been a smooth and enjoyable process. We thank our editor at Agenda Publishing, Camilla Erskine, for her valuable comments and help during the process.

Sami Moisio thanks the Association of Finnish Non-fiction Writers for a grant to write this book. Ugo Rossi thanks the Axpo Observatory of Market Society Polarization at Sciences Po university in Paris, which hosted him in winter 2023 during the writing process.

Some chapters draw on, albeit in rewritten and modified form, previously published journal articles. A section of Chapter 1 draws on: Ugo Rossi & Arturo Di Bella (2017) "Start-up urbanism: New York, Rio de Janeiro and the global urbanization of technology-based economies", published in *Environment and Planning A* (Sage). Chapter 2 utilizes: Sami Moisio & Ugo Rossi (2020) "The start-up state: governing urbanised capitalism", published in *Environment and Planning A* (Sage). Part of Chapter 5 draws on: Sami Moisio & Ugo Rossi (2023) "The value of the urban field in technology-driven knowledge economies: the role of the state", published in *Environment and Planning F* (Sage).

INTRODUCTION: NEO-FEUDALISM OR NEW MONOPOLY CAPITAL?

This is the era of techno-monopoly power in which techno-capitalism has colonized not only the internet, as critics signalled in the early stages of this era (McChesney 2013; Morozov 2013), but increasingly also key aspects of everyday life, with the advent of ubiquitous digital platforms. Cities and larger urban and metropolitan environments have provided fertile ground – or what this book conceptualizes as the urban field – for the rise and fast growth of techno-monopoly power.

What is the techno-monopoly we are talking about? Notions such as "Big Tech", "tech giants", "tech behemoths", "tech titans" and the like, have become customarily used in the public sphere to refer to the rise of a narrow set of technology corporations – operating in the sphere of circulation rather than that of production – that have acquired a monopolistic position in terms of market power. The phenomenon of giant tech monopolies has led a growing number of authors on the academic left and beyond to signal the emergence of a new era of "neo-feudalism", variously defined as "digital feudalism" or "techno-feudalism", characterized by the dominance of rentierism over capitalist profit-making and the rise of a new high-tech oligarchy (Christophers 2022; Dean 2020; Kotkin 2020; Mazzucato 2019; Varoufakis 2023). The techno-feudalism thesis stems from a pre-existing tendency within critical social thought that interprets neoliberal globalization as a kind of neo-medieval order in which transnational technocrats act as novel princes supported by vassals who are subjected to their unaccountable power (Ziegler 2005). Amongst the proponents of the techno-feudalism thesis, Varoufakis (2023) has argued that a historic mutation of capital into "cloud capital" has taken place through the development of technology, the increasing power of tech companies and the ways in which technology and algorithms, for instance, are currently being used by finance corporations and governments. Accordingly, in his view, we are moving from capitalism to feudalism, the way of governing land that prevailed in Europe in the Middle Ages. For Varoufakis, during the

1

past two to three decades, barriers have emerged in the digital space of the internet. What used to be free digital land is now fenced off and privatized by a few large corporations. In this development, technology companies have acquired a position similar to that of governors (landlords) in feudal society. They do not produce goods or products for the world, but they nonetheless extract value through the fenced digital territories and take a great share of their sales. In this perspective, the capitalist market has been replaced by digital trading platforms, and the profit has been replaced by "cloud rent" that must be paid for access to those digital platforms. Hence, the issue of unearned income.

We share the same concerns with Varoufakis and the other theorists of predatory forms of "techno-feudalism" about the erosion of economic and political democracy in contemporary technology-driven societies. However, our analysis differs on a more substantive level, avoiding the kind of ethical-moral criticism that characterizes the techno-feudalism thesis, while offering an understanding of the functioning of existing capitalism in its urban form that is grounded in the critique-of-political-economy tradition. In particular, in this book we argue that the contemporary urban techno-monopoly represents the continuation and intensification of a form of cognitive-affective capitalism (Hardt & Negri 2009) that dates back to the post-Fordist transition of the 1980s (Harvey 1989a), rather than indicating a sudden shift to an entirely new era forged by the revival of feudal forms of economic and political power (for an apt critique of "feudal-speak", see Morozov 2022). What we seek to make visible in the book, hence, is an urban monopoly capitalism that is supported by what we conceptualize as the corporatized state. We thus think about the urban field as the spatial and societal form of techno-monopoly capitalism, a form of political economy that is dominated by technology companies but that is also inherently connected to state power. This is the urban techno-monopoly we analyse in the ensuing chapters.

This book stems from a collaboration between the two authors that started around 2019, leading to joint publications and the participation in common research projects. The book is premised on but also substantially extends the two journal articles that we published together, in 2020 and 2023 (Moisio & Rossi 2020, 2023). In the first article, we put forward the concept of the startup state to examine what we termed the strategic urbanization of the state at a time of heightened inter-city competition over the economization of technology and knowledge. In the second article, we explored the performative dimensions of capitalist urban economies and the role of the governmental state in the business valuation of startup companies as well as in the creation of human capital for capitalist corporations in the technology sector.

The original idea behind our collaboration was to draw attention to the largely unexplored governmentalities of technology-based economies in the context of an increasingly urbanized global capitalism. We noticed that mainstream approaches to the study of technology-based urban economies have substantially ignored the political and institutional factors behind the ascendancy of novel economic-technological complexes and business "ecosystems" at the urban level. In this context, we observed that the attention of mainstream authors, particularly those scholars that revitalized the dormant field of urban economics since the 1990s, has gone almost exclusively to endogenous factors of urban agglomeration and related externalities, such as the so-called "power of place" and the multiplier effects of urban investments. Not only have these authors ignored the institutional and political factors behind today's urban economic revival, but their elitist explanations of the urban comparative advantage, centred on the role of high-skill human capital variously termed as "creative class", "knowledge workers" and the like, have also tended to offer theoretical justification for current socio-spatial inequalities at intra-urban and inter-city levels, as this book will show.

The present book, therefore, is the result of a five-year collaboration in which we have sought to elaborate constructively on the critique of the dominant stream of urban economics. In the economic disciplines, an alternative narrative to the mainstream view has been provided by a more heterodox, left-leaning author such as Mariana Mazzucato, who has emphasized the overlooked role of the "entrepreneurial state" in the ascendant phases of technology districts, particularly in the United States (US) (Mazzucato 2013), and has posed the problem of value measurability in contemporary capitalism (Mazzucato 2018). Even though we agree with Mazzucato's historical reconstruction of the rise of technology-intensive regional development in the US, we also have a different view on some of her key propositions, particularly on her conceptualization of value, wealth and rent in contemporary capitalism (see Chapter 3), as part of our critique of the techno-feudalism theses that have gained wide currency in the academic left and beyond.

We thus offer a different kind of understanding of the urban "innovation complex", as Sharon Zukin (2020) has called it, that is at the heart of global techno-monopoly capitalism in today's urban age. Elaborating on Hardt and Negri's conceptualization of immaterial labour and the "commonwealth" (Hardt & Negri 2009), our work signals the rise of what we have termed the "urban field" (see Chapter 2) as a space that condenses social relations, a wide array of potential and existing collaborations, affects, emotions and a knowledge capital that transcends conventional divisions between high-skill and low-skill labour. At the same time, drawing on Michel Foucault's notion of governmentality (Foucault 1991), we recognize that in late liberal societies such a dense space of immaterial labour and social interaction becomes generative of economic value for capitalist companies – particularly for monopolist technology corporations in the current configuration of global capitalism – through the governmental activity of the national state and local state. In this sense, we use the concept of the "urban field" to make sense of the fertilizing intervention of the governmental state.

The term "urban field" is a key concept that we develop in the book. The concept is due to planners John Friedmann and John Miller, who put it forward in the mid-1960s (Friedmann & Miller 1965), referring to the physical expansion of urban areas beyond the administrative boundaries of cities and metropolitan areas. We find echoes of this expanded conception of urbanism in subsequent elaborations of Henri Lefebvre on urban society and the production of urban space (Lefebvre 2003), as well as in contemporary discussions over "planetary urbanization" (Brenner & Schmid 2014) that aim at getting rid of city-centric conceptions of urban processes. We are attentive to discussions about the expansion of urban processes and, for this reason, our work is intended to shine light on the ways in which this expanded conception of urban society should be linked to the understanding of the operations of technology capital, the state and governmentality in late liberal societies. A more in-depth understanding of the encounter between capital and the state, and the generation of an urban governmentality centred on the economization of knowledge and technology is what we aim to accomplish in this book. We do so by focusing on four sites of capitalist valorization of the economic potential of the urban field: labour, human capital, startups and forms of life.

We hope that the book's main contribution lies, therefore, in its analysis of the role of the governmental state in contemporary techno-capitalism, through the construction and maintenance of the urban field. In doing so, the book exposes how contemporary governmental activity differs from the traditional "cold" industrial policy pursued by the entrepreneurial state and the associated "urban growth machines" (see e.g. Jonas & Wilson 1999) at the time of the Keynesian-Fordist capitalism of postwar decades.

In capitalism at the time of techno-monopoly, state intervention often becomes less explicit and direct; other times it takes the liturgical form of acclamation (Agamben 2011) through its involvement with corporate power. In any instance, governmental power nonetheless remains a decisive factor behind the ascendancy of an economic pattern in contemporary techno-capitalism centred on the expansive socialization of entrepreneurial living, as Michel Foucault presciently diagnosed in his writings on human capital in neoliberal societies (Foucault 2008). Our book therefore offers a conceptually situated critical analysis of the multifaceted governmental activity of the state in the contemporary urban age marked by the unrivalled power of monopolist technology corporations.

OVERVIEW OF THE BOOK STRUCTURE

In addition to this introductory chapter and the concluding chapter, the book consists of six chapters. The first two chapters are intended to offer a historical and conceptual framework for the subsequent chapters, each dedicated to one of the four sites of economic value extraction that characterize the contemporary capitalist conjuncture shaped by what we define as "urban techno-monopoly".

Chapter 1 sets the scene for the subsequent analysis through a rethinking of the political-economic trajectory that has led to the current dominance of what we term the "urban technological paradigm", laying the foundations for today's urban techno-monopoly. In this recounting of a five-decades-long path, we identify two driving technologies, material and immaterial respectively: the invention and commercialization of microprocessors since the early 1970s and the rise in prominence of algorithmic technologies since the mid-2000s. These technologies are at the heart of the information and communications technology (ICT) sector's growth that has so profoundly reshaped contemporary capitalist societies. In the chapter, we focus our attention on the mutating role of the state within the evolution of the urban technological paradigm: from the competition state in the early stages of the ICT sector's ascendancy during the post-Fordist transition, up to the rise of the corporatized state in today's techno-monopoly capitalism.

Chapter 2 introduces the concept of the urban field, presented in its current form as the spatial form of techno-monopoly capitalism. The urban field, in particular, is understood through an analysis of the evolving relationships between the nation-state, the local state (cities), and the operations of capital in the creation and extraction of economic value from existing societies. The triangulation between the urban field, capital and the state is observed in its historical trajectory: from the nationalized urban field of the Fordist-Keynesian times in the twentieth century, up to the contemporary redesign of the urban field as a post-political laboratory for social interaction and test bed for capitalist innovation in startup economies and platform capitalism. In the current configuration of the urban field, we observe the strategic urbanization of the state, a process that ties transnational capital, the nation-state and the local state tightly together in the name of innovation, technology and economic growth. The chapter offers evidence of these processes through a discussion of the digitalization of the Finnish nation-state, where digitalization has emerged – as Foucault would put it – as "a method of government that can procure the nation's prosperity" (Foucault 2008: 13). This is how the process of digitalization marks the rise of the corporatized state.

Chapter 3 discusses the contradictions and possibilities in using labour as the measure of value in contemporary capitalism. In doing so, the chapter challenges urban economists' elitist and exclusionary conception of the knowledge economy, which circumscribes knowledge value to a narrow set of high-skill workers and professionals, variously called "knowledge workers", the "creative class" and the like. We argue that this dominant conception offers justification for the large income and wage inequalities and the consequent wealth polarization that exist within and among cities in present-day capitalist economies. In doing so, the chapter concentrates on the revaluing of the knowledge value of service work and particularly of gig workers in contemporary platform urbanism. Drawing on evidence obtained from fieldwork conducted with food delivery workers in Turin, Italy, the chapter offers a theory of labour value in contemporary techno-capitalism centred on the cognitive value of the urban field. This theorization of the value of the urban field allows us to move beyond a merely ethical stance towards the rights and the status of service workers in contemporary society. In doing so, we intend to offer an understanding of labour exploitation in the platform economy as the continuation of forms of surplus value extraction that have characterized post-Fordist cognitive capitalism in the last few decades, rather than as a novel, merely coercive control over the labour force that has emerged with platform companies, as in contemporary techno-feudalism theses.

Chapter 4 reconstructs the trajectory of human capital theory and its political and intellectual reception since the postwar years up to now with the current configuration of techno-monopoly capitalism. The chapter shows how the theory and operationalization of human capital have acted as key sources for the mutual reinforcement between the urban field and the state. The creation of human capital is instrumental in the economization of knowledge as an investment asset and of the individual as a site for this investment. In standard economic theory, investment in individual human capital is believed to offer increasing returns thanks to knowledge's supposedly intrinsic tendency to spill over across firms and different economic agents that are part of the city's business ecosystem. As illustrative evidence of its theses, the chapter offers a discussion of the contemporary housing crisis as well as of tech-driven projects of futuristic, privately run urban startup ecosystems and cities, variously termed by their proponents as "charter cities", "startup cities" and the like. These examples demonstrate the impact of human capital theorizations on existing societies in terms of production of unprecedented inequalities, entrepreneurialization of living and privatization of societal governance.

Chapter 5 identifies the third site of capitalist valorization of the urban field in contemporary technology monopoly: the startup economy. Showing how the urban field and the startup economy are mutually constituted, the chapter looks at, on the one hand, how the urban field plays out as a key enabler of the startup economy, and, on the other hand, how the startup economy acts as a productive force of the urban field. The mutual constitution of the urban field and the startup economy enables the fast growth of successful startup companies, their market valuation and their eventual designation as unicorns. Through the case study of a food courier company, Wolt, one of the most celebrated startups in Finland, the chapter suggests that the potential of the urban space is an important factor in the market valuation process of startups and that the state contributes to the economic value creation process of the startup economy in many, if implicit, ways. Understanding the startup economy as a productive force of the urban field, closely associated with the market valuation of startup companies, is for us a way to discuss the urban field in such a manner that overcomes the binary between productive capitalism and parasitic/speculative financial capitalism that is based on fictitious capital and the related predatory practices by professional investors.

Chapter 6 looks at place-specific forms of life as a site for economic value extraction in the age of techno-monopoly capitalism. Place-specific forms of life are understood here as locally embedded instances of social practices. These are not necessarily codified in the form of institutions but relatively stabilized and attached to a sense of place belonging, compared with more contingent or ephemeral manifestations of local societies such as ways of life and lifestyles (Jaeggi 2018). In doing so, the chapter continues to delve into the dynamics of the urban field, as it unfolds in the context of the contemporary corporatized state: the governmental orchestration of urban economies, the commodification of popular culture, and related contradictory developments in urban society at the time of techno-monopoly capitalism. As empirical evidence, the chapter offers a study of Naples becoming a mass-tourism city since the mid-2010s, particularly after the advent of digital platforms for short-term holiday rentals. As a demographically dense urban environment and a post-disaster struggling economy situated in the southern periphery of the Global North, Naples is an especially fertile ground for the investigation of the aptly orchestrated ways in which place-specific life forms become commodified and monetized under contemporary techno-capitalism. In particular, Naples can be seen as a laboratory for the extractivist operations of technology capital and the commodification of urban space in the practices of experiential tourism. In the contemporary urban field, the experience economy is no longer a mere niche sector of the entertainment industry, as in the postmodern urbanism of the 1980s, the 1990s and the 2000s, but has come to permeate almost any aspect of the market economy through the platform-mediated economization of place-specific forms of life.

PART I

MACRO-POLITICAL ECONOMY OF THE URBAN FIELD

CHAPTER 1

THE RISE OF THE CORPORATIZED STATE

INTRODUCTION

The extraction of economic value from urban space is a long-term feature of capitalist societies, particularly in relation to the relentless production and reproduction of land rent. The long tradition of understanding economic value and economic growth in the context of urban space as the economic value of land characterized urban studies and cognate fields during high Fordism and Keynesianism – and it remains a key aspect in the present conjuncture of heightened commodification of the housing sector. Economic value extraction from urban spaces and urban living, however, has expanded during the last few decades, in the globalized era dominated by ICT. Urban value extraction and the emergence of algorithmic spaces have become two sides of the same coin. In more recent times, the advent of digital platforms has diversified the extraction of economic value from cities and urban environments, not only from their built environment but from a variety of sectors related to the essential foundations of everyday life, such as infrastructure, mobility, leisure, education. As such, the expansion of the "urban field" (Friedmann & Miller 1965) as it unfolds today can be understood as an intensification and diversification of the urbanization of capital and as a significant response to the various global crises that have taken place since the 1990s in the world economy.

Over the last few decades, the urban field has been closely connected to the urban technological paradigm. In other words, cities and wider urban environments have become primary sites involved in the creation and extraction of economic value in the techno-capitalism era. The last four decades, in particular, have seen the succession of different manifestations of the urban predominance in the economization of knowledge and the technology sector: informational cities, science parks and technopoles in the 1980s and the 1990s, smart cities in the 2000s and the 2010s, startup ecosystems, innovation districts, innovation complexes and the platform economy in the 2010s and the 2020s. By following the logic of Sharon Zukin (2020), we comprehend these spaces as discursive, organizational/institutional and physical.

The mainstream view in urban economics links the urbanization of the knowledge-driven sectors of capitalist economies to the multiplier effect generated by the spatial concentration of a variety of innovation-related factors such as face-to-face engagements, technological spillovers, information flows, knowledge-creating institutions, as well as cultural industries and environmental amenities. According to this view, density is the "wealth of cities", as it enhances worker human capital and entices skilled industries, thus enabling the urban comparative advantage in business innovation and larger human affairs (Glaeser & Gottlieb 2009; Moretti 2012). As Edward Glaeser – a leading exponent of Western "celebrity urbanologists" (Moisio 2018a; Peck 2016; Rossi 2020) – puts it, cities are successful because they epitomize "the absence of physical space between people and companies. They are proximity, density, closeness. They enable us to work and play together, and their success depends on the demand for physical connection" (Glaeser 2011: 15).

From the perspective of mainstream urban economics, the success of urban societies lies not only in the fact of granting a proximity effect to a wide range of value-generating economic activities, but also in their provision of post-material values of cultural pluralism and socio-ethnic diversity. The defining characteristics of urban living explain why, as Richard Florida has famously put it, "place matters" in contemporary economic development (Florida 2012). Enrico Moretti argues in a similar vein that a startup economy, which in short is about generating the next Google, is "possible only in a dense high-tech cluster" (Moretti 2012: 133).

The mainstream economists' view that has become conventional wisdom in urban thinking and in urban policy alike, therefore, tends to portray technology-based economies as self-propulsive economic growth machines. Overall, mainstream scholarship has left the role of state power and larger institutional and political factors unexplored, providing an understanding of urban economies as entities that appear to be – somehow magically – capable of self-generating clusters of high-tech entrepreneurship and innovation-oriented economies as a result of multiple agglomeration externalities.

In this chapter we will offer an alternative explanation of the trajectory that has seen the emergence and evolution of what is defined here as the urban technological paradigm, which has eventually led to the current configuration of techno-monopoly capitalism, particularly interrogating the role played by the state in forging urban forms and governmental regimes. The paradox of state intervention in the context of techno-capitalism is that its visibility is inversely proportional to the grip of technology-driven urban forms and governmental regimes on society and human life. This means that state intervention was and remains tangible in purposely designed high-technology districts, which have an impact on firm creation and entrepreneurship. On the contrary, state intervention becomes less visible but nonetheless highly pervasive in smart cities and platform-mediated service economies, which extract value from the urban field, and, relatedly, from nearly all forms of social life.

In doing so, the chapter will first define the concept of the urban technological paradigm, offering an interpretation of its trajectory that identifies two distinct phases, each shaped by a dominant technology: one based on the semiconductor industry and another based on algorithmic technology. The chapter will then look at the different manifestations of the urban technological paradigm and the qualitatively evolving role played by state governance and governmentality in them. In the final instance, the chapter exposes how the technology-driven colonization not only of the internet but also of key aspects of social life has led to the rise of a corporatized state that is closely implicated with the operations of today's techno-monopoly capitalism.

THE URBAN TECHNOLOGICAL PARADIGM

The emergence of cities as key nodes in today's global techno-capitalism is a decades-long process whose origins date back to the early stages of the ascendancy of the ICT sector after the Second World War. The central role acquired by urban environments in contemporary techno-capitalism can be understood as the spatial manifestation of the technological paradigm centred on the dominance of information and communications technologies. Neo-Schumpeterian evolutionary economists have long theorized how the advent of a technological paradigm stabilizes a certain configuration of the capitalist mode of production, through the encounter between technology innovation processes, economic conjunctures and surrounding socio-institutional contexts (Dosi 1982; Perez 2010).

Within the 50-year trajectory that has led to the current dominance of the urban technological paradigm, two distinct phases can be identified, each characterized by a distinctive technology and related industrial applications. The first phase traces its origins back to the early 1970s, when the commercial production of microprocessors using a silicon-gate technology began, with Intel 4004 being conventionally considered the first of this type. The commercialization of the first microprocessor paved the way to the boom of the semiconductor industry and the related rise of high-tech districts. The second phase can be associated with the rise to prominence of the algorithm-based Google search engine (called PageRank) between the late 1990s and the early 2000s, even though the possibilities of its industrial applications became tangible more clearly in the mid-2000s with the so-called tech boom 2.0. The new technology boom brought about the adoption of cloud computing, the rapid growth of mobile technology services and the explosion of social media during the 2010s (Martin 2013).

In our understanding, these two phases within the urban technological paradigm correspond to different approaches of the state to the governance of technology-based economic spaces. In particular, we observe the shift from their direct control and design through a more conventional industrial policy (what we call here "the competition state") to an increasingly more hybrid governmentality based on collusive state-capital interactions (here defined as "the corporatized state"), which deeply impacts human life and society as a whole. In both cases, the outbreak of economic crises has been decisive in the rise and evolution of the urban technological paradigm. The state has been actively involved in the consolidation of the new accumulation regime after the crisis of Atlantic Fordism. As such, the state – both as a competition state and as a corporatized state – has contributed to the global expansion of capital through the governmentalization of the urban field, and in so doing has shaped the overall development of urban social structures and the lifeworld.

Historically, as Joseph Schumpeter's classic definition of "creative destruction" entails (Schumpeter 2010), structural economic crises have functioned as decisive accelerations in the evolutionary trajectory of capitalism. In times of uncertainty and economic turmoil, entrepreneurs look for new combinations of products, processes, tools and organizations as a response to the destruction and devaluation of capital when the economic crisis takes hold (Holgersen 2015). In this process, a novel technological and economic paradigm emerges, becoming the new normal of the capitalist economy. In this sense, we argue that the urban technological paradigm has become "ecologically dominant" (Jessop 2000) in the post-Fordist economies of cognitive and affective capitalism.

The first phase based on the semiconductor industry and the subsequent phase based on algorithmic technology are distinct but at the same time mutually interlinked, and their succession has not been linear and consequential. As our analysis will show, the trajectory of global techno-capitalism should not be seen as a mere succession of stages of economic development, but as an intricate stratification of constantly evolving state-capital interactions and accumulation strategies.

In the remainder of this chapter we will thus offer a reconstruction of the politico-economic trajectory that has eventually led to the emergence of what in this book is called the "urban field", serving as the dominant spatiality of contemporary techno-monopoly capitalism. In particular, the chapter will show how the long process of urbanization of technology-driven and knowledge-based economies has seen a shift from the visible and normative interventions of the competition state to the more performative governmentalities of the contemporary corporatized state. Both the competition state and the corporatized state are seen as manifestations of the same technological paradigm, which we have already defined as the urban technological paradigm.

THE COMPETITION STATE

The global project aimed at turning cities and regions into specialized districts for high-tech economies dates back to the 1970s, particularly within the context of the rise of economic-technological spatial complexes variously called "informational cities", "science parks", "technopoles" (Castells 1989; Castells & Hall 1994; Massey, Quintas & Wield 1992). In the early spatialization of information and communications technologies, the state played a central and largely visible role, in conjunction with other important actors, namely capitalist firms and universities. In his seminal book published in 1989, Manuel Castells centred his understanding of the constitution of the "informational city" around what a group of researchers in Europe at that time defined as "milieux of innovation" (Aydalot & Keeble 1988), which stemmed from the interaction of a wide range of government-sponsored and corporate-led research-intensive institutions (Castells 1989). The semiconductor industry was central to the development of the high-tech sector in these foundational stages.

Tech-intensive districts originated in the US during the postwar decades. The growing importance acquired over the time by the semiconductor industry with the commercial production of the first microprocessors in the early 1970s became the propulsive force behind the ascendancy of two leading high-tech districts in this country: the Californian region of Santa Clara County, commonly known as Silicon Valley, and the technology district in Massachusetts. The former saw the development of the first silicon-based semiconductor devices since the late 1950s by pioneering companies such as the Shockley Semiconductor Laboratory based in Mountain View. The latter formed around the state highway known as Route 128, experiencing a boom of firm creation in the microprocessor sector since the 1970s, accompanied by the growth of new technology-intensive sectors such as software, robotics and biotechnologies. After the crisis caused by the rise of Japanese competition in the early 1980s, concomitantly with the recession induced by the tightening monetary policy adopted by the Federal Reserve in those years, Silicon Valley resurged over the course of the 1980s, giving rise to a new wave of semiconductor startup firms.

At the time of their ascendancy, scholars who took the lead in the investigation of high-tech districts highlighted the combination of numerous local and regional factors behind their growth in the expansive phases and their economic resilience in the contraction phases. These factors included primarily the existence of regional production networks and of a skilled workforce, the availability of pre-existing technology infrastructures and of venture capital, as well as the collaboration with innovation-oriented universities such as the MIT for the Route 128 district and Stanford University for Silicon Valley (Dorfman 1983; Saxenian 1990).

Along with the importance of local and regional factors, there have been strategic state interests at play behind the ascendancy of high-tech districts in the US. The sector of microelectronics and the semiconductor industry in particular have been at the centre of geopolitical tensions since the advent of the urban technological paradigm over the last few decades, and they continue to be so. The issue of inter-state competition in the semiconductor industry came to the forefront of public debates in the US in the 1980s with the rise of Japan as a global competitor (Ferguson 1988). In more recent times, inter-state industrial conflict has come to the fore again in the popular media with the so-called "global chip war" of 2020–21 and the related trade war between China and the US and the question of Taiwan, where the vast majority of the most advanced microchips are currently produced (*The Economist* 2023). One company in particular – The Taiwan Semiconductor Manufacturing Company (TSMC) – concentrates almost all the production of advanced chips on which the algorithmic architecture that is behind the development of so-called artificial intelligence relies (Toews 2023).

TSMC uses advanced chip-making tools that only ASML, a multinational corporation located in the Netherlands, can provide (Lee & Nellis 2022). The partnership between TSMC and ASML creates unprecedented market power in the semiconductor industry and in contemporary techno-capitalism at large. This concentration of economic power has enormous geopolitical significance, also because the semiconductor industry has always needed government support, as analysts of this sector underline (Coldiron 2022). In fact, today's importance of microchips goes beyond the computer industry with which this technology has long been associated, as microchips enable the functioning of a variety of essential consumer products and strategic services, such as cars, planes, home appliances and advanced military equipment. Their ubiquity shows how microchips are central to economic prosperity, military strength and geopolitical power in today's techno-monopoly capitalism (Miller 2022), even at a time in which in popular discourse their supremacy within the urban technological paradigm has been supplanted by algorithmic technology.

At the time of the rise of high-technology districts in the US, the strategic and geopolitical implications of microprocessors as a technology at the centre of the novel urban technological paradigm became evident with the rapid globalization of the semiconductor industry. East Asian countries took the lead in the global race over this technology. The presence of the semiconductor industry in this region dates back to the early 1960s and was due to the off-shore activities of American producers of semiconductor devices: they began to export technology capital. At this time, the attractiveness of East Asian countries was provided by the availability of large reserves of surplus labour and their low wage levels, but also by accommodating forms of state intervention, including in countries and jurisdictions with a clear free-market orientation such as Hong Kong, Singapore and South Korea (Scott 1987).

Since the 1980s, the knowledge-driven high-tech economy has acquired growing significance in the accumulation strategies pursued by the developmental states of East Asian countries. Japan and Taiwan were the first to embark on an "information society" strategy in the early 1980s as part of their long-term state-driven business conglomerate projects (Jessop 2016). Taiwan in particular can be considered a pioneer in strategies of technological sovereignty, with its Hsinchu Science Park created in 1980, which rapidly became a leading district internationally in the semiconductor industry mainly consisting of homegrown firms (Mathews 1997).

Since the late 1980s, other key countries in East Asia have started planning their own high-tech districts specializing in electronics manufacturing production, supported by transnational intra- and inter-firm connections with Silicon Valley and other technological centres elsewhere in the US and Western Europe, and within East Asia (Yeung 2022). Two examples of state-led strategies at this stage are the "Multimedia Super Corridor" launched in Malaysia in 1996 and the technopole of Zhongguancun near Beijing in China, created in 1988 and expanded in 1999 as a "science and technology zone" (Zhou 2008). These examples expose how the importation of the Silicon Valley model in East Asia and the related formation of transnational production networks are indicative of the role of the state in the integration of national political economies into the global competition over the control of the semiconductor industry and the larger ICT sector (Bunnel 2002).

Singapore is another example of a "developmental state" that turned into a "competition state", as Bob Jessop (2016) has put it, with the advent of neoliberal globalization. The evolution of its trajectory is illustrative of the different phases that have characterized the last four decades of technology-driven economic development. In the 1980s, the government strategy focused on the computerization of the public sector and the development of an export-oriented ICT sector. In 1991, the government started embracing an "intelligent city" strategy in which information technologies were expected to pervade every aspect of society: at home, in the working place and in leisure time (Arun & Yap 2000). The stated aim of the plan was to create favourable conditions for the development of clusters of globally competitive tech industries in different domains, from information technology to the biomedical sector. With the dominance of algorithmic technology, since 2014 government policy has morphed into a "smart nation" strategy, aimed at gathering data and creating what is defined as the "Smart Nation Operating System" (Ho 2017).

In the 1980s and the 1990s, the visible hand of state and local authorities was not confined to the emerging economies of East Asia. State interventionism became a distinguishing feature of technology projects across the world (Castells & Hall 1994). High-tech districts that more or less explicitly drew inspiration from Silicon Valley were scattered across the globe. These included, among others, the technology park of Sophia Antipolis in France; the startup economy that developed around Technion university in Israel; the high-tech cluster in Cambridge, England; the so-called Silicon Glen in Scotland; the ICT district in Bangalore, commonly portrayed as "Silicon Valley of India"; and the "digital island" of Ireland (Cooke & Huggins 2003; Henderson 1987; Roper & Grimes 2005; Rosenberg 2002).

In one way or another, the trajectories of these technology districts are evocative of what happened in previous decades in the Sun Belt, the vast region located in the south of the US. Mainstream, market-oriented economists have drawn attention to local attraction factors in their explanations of the Sun Belt's (from California to Florida) economic ascendancy: from natural amenities (warmer weather conditions compared to the old industrialized northeast of the US, which have attracted high-skilled human capital) to what Edward Glaeser and Kristina Tobio have defined as the "Southern tolerance for new construction" (Glaeser & Tobio 2008: 616). According to these authors, tolerance for new building activity has made housing supply more elastic in this part of the country: "more homes were built, and more people came to live in the South", Glaeser and Tobio contend (*ibid.*: 617). The latter explanation has reverberations on recent discussions on the housing crisis that afflicts cities in the US and across the world, where mainstream economists advocate supply-based solutions to the housing shortage and affordability crisis (see also Chapter 4).

Heterodox economists and social scientists have provided an alternative, demand-centred explanation of the rise of the Sun Belt in the US. These scholars have looked at the political-economic context in the 1960s and the 1970s, when the American south witnessed intense economic growth that benefitted from Federal defence programmes, which helped establish the region as a national leader in aerospace, electronics and "business climate" (Schulman 1991). The "entrepreneurial state", therefore, played a key role in the rise of what is customarily known as the post-Fordist Sun Belt, bringing together a Schumpeterian emphasis on technological innovation as a motor of economic growth with a demand-driven, Keynesian approach to economic development (Eisinger 1988; Mazzucato 2013).

According to the latter interpretation, three common characteristics of the emerging technology-driven districts can be identified. First, the majority of these districts revolved around a threefold university–industry–government interaction, or the "triple helix", as it was famously defined (Etzkowitz 2008). In this context, the process of technological innovation relies on spatially contained processes of knowledge spillover, networking and institutionalization, as in the cases of technology clusters, science parks, business accelerators and university incubators. Second, in spatial terms, even though a limited set of powerful metropolitan areas such as Tokyo, Paris and London with economically and socially "innovative milieux" have already witnessed endogenous dynamics of technology-led economic development (Castells & Hall 1994), private and public investment and related "high-tech fantasies" remained focused on a select circle of college towns, suburban areas and semi-rural environments. At this time, the adoption of a hierarchical and spatially selective innovation model led to leaving off the map both conventional manufacturing spaces and the vast majority of inner-city areas (Massey, Quintas & Wield 1992). Third, even though economic-political conditions substantially differed from one place to another, informational cities, technopoles, science parks and other experiments inspired by Silicon Valley were generally "planned developments... resulted from various kinds of cooperation or partnership between the public and private sectors... promoted by central or regional or local governments, often in association with universities" (Castells & Hall 1994: 1).

The late-Keynesian pattern of state entrepreneurialism pursuing projects of high-tech clustering has revived in recent years, particularly within the framework of the purported "return to state capitalism" that has been observed in different countries across the world, including Western capitalist countries. The Covid-19 pandemic, especially in its early stages, has provided further evidence of the emergence of a "new state capitalism". The idea of a return to a "new state capitalism" originally emerged in the late 2000s, with reference to non-Western economies, such as Russia, China and other so-called "emerging markets" (Bremmer 2008). With the unprecedented impact of the Covid-19 pandemic on societies and economies, national states were called to play a leading role in the political and economic response to the pandemic (Tooze 2021).

Ironically, despite the social distancing measures that characterized the pandemic, Covid-19 has only modestly altered the conventional belief in the economic advantages of human-capital density and the physical proximity of technologically innovative activities that are associated with a select set of urban places and their socio-cultural composition. In the immediate aftermath of the emergency phases of the pandemic, local and national governments have continued to invest in science cities, technology-oriented ecosystems and innovation districts in their post-Covid recovery programmes. These initiatives have occurred despite the widespread diffusion of remote work that has emptied downtown business districts across the world, including in those urban centres whose central city entrepreneurial ecosystems have been at the forefront of the digital technology boom, such as New York and San Francisco in the US (Dougherty & Goldberg 2022). In this country, the coronavirus pandemic has led to historic population losses in a large number of big cities, while it has slowed down the demographic growth of suburban areas (Frey 2022). At the same time, the fact that the companies that have taken the lead in the provision of Covid-19 vaccines are located in urban areas in the US that specialize in applied research and capital investment in the life sciences (namely, Boston, New York, San Francisco) has reinforced the commonly held belief about the advantages of physical proximity and institutional density on firm performance, human capital attraction and economic productivity (Savage 2022).

In conclusion, the long wave of high-tech investment led by what Bob Jessop defined as the "competition state" is indicative of what is customarily known as the "late-Keynesian era", whose main features are the following: a process of economic value creation and extraction emanating from the university–industry–government interaction; a highly selective locational logic; and a normative role of public policy. The urbanization of venture capital investment since the second half of the 1990s will not only change the geographies of high-tech districts, strengthening the role of multi-sectoral business ecosystems in central city districts, but will also transform the characteristics of state intervention in the ensuing years, as we will see in the next section of this chapter.

THE CORPORATIZED STATE

The second half of the 1990s saw the first boom of digital startups. These were the pioneers of the internet that could benefit from the low cost of money guaranteed by the expansionary monetary policy adopted by central banks at that time. However, the bust of the so-called "dot-com bubble" in 2000 and subsequent technological changes led to the end of the internet economy as it became known in the 1990s. This first stage of the startup boom saw the emergence of a select circle of urban and regional spaces attracting newly formed firms and venture capital in the digital sector (Massey, Quintas & Wield 1992).

The sudden end of the so-called "dot-com boom" of the late 1990s led to the rapid dissolution of the first startup era in the early 2000s. In the US, venture capital investment and startup clusters started to grow again from around 2003 onwards (Center for an Urban Future 2012). However, the financial crisis of 2008–09 led to another postponement of the long-awaited startup boom. In the aftermath of the late 2000s "great contraction" and the concomitant popularization of the web 2.0, the so-called "tech boom 2.0" allowed the second outbreak of entrepreneurship and consumption linked this time to algorithmic technology.

The tech boom 2.0 that has followed the financial meltdown of 2008–09 therefore represents a decisive turning point in the trajectories of urban economies. The widespread adoption of "radical technologies" (Greenfield 2017) in the digital sector has played a key role in this process. In the first place, the planetary expansion of social media has opened the way to the cultural hegemony of digital technologies and of the large firms that represent this sector in the public realm. The fast growth of social media has contributed to spreading a popular culture with a strong urban technological characterization. When social media such as Facebook, Twitter and Instagram were created, their founders were based in technology-intensive urban areas such as Boston and San Francisco in the US. The constitutive values of this culture are rooted in both communities of practice (social media favour the multiplication of affinity groups and intentional communities) and individual identity (social media and digital platforms encourage the exhibition of the self and of personal achievements). Arguably, this culture has become one of the dominant appearances of the urban technological paradigm.

In the second place, the adoption of infrastructures of cloud computing capable of storing huge, potentially unlimited quantities of data has allowed the development of the so-called Internet of Things. The "smart home" and at a larger scale the "smart city" are based on biometric sensors that extract data from everyday movements and behaviours (Gabrys 2016). The digitalization of social life and increasingly of biological life, too, has increased the commercial attractiveness of densely populated urban areas as the concentration of residents and consumers offers almost unlimited opportunities for data mining.

Finally, closely linked to the advent of big data, there is the invention of machine learning, a term that indicates the ability of algorithmic technologies to constantly improve their performances on the basis of the data obtained from their own performances. Urban environments offer unique opportunities for machine learning and its utilization in the creation of economic value, allowing consumer-oriented platforms to function in flexible and adaptive manners. These innovations – which are at the same time socio-cultural, technical and organizational – are at the heart of the platform revolution (Parker, Van Alstyne & Choudary 2016) and the consequent platformization of global capitalism (Srnicek 2017) and urban life (Barns 2020).

Despite the perception of a de-territorializing global economy, the tech boom 2.0 has therefore led to an intensified relationship of digital technologies to society and the urban economy, most particularly through the algorithmic management of a growing number of human activities and social domains. While in the early stages of the information society there was a clearly demarcated boundary between the "real world" and the internet's virtual sphere, the ubiquitous application of algorithmic technology has made increasingly obsolete the distinction between the real and the virtual, leading to an increasingly inextricable intertwining of social life with the digital space. This development, in turn, has opened up novel possibilities for the creation and extraction of economic value in and through urban spaces. In short, urban digital platforms are now conventionally understood as entities providing a fundamental basis for firms' capacity to grow in order to meet increasing demand, or what is known in managers' lexicon as the "scalability of business".

As a result, the 2010s saw concomitantly the worldwide spread at an unprecedented pace of social media (Facebook, YouTube, Instagram, WeChat, TikTok, etc.), of online retail services (Amazon, eBay, Walmart, AliExpress, etc.), and in recent years of the on-demand services of the so-called sharing economy (Uber, Lyft, Airbnb, etc.) and the food delivery market (Uber Eats, Deliveroo, DoorDash, etc.). It is not by coincidence that the consumption and lifestyle revolution brought on by the advent of the so-called "platform society" has taken form in the aftermath of the financial crisis of 2008–09.

As we said, the business application of algorithmic technology began with the rise to prominence of the algorithm-based Google search engine (called PageRank) between the late 1990s and the early 2000s. In doing so, Google became the first "global rentier" of data extractivism (Pasquinelli 2009). However, the "normalization" and extension of algorithmic technology as an extractivist apparatus occurred during the 2010s, after the economic turbulences of the late 2000s.

After having played a key role in the early stages of the post-Fordist information age as sites for venture capital investment and for industry-company-government interactions (Castells 1989), the role of cities and urban environments has significantly expanded in post-2008 techno-monopoly capitalism. Since the early 2010s, it has become customary to signal in one form or another the rise of a newly monopolist form of capitalism based on an intensified extraction of economic value by tech corporations from and through urban spaces. Starting in the late 2000s, a growing number of smart-city projects in the field of infrastructure (energy, transport, real estate) and broader urban affairs (citizen participation, leisure) led by iconic capitalist corporations such as IBM, Cisco and Siemens, opened the way to the algorithmic transformation of urban societies. Smart-city initiatives apply artificial intelligence and machine learning-based devices to the social foundations of everyday life, such as mobility, housing, education and leisure. For instance, IBM's Smarter Cities Challenge, launched in 2009 and officially registered as a trademark in 2011 as part of the company's broader Smarter Planet initiative, was intended to apply algorithm technology to disparate sectors of urban life: public safety, health and human services, education, infrastructure, energy, water, and environmental services and citizen participation (https://www.ibm.com/smarterplanet/us/en/).

Between the late 2000s and the first half of the 2010s, cities across the world witnessed the proposal of smart-city initiatives based on public-private partnerships involving local administrations and multinational corporations in the ICT sector. National states have been either explicitly or implicitly involved in smart-city projects. In these initiatives, cities are being governed through contractual agreements signed by city governments with corporate actors such as IBM, which deliver the requested services or subcontract them to other global firms or local companies (McNeill 2015). The smart city governance model is illustrative of a regulatory form of capitalism at a time when information technology allows the decentralized retrieval of information about market dynamics and the integration of this information into flexible systems of strategy-making and flexible production systems (Braithwaite 2008). In the more articulated smart-city strategies (Coletta, Heaphy & Kitchin 2019), the local state commits itself to creating markets for service delivery, operating as a hub of the networked system of contractual relationships that involve different partnerships with private actors. The result of this process of regulation has been a hybrid model of state-capital interaction – which has prepared the ground for the rise of what is defined here as the "corporatized state" – in which it is hard to distinguish between the privatization of the public and the publicization of the private (Braithwaite 2008).

The corporatized state that has followed in the wake of the smart-city era takes form with the emergence of techno-monopoly capitalism in the 2010s, along with the multiplication of technology-driven startup ecosystems in a growing number of cities across the globe. The commercial explosion of digital platforms during the 2010s has given rise to a variety of economic and social arrangements, variously termed as "platform economy", "sharing economy", "platform urbanism" and the like. In this context, tech corporations have increasingly urbanized their operations, resulting in further intensification and diversification of the urbanization of capital. At the same time, a select circle of giant technology corporations has become more powerful than most large developed economies and their governments in terms of market control, regulation and arbitrage (Tepper 2018). These corporations now have the capacity to create their own proprietary systems of law and insulate themselves from public regulation (Stone & Kuttner 2020). What is defined here as techno-monopoly capitalism is therefore the result of concomitant forces of urbanization and monopolization of corporate power.

In different ways and forms, urban environments become closely implicated with the wide range of economic value-generating activities that the most powerful companies engage in on a daily basis in order to increase the market value of the enterprise and earn a profit. For capitalist firms, densely populated areas represent at the same time sites for data extraction, reservoirs of variously skilled workforce and unrivalled markets for their goods and services. For its part, the capitalist state (both the national and the local state) orchestrates the urban field as the arena in which it constantly performs a multifaceted activity of persuasion and ingratiation of corporate interests. This performative activity comprises business-sensitive legislation, ceremonial acts, collusive arrangements and other "constitutive practices" that create conditions for interaction and conditions of trust between corporate investors and local stakeholders (Moisio & Rossi 2023).

As we argued earlier, what we call in this book techno-monopoly capitalism treats contemporary cities and urban spaces as "living laboratories", as a test bed for conducting its value-extraction operations thanks to the unrivalled market opportunities that they offer to corporate investors. In this context, the relationship of techno-monopoly capitalism with urban environments goes even beyond conventional patterns of market economies. Smart-city initiatives and platform-mediated economies establish an intimate connection with the governmentalized urban field. As a result, given the unprecedented osmosis between the dominant pattern of capitalist companies and urban environments, tech corporations and digital platforms become a significant constituent of the contemporary urban field. At the same time, the urban field appears as a huge business potential for both companies (profits) and states (tax revenue).

Today, digital platforms are widely debated due to their pervasiveness and their uneven impact on contemporary life. On the one hand, online platforms are believed to improve the quality of living, by making the consumption of public and private goods and services more accessible, as in the previous smart-city model. On the other hand, these platforms are generative of social inequalities and dynamics of exploitation that reiterate, in new forms, long-standing problems associated with capitalist societies. However, this very essence of digital platforms is effectively concealed in contemporary business and policy discourse. It is therefore worth focusing in greater detail on the reproduction of the corporatized state in today's platformization of urban life and particularly on the ambivalence of capitalism-society relationship in the platform conjuncture. Ambivalence is understood here as a gap between the potentiality and actuality of a social formation (Virno 2008). Capitalist societies epitomize this ambivalence in the form of a permanent tension between human living labour as the potentiality to produce value and capital as the force that attempts to steer this potentiality towards the production of surplus value for the capitalist corporation (Treiber & Christiansen 2021). In today's techno-monopoly capitalism reorganized around algorithmic platforms, this tension is reflected in the ability of urban environments to enable value creation and in the capture of this value by high-tech corporations that have a monopoly position in the capitalist market.

Digital platforms therefore epitomize the ambivalence that is distinctive of contemporary capitalist societies. As critical urbanist Maroš Krivý has argued, the concept of platform contains an intrinsic paradox: a platform is characterized by a plain and horizontal surface, but at the same time it relies on a vertical and stratified logic of functioning (Krivý 2018). In this sense, the advent and techno-political dominance of the platform is a powerful confirmation of the ambivalence of contemporary techno-capitalism that produces politically and ideologically ambiguous phenomena like the economic populism that we have observed in recent years. These ambiguities are reflected in the work of mainstream urban economists such as Richard Florida and Edward Glaeser ("celebrity urbanologists" in Jamie Peck's [2016] definition), who have recently reformulated their previous positions on creative cities and urban economic development to address the problem of sociospatial inequalities; however, without substantially revising their conceptual assumptions (Rossi 2020).

Contemporary techno-capitalism oscillates between the rhetoric of consumers' satisfaction, worker autonomy and value creation that informs public discourse around business and technology, on the one hand, and the apparent reality of what a growing number of authors on the academic left have interpreted as "new feudalism", on the other hand, as rent and debt seem to feature as or more heavily in accumulation than profit, and work increasingly exceeds the wage relation (Dean 2020). Again, this points to the stark contrast between appearance and essence that historically characterizes capitalist societies. The latter is today illustrated by the emergence of powerful monopolists of value capture and extraction, such as the big high-tech corporations owning the digital platforms with their social control techniques based on mass surveillance, automation of production, artificial intelligence and the Internet of Things (Ettlinger 2022). The softening or cancellation of antitrust legislation in previous years (Longman 2015) has paved the way to the rise of novel corporate giants and their monopolistic market power.

In speaking of the monopoly power of platform-mediated business and economic value extraction, one cannot avoid thinking about the conventional extractive platforms in the hands of powerful oil companies. Oil platforms stretch vertically downwards in order to dig in the underwater depths and obtain raw materials that were formed in the distant past. Likewise, the digital platforms operated by high-tech corporations penetrate the urban ground of social relationships (which potentially have relatively preserved local histories) in order to extract economic value. As extractive companies are known for not adequately redistributing oil, gas or mineral revenues with local communities, corporations operating digital platforms are similarly known for not returning an adequate proportion of their earnings to local societies. This is irrespective of the fact that urban populations in these places arguably work for these corporations. Rather, these companies often escape national taxation systems by locating their headquarters in fiscally permissive countries, such as Ireland, the Netherlands and the United Kingdom (UK). In 2023, in Italy, Milan's public prosecutor office ordered the seizing of about €779 million ($835 million) from the home-sharing company Airbnb for unpaid taxes. This decision has followed in the wake of closely related actions undertaken in that country by tax authorities against iconic tech corporations such as Meta and Netflix (Fortune 2023).

It is therefore common wisdom today that digital corporations are illustrative of predatory or parasitic economies, as they exploit local resources, both tangible (built environment, infrastructure, etc.) and intangible (local culture, forms of life, social practices, etc.), and operate under conditions of dubious legality. However, the emphasis on predatory economic practices, or the actions undertaken by fiscal authorities in some countries, should not lead us to think about local and national states as mere victims or as external agents with respect to the monopolistic market power of companies in the energy or technology sectors. On the contrary, in today's neoliberal societies, corporate power and political power are constitutively interlinked (Barkan 2013). As Michael Watts has shown with reference to oil companies, extractive companies are central to what – drawing on the work of Michel Foucault and Nikolas Rose – can be defined as "governable spaces" in which local actors and the state are involved, partaking in heterogeneous forms of rule and authority that all together are generative of governmental apparatuses (Watts 2004). While extractive companies in the energy sector rely on forms of "authoritarian governmentality" and even explicit violence, extractive companies in the digital sector that have become hegemonic across the world exist in a kind of "ethical and legal purgatory", as it has been defined in the mass media (Scheiber 2017). The continuous oscillation between the legal and the illegal spheres reiterates in a new form the long-standing disrespect for the law that characterizes capitalist governmentality in its monopolistic tendencies (Stoller 2019), showing how the corporation and political power "are founded in and bound together through a principle of legally sanctioned immunity from law" (Barkan 2013: 4).

Today, a key concern for the tech industry is indeed the pursuit of a novel form of "legally sanctioned immunity from law". As business law scholars have pointed out, the leading companies in the digital sector cultivate a subtle relationship to legality, as for them changing the law has become a key part of their business strategy, trying to change or shape the law according to their business model (Pollmann & Barry 2016). To do so, popular technology firms normally engage in political activity, organizing local actors, in addition to lobbying work as in conventional corporate practice. Politics thus becomes a constitutive element of techo-monopoly capitalism, and hence of the urban field. For instance, in 2016 Airbnb – the leading firm in the short-term rental platform business – launched an initiative called "Airbnb in action", based on the creation of "independent home sharing clubs" that involve Airbnb hosts in order to "leverage the power of their voices". This strategy is instrumental in the creation of a novel "platform-mediated citizenship" (van Doorn 2020) that aims to supplant democratic forms of political representation.

The ride sharing company Uber – perhaps along with Airbnb the most representative firm of the platform-mediated gig economy – has been reported to undertake similar practices of "corporate-sponsored grassroots lobbying" (Yates 2021). Moreover, in 2022 the disclosing of leaked data showed how Uber exerts pressure on government leaders of economically powerful countries (including the US, the UK and France, with proof about the latter having aided the company). The intent is, as *The Guardian* reports: "to rewrite laws to help pave the way for an app-based, gig-economy model of work that has since proliferated across the world". On the other hand, Uber also has "heavily subsidised journeys, seducing drivers and passengers on to the app with incentives and pricing models that would not be sustainable" (Davies *et al*. 2022).

Tech firms' lobbying practices, therefore, end up in collusive relations with government leaders. In 2022, French President Macron replied to the allegations of having been involved in collusive practices with Uber by saying that he was proud of supporting the cab-hailing company to lobby against France's closed-shop taxi industry and that he would "do it again tomorrow and the day after tomorrow" (Chrisafis 2022). These revelations are indicative of a more general orientation of the French government, which in turn can be seen as illustrative of a broader transformation of governments' approach to economic and societal governance in techno-monopoly capitalism. In

Macron's intentions, as institutional political economists Bruno Amable and Stefano Palombarini argue:

> … the gradual Uberization of the main sectors of the economy, the development of startups – or, more modestly, of small businesses and even sole traders – are all called upon to increase the numbers of the self-employed, whether their work is genuinely autonomous or, in reality, directed externally.
> (Amable & Palombarini 2021: 171)

In this sense, the "Uberization" of the French economy and its society is instrumental in the construction of a new hegemonic project by the corporatized state based on the entrepreneurialization of living and the exclusion of labour unions from the governing process. The complicity of the state with monopolistic corporate power in the technology sector is of course not limited to France, particularly among Western countries. In the US, the close relationship between President Obama's administration and tech corporations was widely noticed. Mullins and Bykowicz (2021) report how, as his second term drew to a close, Obama organized a party at the White House in honour of Silicon Valley. According to these authors, some of those involved compared the occasion to a recruitment event for the departing administrators. Indeed, many officials became lobbyists for technology companies. In 2020, 334 people were registered as lobbyists for Apple, Amazon, Meta and Google. More than 80 per cent of these officials had previously worked for either Congress or the White House (*ibid.*). All these developments disclose the presence of the corporatized state.

While lobbying activities have been a long-standing feature of corporate behaviour in capitalist societies, the ways in which governments and technology corporations today converge in the pursuit of capitalist interests and behave in the public domain are evocative of what Maurizio Lazzarato, Christian Marazzi and other theorists of cognitive capitalism argued about the post-Fordist transition of the 1990s. Lazzarato, in particular, put forward the idea of the "political entrepreneur" as a distinguishing trait of this new politico-economic stage: the fact of being an entrepreneur comprises acting and making claims in the public sphere (Lazzarato 2007). In his analysis, Lazzarato referred to the political ascent of Silvio Berlusconi as well as Benetton, at that time an emerging firm in the fashion industry in Italy and internationally. Both Berlusconi and Benetton were examples of what Marazzi in the same years defined as the "linguistic turn in the post-Fordist economy" (Marazzi 2008), with economic actors increasingly embracing communicative action within the public sphere.

Today's political agency of technology firms such as Airbnb and Uber goes beyond the corporate storytelling pursued by the multinational corporations of the post-Fordist transition of the 1990s and even of the more recent smart-city era, centred on the moral imposition of technological solutions on urban societies (Söderstrom, Paasche & Klauser 2014). In techno-monopoly capitalism, the presence of tech corporations becomes rooted in the public sphere, through their active engagement in corporate-sponsored grassroots organizing. This political activity becomes an essential part of the tech companies' business strategy, which national and local governments are willing to recognize and even support. For instance, all across Europe local authorities have agreed different deals with tech corporations specializing in the short-term rental sector, such as Airbnb and Booking.com, in the attempt to moderate the societal distortions of this sector (Taylor 2020). In many cases, however, rather than providing stricter regulations, these agreements have ended up legitimizing the destabilizing effects of the short-term rental business on local housing markets and their social ecosystems. The politicization of corporate agency and the accommodating role of governments is illustrative of how contemporary economies and specifically urban economies are intrinsically political constructs in techno-monopoly capitalism. Their essence is thus political and constitutive of what we conceptualize as the urban field.

Finally, another essential manifestation of the corporatized state is what can be defined as the corporatization of state sovereignty. In this sense, the widely debated "return of state capitalism", particularly in relation to the pursuit of "technological sovereignty", and the policies of the corporatized state – policies that are premised on the implicit adoption of a kind of Silicon-Valley libertarianism – are not opposing developments. For instance, the recent negotiations of the Artificial Intelligence Act in the European Union (EU), in which key EU countries such as France and Germany have embraced subtly anti-regulatory arguments (Henshall 2023), have showed how the idea of technological sovereignty can be associated with a minimalist approach to the regulation of the tech sector, in the name of the hope to effectively nurture new startups that would grow very rapidly and become national champion firms. As such, "state capitalism" does not inescapably signal increasing regulation or the erosion of the corporatized state. Indeed, the governments of the corporatized states reason that an excess of regulation prevents the rise of national champions. In this respect, one may argue that the contemporary version of the corporatized state (and the gradually emerging state capitalism) is eager to finance but not to effectively regulate the technology companies.

Mistral, the recently founded French startup that builds technology that other businesses can use to deploy AI-driven products, is indicative of this development. Moreover, it is noticeable that this kind of corporatized state – eager to develop a sort of start-up nation – is also deeply geopolitical in nature, connected to an effort to master territories of technology in global competition. A journalist reports, revealingly, how "Mistral's fate has taken on considerable importance in France, where leaders like Bruno Le Maire, the finance minister, have pointed to the company as providing the nation a chance to challenge U.S. tech giants" (Metz 2023).

CONCLUSION

This chapter has shown how the emergence of the urban technological paradigm over the last five decades, since the 1980s in particular, signals a simultaneous intensification and diversification in the urbanization of capital based on a novel kind of naturalized "capitalist imperative" (Storper & Walker 1989): the economization of cities and urban spaces as innovation machines. In short, the urban technological paradigm has constituted the urban field in such a manner that enables the expansion of techno-monopoly capitalism in society and has entailed the involvement of the corporatized state in this societal project. In the last section of this chapter we have surveyed three fundamental ways in which the corporatized state becomes implicated in techno-monopoly capitalism: first, through collusive engagements with technology corporations and their lobbying practices; second, through the accommodation of the political agency of contemporary tech corporations; third, through the corporatization of the state policy agenda in the name of "technological sovereignty".

In the resulting state-corporation complex, the construction and maintenance of the urban field is a fundamental political concern in advancing economic growth and societal prosperity that are at the heart of today's economic governmentality.

It is against this backdrop that this book starts from the idea that the economic value acquired by cities and urban societies in today's techno-capitalism cannot be explained only with their "natural" agglomeration characteristics, as the common wisdom in urban economics and the popular media holds. Chapter 2, which more specifically will deal with the role of the state, discusses the ways in which the state–city–capital relation has fluctuated since the nationalization of urban development in the twentieth century, and argues that the deepening capitalization of the urban field does not indicate that the state is withering away in the transnational urbanization process. The ambiguous relationship between the state and the digital platforms of the high-tech sector is revelatory of the less direct and visible involvement of the former in the governance and management of the urban field at the time of techno-monopoly capitalism.

In general, the ensuing chapters aim to show how tech-intensive urbanization is a spatially selective political construction constitutively aligned with the construction, governance and maintenance of techno-monopoly capitalism. In particular, the book will expose how, through different visible and invisible interventions, the governmental state – both the local state and the national state – fills the gap between capitalist firms and the economic value ingrained in the four key sites for value extraction that we have identified in this book: labour, human capital, startups and place-specific forms of life.

CHAPTER 2

THE URBAN FIELD AND THE STRATEGIC URBANIZATION OF THE STATE

INTRODUCTION

The politics of urban revival has characterized neoliberal societal and political regimes and experimentations since the late 1970s and the early 1980s. This process has taken place in several nation-states across the globe, and it has been marked by an intensive technologization and monopolization of the urban field in the operations of capital. In this chapter we first discuss the concept of the urban field. Second, we go on to argue that the urban field is a phenomenon that should be approached through an analysis of the changing relationship between the nation-state, the local state (cities) and capital. In so doing, we highlight the conjunctural nature of the urban field and its character as an open, politically constructed and connective societal phenomenon. In short, this is not only a strategic-relational field of struggle through which different social actors and factions of capital seek to operate, but also a field of action that reconstitutes the urban fabric at a given historical conjuncture in a specific manner. In the third part of the chapter we discuss the fluctuating essence of the urban field.

The nationalization of the urban field during the twentieth century indicated a specific coming together of capital, the local state and the nation-state. During the past few decades, the urban field has been increasingly constituted in the strategic urbanization of the state, a process that ties transnational capital, the nation-state and the local state tightly together in the name of innovation, technology and economic growth (see Moisio & Rossi 2020). In this process, the nation-state has been a constitutive force, as our discussion on the digitalization of the Finnish nation-state demonstrates in this chapter. Here, digitalization has emerged as "a method of government that can procure the nation's prosperity" (Foucault 2008: 13). We believe that the Finnish case is relevant in disclosing some of the key processes of the corporatized state, not least because the "neoliberal revolution in Finland"

(Patomäki 2007: 13) has been characteristically a technocratic process whereby technological knowledge, and the whole techno-industrial complex, has assumed a pivotal role. Neoliberalization in Finland has thus been centred around the idea of constructing a new state form that would fundamentally embrace technological development and productivity (*ibid.*: 67; Moisio & Paasi 2013).

We argue in this chapter that it would be misleading to assume that absence of state intervention has underpinned the technology industry's growing political-economic power in the urban field. Rather the opposite is true. Interrogating the role of the state in the context of urban and regional economies is one of the key ideas of geographical political economy (Bok 2019). This focus substantially differentiates geographical political economy from mainstream urban and regional economics, which customarily rejects any relevant role of the state in the technology-based revival and centrality of contemporary urban economies. However, when the role of the state is taken into scrutiny within more applied scholarship variously inspired by geographical political economy, a common approach is to examine the spatially selective state strategies and related movement of investments that benefit certain cities and regions more than the other locations.

Literature dealing with the so-called "geographies of discontent" and "left-behind places" (MacKinnon *et al.* 2022; Rodríguez-Pose 2018) is illustrative of this stance. This literature on the one hand emanates from the pre-existing idea in urban and regional political economy that the state has a tendency to privilege certain places through accumulation strategies, state projects and hegemonic projects (Jones 1997), but on the other hand views the state as an exogenous actor that is in a kind of external position with respect to the governmentality of cities, urban spaces and regions. For its part, through the concept of the urban field, the remainder of this chapter aims to show the internalization of the governmental state into the urban field (or what we call "the strategic urbanization of the state") as a key site for economic value extraction in contemporary techno-monopoly capitalism.

THE URBAN FIELD

The concept of the urban field was originally coined by John Friedmann and John Miller (1965). These authors sought to develop what they called "fitting city concepts" for regional policy and spatial planning practices in a purportedly new historical conjuncture. Their idea was that the separation between the city and the countryside no longer held true. Accordingly, popular concepts in urban planning studies such as megalopolis or spread-city did not grasp the central tenets of the then urbanization process, which according to the authors unified both urban cores and inter-metropolitan peripheries to a single functional whole. The urban field, in their conceptualization, hence denoted an enlargement of the space for urban living that extends beyond the administrative borders of metropolitan areas into the inter-metropolitan periphery that was supposed to experience revival. The concept of the urban field, therefore, signalled the reversing of the basic trends of the urbanization process at that time. Friedman and Miller (1965: 313) suggested that this kind of urban field is a new spatial order or "new ecological unit" of "America's" post-industrial society".

We find the concept of the urban field a fitting spatial concept in its capacious expansiveness, but not in the physical sense proposed by Friedman and Miller (1965). For our purposes, one of the most important elements of the paper is a quote with which the authors begin their treatise. It is a quote written by the urban sociologist Don Martindale, who in an extensive introduction to the translation of Max Weber's classical text *The City*, argues the following: "The modern city is losing its external and formal structure. Internally it is in a state of decay while the new community represented by the nation everywhere grows at its expense. The age of the city seems to be at an end" (quoted in Friedmann & Miller 1965: 312).

The entanglement of the nation-state and the city is one of the grand themes of modernity. Much of nation-state history and national identity has been construed and contested in cities. Moreover, "national" political forces have had a crucial impact on the development of urban politics, on the idea of modern city and on the forms of cities in different state contexts. Cities have not only represented a challenge for national political regulation and the maintenance of social order, but have also been constituents of state power, not least because of their role as strategically, materially and symbolically important spaces of capital accumulation and wealth generation (Moisio 2018b). In short, capitalist cities have been utterly important for the capitalist states. The urban field has not been a passive outcome of state territorial formation processes, but instead has occupied a pivotal role in the geopolitical processes of the nation-state.

The discipline of sociology has long engaged with field theory. Three senses of the field, in particular, can be discerned in the scholarly literature: first, the field conceived as an analytic area in which one can observe the social positioning of individual and collective actors; second, the field understood as an organization of forces; third, the field understood as a field of contestation, a battlefield (Levi Martin 2003). All of these three conceptions permeate our understanding of the urban field as an economic-juridical notion, to put it with Michel Foucault's definition of the field as a spatial concept (Foucault 1980: 68). Indeed, in our perspective the urban field is the "ground" (Mezzadra & Neilson 2019) of today's techno-monopoly capitalism, which is based on the economic and legal power of technology corporations, as we have seen in Chapter 1.

From the perspective of what is said above, it is useful here to draw on the strategic-relational state theory by Bob Jessop (2007). Accordingly, the state is a complex and strategic-relational political actor, the power of which is constantly mobilized by competing factions of capital and other social forces in the pursuit of possessing state power over the entire political community. In such a view, the state is a political formation forged by politico-economic elites in their efforts to support specific accumulation strategies that are consonant with the existing mode of capitalist production (Jessop 1997). In a similar vein, we suggest that the urban field is characterized by strategic relationality and associated governmentalities: the strategies, calculations and interactions of state management and capitalists come together in the context of the urban field. Moreover, the urban field can also be understood as "a social relation that can be analysed as the site, the generator, and the product of strategies" (Jessop 1990: 260). Technology corporations operating in and through the urban field operationalize the power of the state for several reasons, most importantly but not solely to enable economic value extraction. This operationalization is at the core of the corporatized state. Simultaneously, the power and legitimacy of a given state's management is fundamentally dependent on the generation of economic value in the process of capital accumulation through the urban field.

The urban field can also be conceptualized from the Foucauldian perspective as a process of "statification" (Foucault 2008: 77). From this angle, the urban field is bound to governmental reason. Foucault himself believed that the state is not a universal nor in itself an autonomous source of political power (*ibid*.). Rather, the state is a process whereby numerous governmental rationales and practices are bound together and articulated from a combined, unitary perspective in what we call and understand as the state (Jessen & von Eggers 2020). In a similar vein, Timothy Mitchell has argued that "the state should be addressed as an effect of detailed processes of spatial organisation, temporal arrangement, functional specification, and supervision and surveillance, which create the appearance of a world fundamentally divided into state and society" (Mitchell 1991: 95).

The urban field is constantly produced in the process of statification and the associated governmental performativities that constitute the urban field. In this constitution, the state plays a central role as an imaginary, fictive or discursive object that links the multiplicity of governmental performativities together and makes them appear as a given entity (Agamben 2011; also Lemke 2007). One important empirical and theoretical question is then what role the state plays in the multiplicity of governmental practices of statification that constitute the urban field in different temporal and geographical

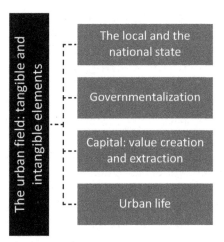

Figure 2.1 The urban field

contexts and how we can understand the corporatized state in an analysis of contemporary governmental performativities related to the capitalist urban transformation in the age of techno-monopoly.

An inquiry into local state/national state relations is particularly pertinent for any critical analysis of contemporary conditions. The geographical imaginaries of techno-capitalism are highly city-centred, and they often present cities as solutions to all kinds of economic and political crises. In political debates in corporatized states, as well as in mainstream scholarly work in urban economics, management studies and in related fields, and in the work of all kinds of consultant companies and guru scholars, issues such as technology, innovation, productivity, internationalization, growth and creativity are increasingly brought together and associated with the urban fabric. These debates are not only descriptive but also prescriptive – constitutive of the corporatized state. In short, the urban field is constituted and transformed in ideational processes and hence anchored to ideas as well as to ideational change (Moisio 2024).

The concept of the urban field also refers to the operations of capital: the creation and extraction of economic value. By using this concept, we underscore the ways in which what Mezzadra and Neilson (2019) conceptualize as the operations of capital shape the spatialities of contemporary capitalism. Indeed, our concept of the urban field comes close to what these authors term as "ground":

> ... we use the word ground in a sense that is at once material and prospectively constructed as an operative surface on which capital intervenes. While ground is neither merely terrain not land, it

> registers the specificity of spatial, social, legal, and political formations with which capital must grapple as it becomes enmeshed in a dense constellation of flesh and earth ... We understand space at large as a field of tensions and struggles, where established spatial formations are far from passive with respect to operations of capital, while those operations often have a disruptive effect on the production of space. (Mezzadra & Neilson 2019: 3)

In our conceptualization, the urban field is a conjunctural phenomenon that accommodates different entities together (see Figure 2.1). It does not refer to a clearly delineated city in an administrative sense. Rather, the urban field comprises a set of heterogeneous elements such as labour, institutions and modes of regulation, the built environment, forms of governing, urban life, intellectual ideas regarding cities and their success and failure, investments, and the various operations of capital. As such, the urban field not only brings together the material, the symbolic, the social and the discursive, but also provides different actors with notable "potentials" that can be utilized in multiple ways. As such, the concept of the urban field underlines the need to examine the essence (or the "content") of urban space: the unity of various appearances in a given historical conjuncture.

The concept of the urban field seeks to demonstrate the ongoing political construction of cities and urban areas in techno-monopoly capitalism, and the ways in which in this particular context the corporatized state – both the local and the national state – attempts to turn urban society into a kind of living laboratory for capitalist innovation (Moisio & Rossi 2020). In doing so, we underline the role of governing practices in the moulding of social life that is constitutive of the urban field.

Given the tendency of capital to rely on movement rather than fixity, we adopt the idea of the urban field in a literal sense of the field being conceived as an "open" land area. In the current platform conjuncture, the refashioning of urban societies as an open land is instrumental to the value-extraction mechanisms of techno-capitalism. Capitalist corporations derive from the urban field the living labour, the diffuse knowledge, the social infrastructures and material logistics that are at the heart of their business activities. As such, the contemporary urban field is the spatiality of capital that structurally exceeds the nation-state as a bordered space but at the same time reconstructs the state as a political territory (cf. Mezzadra & Neilson 2019).

In today's current politico-economic landscape, the existence of a truly open land area remains a corporate ideal, as the urban field is punctuated and demarcated by a complex set of physical or intangible enclosures and market monopolies that are characteristic of the economic-political conjuncture that we live through. In our understanding, therefore, the contemporary urban field is an essential element of techno-monopoly capitalism and the reworking of national and local states as corporatized states. As a political construct, the contemporary urban field is characterized by pervasive economic instrumentalization: developing urban social life, the environment, land and the built environment, to mention but a few, primarily from the perspective of exchange values and profits. For us, an analysis of the urban field is thus inescapably a study of the creation and extraction of economic value in the contemporary conjuncture, the latter understood as "a period during which the different social, political, economic and ideological contradictions that are at work in society come together to give it a specific and distinctive shape" (Hall & Massey 2010: 57).

The concept of the urban field thus is intended to highlight the contemporary articulations and diversification of the politico-economic process that David Harvey termed as the urbanization of capital (Harvey 1985a). By using this concept, Harvey originally sought to analyse capital switching: the ways in which the urban built environment was central in absorbing surplus capital in the context of economic crises in basic production in the 1970s, and in so doing to tackle the crisis in manufacturing.

The construction and maintenance of the urban field as a key site in the intensive and multifaceted quest for value that characterizes contemporary capitalism involves both tangible and intangible elements. Two main economic complexes are central to the urban field in today's extractivist form of techno-monopoly capitalism. The built environment and the real-estate industry have, of course, remained crucial. On the one hand, the technology-based economy has become significant over the past few decades. Inspired by the seminal analyses of key authors in critical urban theory such as Henri Lefebvre and David Harvey, urban scholars have customarily focused their attention on the built environment and the real-estate sector (the "secondary circuit of capital" and the related growth machines) as crucial sites of economic value extraction in financialized capitalism. This approach has been revived by studies on the ways in which local governments have come to depend on dynamics of "value capture" in the real-estate sector, in order to finance their everyday activities and structural investments (Robinson & Attuyer 2020).

On the other hand, what Harvey (1979) defined as the "tertiary circuit" of capital, which comprises investment in science, technology and labour power, has long remained relatively overlooked in critical urban studies investigating neoliberal urban societies. This is irrespective of the fact that the transformation of the urban field is ultimately about what Harvey (1985a) conceptualized as capital switching. From this perspective, the transformation of the urban field is constituted in the process of solving the problems of the existing mode of accumulation. If the urban built environment was central in absorbing surplus capital in the context of economic crises in basic production in the 1970s, the tech-driven economy can similarly be understood as a process of securing capital appreciation, and in so doing averting the crisis that became evident in the late 1980s. The state has been central in this development.

However, with the advent of algorithmic technologies and the subsequent explosion of digital platforms in the 2010s, urban scholarship has started paying attention to the urban manifestation of what Harvey termed the "tertiary circuit of capital". The phenomenon of "capital convergence", in which real-estate capital and tech-oriented venture capital together contribute to the rise of a new "real estate/financial/technology complex", has particularly attracted the attention of critical scholars of platform urbanism (Sadowski 2020; Shaw 2020; Zukin 2020). This scholarship, for instance, has shown how processes of capital convergence have opened the way to the ascent of global corporate landlords such as private equity firms that through operations of algorithmic management are able to securitize rental income from thousands of rental properties that are geographically dispersed: the so-called "automated landlord" phenomenon (Fields 2022).

Beyond two key sectors such as the real-estate industry and digital technology, from a wider perspective the urban field becomes crucial as a provider of what in the sociology of markets is known as the "shared lifeworld" that is behind knowledge production in today's economy (Aspers 2006). This socially produced knowledge is created both within institutions explicitly designed to knowledge creation (universities, research centres, etc.) and within the framework of unstructured social relations (May & Perry 2018). The production of knowledge that emanates from either organized or unstructured modes of social interaction is instrumental in the creation of the intangible assets (design, branding, research and development, software, etc.) that are at the heart of today's capitalist economies and societies (Haskel & Westlake 2018).

ON THE "NATIONAL" URBAN FIELD

Max Weber stressed in his book *The City* (1921) that the rapid process of industrial urbanization in the nineteenth century, and the associated phenomenal population growth and physical expansion of cities in Europe and in North America in particular had not led to the growth of cities in a "sociological sense". By this Weber meant that some of the earlier city forms were being replaced by increasingly national cities. These latter cities were dominated by national governments, and characterized by inter-local activities and planning schemes of the nation-state and its "statist" interests. Weber further argued that the modern city was losing its previous external structure and that a new nation-state community was growing at its expense (Weber 1958). One may argue that this development culminated during the peak of spatial Keynesianism in postwar Europe when cities and urban regions became firmly connected to the functional geographies of the nation-state (Brenner 2004). This was the era of the urban field when "the state acquired a monopoly over the making of territory" (Mezzadra & Neilson 2019: 25).

Under Fordism, the urban field united certain nationally scaled institutional mechanisms for reproducing semi-skilled labour, wage relations and forms of mass production of standardized goods and related consumption patterns (cf. Jessop 1992). Demanding a specific state-society relationship to confine capital circuits within national borders, the Fordist-national urban field was both produced by and productive of a particular kind of national state. The urban field was characterized by the central priority of the government to produce economic growth with the help of nationally scaled political structures and social welfare. It was a model of economic nationalism that was characterized by a state-led and corporatist growth model and involved a division of labour between different sectors of society as well as the state taking on an active role in bridging conflicts through a celebration of the virtues of collectivism and national integrity. The local state and the national state launched distributive planning schemes – which were based on progressive forms of income taxation and transfer payments – by positioning localities within a national place hierarchy, and by controlling the land question.

The design of the Keynesian-Fordist welfare state thus involved constituting local governments and the urban field as extensions of the national state and instituting a particular political-institutional framework centred upon municipalities. This framework increased the reliance of local government on the national state, and it consequently decreased the power of local business communities. Taken together, the state became a centralized institution located "above" localities (cf. Ferguson & Gupta 2002). The welfarist policies that characterized the nationalized urban field in the 1960s and 1970s were both growth-oriented and redistributive, and they represented a high degree of consensus among capital, unions and the leading political forces about the need for a universalistic state. So, the statification of the urban field took the form of a "national coalition" within which political projects and processes were first and foremost articulated in the name of national consensus and integrity. In so doing, the urban field in most of the Western European states represented a specific "distribution regime" based on principles of social and spatial universalism (see Esping-Andersen 1990).

The national era of the urban field was predicated on the dominance of national-scale regulation, with local governments acting as intermediaries for centrally determined policies (Brenner 2004: 152). It was a national assemblage that brought together the government, "national" yet private banks, foundations and insurance companies as well as trade unions; an assemblage that was characterized by a system of "patient" and ultimately national capital. This form of capital was also locally anchored and thus inescapably associated with the state's spatial planning agendas in which each location (town, city or even village) was viewed as having a particular position in the national hierarchy of places.

The construction of the national urban field involved the nationalization of finance and production and the subsequent rise of "national industries" that operated under the guidance of "national money" and the complicit banking sector. The political economy of the Keynesian state was associated with demand-side interventionism and welfarist social policies (see Peck 2002) that operated on the basis of nationally scaled political mindsets and a nationally scaled public sector.

During the Keynesian-Fordist era, economic value creation in urban space was tightly bound to urban land uses. The national and local state coordinated the economic value creation through urban land with various regulative mechanisms, and in so doing sought to restrict all kinds of speculative operations of capital. At the same time, the logistical operations of capital in the urban field were ultimately bound to physical infrastructures, such as roads, rails, bridges and electricity systems, which enabled the circulation of commodity capital, for instance.

THE URBAN FIELD IN THE AGE OF NATIONAL COMPETITIVENESS

The Fordist mode of accumulation began to unravel in the 1970s and was gradually replaced by "flexible" processes dealing with labour, finance and production. Ever since, with circuits of capital no longer confined within state borders, the post-Fordist regime of accumulation has hastened the geographical mobility of financial capital and highlighted city entrepreneurialism, information and communications technologies, and the role of skilled labour in the generation of economic value (Jessop & Sum 2006).

From the 1980s onwards, the transformation of the urban field has had a productive relationship with the idea of fierce global inter-spatial competition. This idea is customarily articulated with the notion of international competitiveness of states, regions and cities. In the OECD (Organisation for Economic Co-operation and Development) world, the discourse of national competitiveness emerged in the 1980s when the notion of competitiveness shifted from reflections on how to manage a firm to reflections on how to govern the state (Fougner 2006: 165). Today, competitiveness is often presented both as the primary goal of state policies and as a means of resolving the problems that confront the state. This form of political reasoning dominates political and economic discussions in the contemporary world order; it has been celebrated by international business and also promoted by state governments (see also Laffey & Weldes 2005) prior to and after the global stagnation that broke out in 2008 (Summers 2016). Since the late 1980s, the competitiveness problem, therefore, has become a key policy concern that permeates the entire policy-making field in the advanced capitalist states. This has resulted in increasingly selective state strategies that seek to connect the territorial state to the global spaces of money capital, talent, innovations and ideas.

Neil Brenner points out how "it is no longer capital that is to be molded into the territorially integrated geography of state space, but state space that is to be molded into the territorially differentiated geography of capital" (Brenner 2004: 16). Bolting the state to the global geography of capital through cities has been a notable phenomenon. The rise of the post-Fordist economy has hence been defined by the growing importance of cities in the accumulation process that occurs through global value chains. The increased power of financialization and the heightened role of consumption have also heightened the role of urban spaces in the global accumulation of capital. Moreover, as contemporary techno-capitalism requires an intensive extra-economic management of the workforce by the state in terms of social reproduction and skills production, the post-Fordist regime of accumulation as a particular type of governmentality has been characterized by a qualitatively novel entanglement between the urban field and the state's entrepreneurial strategies (e.g. in the field of education, see Pyyry & Sirviö 2023).

The making of "international competitiveness" as the ultimate governmental problem and concern has since the late 1980s brought the urban field closer to neoliberal rationalities and governmentalities. The ongoing attempts of state authorities, as well as local and regional authorities, to sell and market their locations as innovative environments for economic value creation and profit-making is a testament of this process. This process denotes an active production of polity for effective economic competition, or a penetration of market rationalities to the practices of the state itself (Cowen & Smith 2009). In this rationalization, both the national and the local states must reconstruct themselves in market terms. The corporatization of the urban field thus displays a will to generate the state increasingly as an enterprise association; that is, as a purpose-governed community (Cotton 2000: 155) promoting the instrumentalization of its own activities and structures with the aim of creating a competition state (Cerny 2003: 216).

Over the past decade, state apparatuses across different geographical contexts have become increasingly oriented towards facilitating capital accumulation for the most internationalized investors, regardless of their nationality. In this process, the urban field has been closely constituted in and intertwined with the global logistical functions of techno-capitalism, hence resulting in its peculiar transnationalization. The corporatized state operates through a dual logic in this context. On the one hand, it is charged with stepping aside and setting the stage for market functions, but on the other hand, the state needs to be active in creating an optimal business climate, foster competition within society and "behave as a competitive entity in global politics" (Harvey 2005: 79).

During the past two decades, we have not witnessed the rebirth of city-states but rather what can be understood as the strategic urbanization of the state and the concomitant corporatization of the urban field. This process highlights the importance of large cities and dense urban spaces in particular in the reworking of capitalist states as economic territories, in terms of common national interest (Moisio 2018a).

Since the 1980s, the qualitative transformation of the state towards an entrepreneurial form characterized by supply-side policies, together with a widely shared understanding of the role of the state as a facilitator of economic processes, involved significant urban transformations that became both constituents and expressions of broader processes of neoliberalization of space (cf. Brenner & Theodore 2002). The shift in focus from an emphasis on national champion firms to national champion cities (Crouch & Le Galès 2012) is a good example.

Growth-first based competitiveness reasoning – coupled with the imperative of inter-spatial competition – has not only touched upon changes in the ways in which states are governed and organized spatially. Cities, too, are shifting from the entrepreneurialization of governance (Harvey 1989b) to an entrepreneurialization of urban living (Rossi 2017; see also Hardt & Negri 2000), up to the present-day corporatization of the urban field that we investigate in this book. This form of corporatization seeks to harness urban social life for the extraction of value, and results in a massive economization of the urban field. Pre- and post-Covid developments have intensified the entanglement and co-constitution of corporatized "tech-cities" and the corporatized state. In this context, the urban field has emerged both as a site for economic investment in innovation districts (incubators, accelerators, co-working spaces, etc.) and as an arena for the rise of a governmental rationality constitutive of and shaped by the culture of urban techno-capitalism (Cirolia & Harber 2021; Kayanan 2021; Pollio 2020). The urban tech-driven economy has become a central concern in the political agendas of national states and cities across the globe (Pollio & Rossi 2024; Zukin 2020).

Despite being commonly overlooked in mainstream analyses of tech-driven economic processes, the engagement of the national and local state actors in the techno-capitalist economy has become increasingly manifest in global trajectories of "startup urbanism", especially in aspiring startup hubs in the global periphery (McNeill 2021; Rossi & Di Bella 2017). In both emerging and wealthier economies across the globe, policy initiatives now build on the assumption that organizing knowledge-intensive businesses and human capital into urbanized innovation systems is a guarantee of an increase in their economic value (Drucker, Kayanan &Renski 2019; Katz & Wagner 2014; Wagner, Katz & Osha 2019).

In tech-driven economies, capital largely stands in a position of externality to the social relations that are behind economic value generation, but at the same time is eager to enable the realization of this value through the abstraction of financial metrics or the incorporation of its human capital as fully as possible into the new economy (Hardt & Negri 2009: 142). It is in this interstitial space that the state "intervenes", acting as a facilitative gatekeeper, fertilizer and mediator between corporate investors and urban society through a variety of technologies of urban valuation that enable the organization, measurement, calculation and representation of the urban field and its potential.

In the age of urban techno-monopoly, the state acting as an urban valuation engine pursues an activity of persuasion and ingratiation with corporate investors and local stakeholders that varies according to place-specific institutional conditions, governance structures, local cultures of capitalism and urban imaginaries. The characteristics of ingratiation tactics aimed at attracting corporate investors also depend on the positionality of cities and metropolitan areas within the larger economic development landscape of contemporary globalization (Sheppard 2002). The heterogeneity of these processes, therefore, reflects existing conditions of uneven development within and among cities and regions.

DESIGNING THE FINNISH NATION-STATE AS A DIGITAL SPACE

As we have discussed in Chapter 1, the state – both as a competition state and as a corporatized state – has contributed to the global expansion of capital through the governmentalization of the urban field, and in so doing has shaped the overall development of urban social structures and the lifeworld. A shift from the visible and normative interventions of the competition state to the more performative governmentalities of the contemporary corporatized state is hence ultimately connected to the urban field. In the context of the corporatized state, the urban field involves both states and corporate actors in a complex relationship. In other words, the corporatization of the urban field and the corporatized state are co-constituted. In the age of techno-monopoly power, the state contributes to the production of the urban field as an entrepreneurial, financialized and increasingly digitalized domain. The power of the state is thus productive of the corporatization of the urban field in a historically contingent manner. As such, the urban field is an effect of political strategies and governmental rationalities.

Since the 1990s, the ideological path on which the Finnish state has come to depend on technology and entrepreneurialism has been predicated upon a particular narrative of globalization as an instigator of severe risks, threats and possibilities alike for the nation-state. In the early 1990s, a key symbol of this concern was the domestication of the idea of "national innovation system" (NIS, originally an idea formed in the context of the OECD, see Godin 2009) at the high state level (see Miettinen 2002; Sharif 2006). Ever since, the technology-centred view of Finland has been about seeing and understanding the present condition of the "welfare state" in terms of a "crisis" that is then used to legitimize state transformation.

In this section, we argue that in the contemporary context the nation-state has played a fundamental role in generating technological framework conditions for the urban field and the related operations of technology capital. At the same time, the technology industry has been increasingly entwined with the activities of the nation-state. We illustrate this argument with a brief analysis of the development in Finland as a digital space after the global economic turmoil that broke out in 2008.

In Finland, the formation of the corporatized state has proceeded in tandem with emphasis on economic competitiveness, economic efficiency and entrepreneurialization. The most recent government programme by Prime Minister Petteri Orpo (Finnish Government 2023) effectively confirms the trend that has continued already for nearly two decades. The consecutive two governments elected during the post-2008 recession years, together with the centre-left government of Sanna Marin (2019–23), all placed high hopes on innovation-based policies of economic growth. In fact, all the government programmes since 2007 place technology-driven competitiveness and entrepreneurship as the pivot of national success and survival. This is hardly surprising given that since the 1990s the gradual neoliberalization of Finland has been characteristically a technocratic process whereby technological knowledge, and the whole techno-industrial complex, has assumed a crucial role. Indeed, the government programmes of 2011 and 2015 are premised on the idea of constructing a new state that would embrace technology-intensive development and productivity across social spheres. In 2011, Prime Minister Jyrki Katainen's programme (centre-right National Coalition Party and the Social Democratic Party as the leading groupings) rested fundamentally on the idea of building a link between entrepreneurship, education, technology and innovation. The latter, a highly technocratic government consisting of the centre-right Centre Party, the National Coalition and the national revanchist Finns Party, made a similarly pervasive connection between the culture of entrepreneurship, the nation's innovation and technological capacity, policy experimentation and education as central means to foster national competitiveness and economic growth.

The following quotes from the government programmes and implementation plans in 2011 and 2015 reveal a great deal of the dominant political rationality of entrepreneurialism during the post-2008 recession years in Finland:

> Links between education and the working life, and employee and entrepreneurship education providing information about the rights and obligations of citizens, employees and entrepreneurs will be enhanced at all levels of education … Efforts will be made to increase interest in and preparedness for entrepreneurship by means of training at various levels of education.
> (Programme of the Jyrki Katainen Government of Finland 2011: 65)

> Expertise is not being converted into innovations, innovations are not commercialised. We are losing our expertise-based competitive edge. We must set people's resources free to engage in creative activity, entrepreneurship … Finland must become a society founded on know-how, entrepreneurship, equality and caring.
> (Programme of the Juha Sipilä Government of Finland 2015: 8)

> Experimentation will aim at innovative solutions, improvements in services, the promotion of individual initiative and entrepreneurship …
> (Programme of the Juha Sipilä Government of Finland 2015: 28)

The entrepreneurial language that is at the core of the corporatized state and that is customarily associated with technology-centred startup economies is highly visible in all the government programmes since 2011. The programme of the Juha Sipilä's "austerity government" (2015–19), for instance, explicitly articulates that in order to "enhance the funding, equity capital and risk-taking capacity of businesses, the government will implement measures that will impact the needs of startups, fast-growth companies, and change-of generation businesses" (*ibid.*: 10). In summary, in the formulations of the government programmes and their implementation plans since 2011, the technology-centred economic imaginary emerges as a fundamental political strategy of the state, as well as a broad cultural political agenda to bring about societal change within and beyond the state apparatus.

From the perspective of the urban anchoring of corporatized state strategies, it is notable that the latest governments have sought to promote a change in the role of local states in the future, "from an arranger of services to increasingly a promoter of vitality, entrepreneurship and employment" (Programme of the Juha Sipilä Government of Finland 2015: 32). Juha Sipilä's government used the language of "ecosystems" rather than cities in spatializing innovation-based economic growth. The "ecosystem forum model" (Implementation Plan of the Government of Finland 2018: 47) was nonetheless a revealing example of how economic growth at the scale of the state was understood as being firmly rooted in the urban field. In sum, the last four governments in Finland have built a peculiar link between the future of the nation-state, education, technology, entrepreneurialism, internationalization and innovation. This has implicitly signified an increasingly pervasive urban anchoring of the future of the Finnish nation-state.

But the process has been highly uneven spatially, as Figure 2.2 demonstrates. In 2019, 49.8 per cent of all the private and public investments in research and development concentrated in Finland into one of the 19 provinces, and into the capital city-region more specifically. The research and development expenditures are over ten times higher per capita in the Helsinki city-region than in the lagging regions. This uneven geographical development is important given that intangible investments such as research and development have become important to the national economies across different geographical contexts, especially during the post-2008 recovery (Haskel & Westlake 2022: 43). In general, therefore, the role of the state in the spatially uneven distribution of resources is an important phenomenon that merits attention in an analysis of the urban field in the context of the corporatized state.

One notable dimension in the recent four government programmes in Finland has been the tendency to approach state functions primarily as service commodities. This commodifying perspective is enabled through the imaginary of integrated "digital state architecture" and the different market-emulating constructions built to support it. Since 2011, digitalization has denoted the possibility of integrating the singular local information societies of the state into one coherent service platform, a sort of digital service state (Ahlqvist & Moisio 2014).

The digital service state is about building a close alliance between technology capital, the nation-state and the local state. It can be understood as the turn to "dataist statecraft" that facilitates "a corporate reconstruction of the state" (Fourcade & Gordon 2020). The digital service state is ultimately

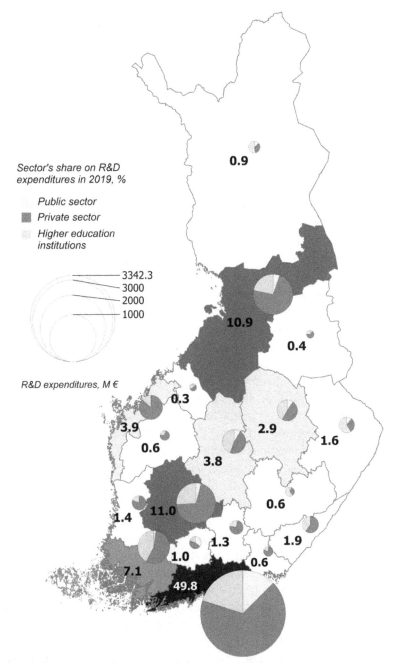

Figure 2.2 Research and development expenditure in Finland across economic sectors and regions

Source: prepared by Heli Kurikka and reprinted with her permission.

constructed upon an idea that once the integrated state "service platform" is set up, private actors are then able to take responsibility for service provision together with the public sector. In the right-wing techno-governmental articulation in particular, this idea is supported by underlining the potentials of cost-efficiency and attainability. Moreover, this idea translates the dominant view of the transition from material industry to service industry on to the state context and imagines the state as a monopolistic entity that impedes an immense potential market (Ahlqvist & Moisio 2014). In the national digitalization process, the primary role of the state is to act as a system administrator for the digital service platform, and to function as a "grand procurer" that sets the outlines for private service provision. During the past two decades or so, the digital service state has been widely discussed, developed and furthered in Finland (e.g. Arantola 2010).

After the global economic downturn in 2008, arguments about the need to deepen and reorganize the state's digital functions have been widely acknowledged and disseminated in the key documents of numerous influential organizations in Finland; for example, the Finnish Technology Industries (Hernesniemi 2010: 24, 81, 99–100) and the Finnish Innovation Fund Sitra (Määttä 2010). The digital service state thus represents a prime example of "capillary neoliberalization": a neoliberal political perspective is endorsed yet the message is dispersed by way of the seemingly non-ideological technology- and competitiveness-centred argumentation on the future of the nation-state (Ahlqvist & Moisio 2014). As such, the digitalization of the state can be understood as a method of government "that can procure the nation's prosperity" (Foucault 2008: 13). Simultaneously, the digitalization process connects the state, its citizens and locations to technologies and tech capital: a key process in the operations of the corporatized state.

The construction of Finland as a digital space has been partly premised on an idea to open up "state functions" to market practices. One of the Finnish pro-market think tanks revealingly suggests that the spread of digital practices is creating a gap between "forerunning" and "lagging" countries (Turkki 2009: 28). "Forerunners" are those countries that have "updated" their information societies, and quickly undertake public reform by embracing ICT (e.g. Rainisto 2010). Already, more than a decade ago, this logic surfaced on the notion that the opening of public service provision would make the municipal structure not only more cost-effective but also more "fit" for integrated strategic management. In these and later debates, digitalization and digital service provision have been portrayed and articulated by the proponents of the ICT industry as means through which the state may be reconstructed as an economically efficient and flexible political entity (Leino 2009).

A key motivation for driving the idea of the digital service state is the mass of information on citizens that is currently under the public system, but with restricted access. From the perspective of digital business, this appearance of the civil society in a digital form is an untapped reservoir of business potential. Over the past decade, several actors have recommended that the state should open its masses of digital information to multiple economic uses, including business activities ranging from health to social services, security and finance.

The programme of the right-wing government of Finland elected in June 2023 is impregnated with the rhetoric of digitalization in a context of austerity imposed by the turbulent geopolitical and macroeconomic conditions. Again, digitalization appears as a "great potential" in the context of all kinds of things, ranging from governing to business. The programme states, for instance, how the "government will implement a central government productivity programme to support the government's objective of economic sustainability in public finance. The implementation of the productivity programme utilises, in particular, the potential of digitalisation to make the public sector more efficient" (Finnish Government 2023: 57). In addition to that, the corporatized state programme articulates that the "growth formula" of Finland is today and in the future increasingly connected to "data economy" and "digitalisation" (*ibid.*: 97).

This way of conceiving the future of the nation-state is in line with the contemporary work of the EU, which highlights the role of digitalization as an essential element in securing the economic and geopolitical status of the EU in the middle of fierce international competition between China/Asia, the US and the EU. As such, the EU is a significant digitalizing force in Europe and contributes to the operations of the corporatized state in Europe. For instance, the 2030 Digital Decade policy programme of the EU sets out all-embracing technological ambitions, which cover and connect skills, government, infrastructure and business in a revealing manner (Figure 2.3).

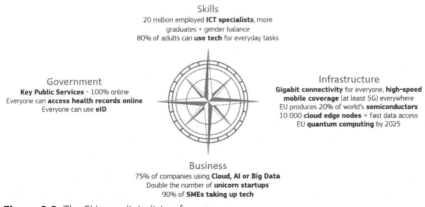

Figure 2.3 The EU as a digitalizing force
Source: European Union, 2023 European Commission, Digital Strategy.

The digitalization of the nation-state lays the technological and techno-cultural foundations for the intensification of the relationship between capital and the state in the context of the urban field. In so doing, the digitalization of the national state is one of the prerequisites for the pervasive technology-oriented processes of generating and extracting value in the urban field. It does not come as a revelation, therefore, that powerful tech firms have sought to mobilize the state, the local state, universities and various other institutions such as the EU to support the spread of algorithmic technologies.

In the Finnish context, the state has established an innovation ambassador who has been supporting the expansion of the Finnish tech service companies in the US, for instance. The Finnish experience resonates with a more general trend whereby both the explicit and implicit lobbying practices enacted by large tech firms have become salient and, one might argue, successful over the past two decades (see Chapter 1); many high officials of the state have become lobbyists for technology companies across geographical contexts. The digitalization of the state discloses broad and deep connections and contributions of the state to the expansion of techno-monopoly power, whether this is called "uberization" or something else. Today, the urban field provides the living labour, the infrastructures, services and logistical functions, the diffuse knowledge and the wide array of social interaction processes upon which contemporary technologies of information and communications and the associated capital rely. Bhagat and Phillips (2021) discuss the ways in which governments and Big Tech currently converge in the pursuit of capitalist interests, thus enabling the Big Tech to operate in the public domain. Their conception of the techfare state seeks to make visible some of the ways in which Big Tech capital evades state control and becomes entwined with the activities of the neoliberal state apparatuses both in the domains of finance and security-discipline. The digitalization of the Finnish state; that is, generating the state as a digital platform, demonstrates the same process.

CONCLUSION

The role of the state in urban techno-monopoly capitalism is a significant, albeit customarily overlooked phenomenon. In this chapter we have discussed the concept of the urban field and its connections to the operations of capital and the state. In the twentieth century, the state played a crucial role in the constitution of the urban field in the context of Fordist-Keynesian capitalism. This is equally true today at the time of urban techno-monopoly.

The Keynesian-Fordist design of the welfare state was essentially associated with the political production of the "national" urban field. During that era the state was rooted in place through extensive redistributive mechanisms that localized the state. This process was characterized, for instance, by a complex national transfer payment system between the state and municipalities and between municipalities themselves. Local governments were effectively subordinated to the national process and functioned as an extension of the nation-state in implementing welfarist policies through the "national" urban field. The tendency towards social and spatial equalization and cohesion through a balanced distribution of socioeconomic capacities through the urban field also regulated the operations of capital and constrained the extraction of economic value through the urban field. The urban field was characterized by social and economic processes related to land and the built environment and was subsumed into the nationalizing growth machine (e.g. Terhorst & Van De Ven 1995).

Within the advanced capitalist states, the state-orchestrated late-Keynesian policies of the 1980s and 1990s were increasingly structured around local competences, entrepreneurialism and technological know-how. This was a peculiar setting that brought together some of the basic tenets of spatial Keynesianism and neoliberal policies of states' international competitiveness. The rise of the discourses and policies of state international competitiveness nonetheless gradually affected the ways in which major cities, in particular, were understood as having an essential role in the production of economic competitiveness in global techno-capitalism. As the states' international competitiveness was increasingly related to inter-spatial competition between the high-tech capacities of cities, the discourses of inter-state competition contributed to the construction of entrepreneurial cities and related governance forms.

The latest phase of tech-driven capitalist restructuring has become increasingly salient not only in the foundational processes of startup economies but also in the processes of digitalizing the state. These political processes of the corporatized state disclose some of the ways in which the operations of global techno-monopoly capital and state power are intertwined in the contemporary conjuncture, showing in the last instance how the processes of corporatization of the urban field and what we call the strategic urbanization of the state (Moisio & Rossi 2020) have become mutually constitutive.

From our perspective, the state has been an active agent in the process of transforming the state into a digital form that lays the economic, cultural and logistical foundations for the operations of capital in the urban field. This discloses how – in order to extract value and exploit resources, labour, data and forms of life – capital is today in a close relationship with the state (see Mezzadra & Neilson 2019). It would be therefore misleading to assume that some sort of absence of state intervention has underpinned the technology industry's growing political-economic power in the urban field. Rather, the opposite is true. The entrepreneurial and urban nature of such a digital and tech-driven nation-state is produced in state-orchestrated processes that seek to reinvent the state as a national economic territory.

It must also be noted that, in Europe, the EU has significantly contributed to the strategic urbanization of the state during the post-recession transition since the early 2010s. The EU has been a notable engine of digitalization. As such, the strategic urbanization of the state intensified at a time in which European economic and political elites were struggling to leave behind the spectres of "secular stagnation" and related anxieties within the middle class that had become generalized with the crisis of the Eurozone and the subsequent low-growth performances of national economies. As such, the digitalization and strategic urbanization of the state can also be understood as by-products of the age of austerity in the early 2010s. The digitalization of the state, for instance, was closely associated with the promise of technology in experimenting with new ways to cut public spending. This, in turn, tied together high-tech capital and the nation-state in an intense manner. In our view, the formation of the alliance between the nation-state and the operations of techno-monopoly capital result from the active discursive construction of the "nation-state in crisis", a crisis narrative that began to take shape in the 1990s in concomitance with the rise of the internet.

By generating entrepreneurial and digital capacities and orientations of the populace through education and other governmental technologies, the state instrumentalizes urban life in the contemporary capitalist conjuncture in the name of "national interest". Today's corporatized "startup state" (Moisio & Rossi 2020) not only valorizes urban environments as interactional economic contexts, but also rearticulates national welfare and societal expectations of prosperity in terms of an all-embracing entrepreneurial tech economy and its associated production of value. The realities of high-tech economies in the urban field show a qualitatively transformed role of the state, one which goes beyond the conventional "direct intervention versus coordination" dichotomy associated with Keynesian and neoliberal approaches to the governance of economic development, respectively.

Finally, the reworking of the urban field in late techno-capitalism has also contributed to the spatial reconstruction of the nation-state as the corporatized state. During the past few decades, the state has hence figured prominently in the constitution of the economized urban field that differs from the Keynesian era marked by the construction of the spatially consolidated welfare state and urban managerialism. In short, the state has become central to the contemporary creation and extraction of economic value through the urban field that is increasingly forged by techno-monopoly power.

PART II

MICRO-POLITICAL ECONOMY OF THE URBAN FIELD

CHAPTER 3

LABOUR

INTRODUCTION

The advent of the platform economy with the eruption and rapid growth of digital platforms and related technology-based economic forms since the early 2010s has revived the political and scholarly interest in cities and urban areas as reservoirs of an economically undervalued service workforce. Despite their devaluation, service workers provide goods and services that are crucial to the pursuit of individual and societal well-being in today's capitalist societies. The outbreak of the Covid-19 pandemic in 2020 and the multiple crises that have followed it have further deepened the perception that contemporary societies increasingly depend on a reserve of low-paid, overworked "essential workers", or "key workers", as they have been variously defined during the emergency phases of lockdowns and sanitary restrictions. These workers not only provide crucial goods and services, but their presence is ubiquitous across the economic sectors, starting with health, food, transport, environmental services and education.

The notion of gig workers and that of essential or key workers are distinct but complementary in significant manners. The term "gig workers" refers to people working on a part-time basis for online platforms and other tech-based economic entities. These labourers are characterized by the fact of being in a variety of casual employment relationships, as they can be recruited as independent contractors, as temporary staff or in other mixed arrangements such as freelance and on-call workers. In terms of income, gig workers are among the worst-paid service workers, as several analyses have shown (e.g. Zipperer *et al*. 2022). For their part, essential workers, and the sub-group of "essential critical infrastructure workers", as they have been defined by the Federal Government in the US during the pandemic, are "those who conduct a range of operations and services in industries that are essential to ensure the continuity of critical functions" (https://www.cdc.gov/vaccines/covid-19/categories-essential-workers.html).

Gig workers and many of the essential/key workers are frontline workers, which means that their work entails continuous interaction with the general public as either customers or recipients of their services. Unlike gig workers, essential/key workers are likely to be regularly employed with permanent or full-time contracts, even though their working conditions can be challenging and their wages can be low compared with more "valued" professions and jobs in today's capitalist society.

Even though the Covid-19 pandemic has brought to light the condition of both gig workers and essential/key workers in unprecedented ways, service interactional workers had already attracted the attention of public and scholarly debates in previous decades. Frontline service workers came to the fore of public debates in the 1990s with the global diffusion of the fast-food industry (KFC, McDonald's and the like), which reached countries such as Russia and China that had just opened their doors to foreign investment (Rossi 2017). At that time, routinization, deskilling, strict management control, casualization and low wages were seen as defining characteristics of service workers (Leidner 1993). In subsequent years, the rapid growth of retail chains characterized by physically large stores, such as Walmart in the US or H&M and Zara in Europe and globally, gave another major impulse to the expansion of low-paying jobs in the service sector (Ehrenreich 2002).

In many respects, service workers employed in chain stores and restaurants can be seen as precursors to gig workers, particularly those in the food delivery industry, which started proliferating in the mid-2010s. One important difference is that the former are sedentary in their workplace, while the latter are moving across urban space, with all the implications and experiences in terms of engagement with the urban environment. Another significant difference is their contractual condition, as traditional service workers are normally hired as employees, although often on a part-time basis, while gig workers are customarily recruited as "independent contractors".

The abovementioned differences aside, all these kinds of service workers, such as retail chain workers, gig workers and essential/key workers, are largely coincident with what Richard Florida in his bestselling book on *The Rise of the Creative Class* defined as "the service class", which he distinguished from the knowledge-intensive "creative class" as well as from the "working class" employed in the manufacturing sector (Florida 2012). In his book, Richard Florida associates the service class with "low-end, typically low-wage and low-autonomy occupations", such as "food-service workers, janitors and groundskeepers, personal care attendants, secretaries and clerical workers, and security guards" (Florida 2012: 47). All these occupations are absolutely central in maintaining and reproducing the contemporary urban field and its populace. Even though Florida expresses his regret at their hard working conditions, Florida views the inferiorized status of the service class as inevitable, as members of this class are not part of the innovation-driving "creative class" made up of "talented people", which is the focus of his apologetic analysis of the post-Fordist era.

As Richard Shearmur has argued in one of the most incisive critiques of Richard Florida's creative-class thesis, this selective view has a specific policy implication; that is, redesigning urban social welfare at the service of its professional elites:

> The "creative class" must necessarily be constituted in opposition to a "non-creative class". This other class – which, according to Florida, comprises about 70 per cent of the population – is not addressed by his theory. The notion of "creative class" immediately raises the issue of this class's interests – interests that Florida actively encourages cities and regions to promote. The message that he sends to municipal and regional politicians and policy-makers is that cities should modify their local policies, their planning and their budget, in order to respond to the preferences of this creative class. Given that by definition this class comprises those people best suited to succeed in the "new" or "knowledge" economy – the knowledge aristocracy – this message boils down to saying that municipalities and regions should reinforce and subsidise their elites. Such "talent welfare" is reminiscent of "corporate welfare" policies relied upon by certain jurisdictions to attract companies. (Shearmur 2006–07: 36–7)

Similarly to Richard Florida, Enrico Moretti – another popular urban economist – in his bestseller *The New Geography of Jobs* briefly mentions what he defines as "service workers with limited education", only to demonstrate "the multiplier effect" of the booming high-tech economy, namely the fact that service workers cluster around high-tech workers, with the former supporting the personal needs of the latter (Moretti 2012). The exclusive association of talent and knowledge with an elite of creative or highly educated people and the emphasis placed on the "clustering of talent" in urban places as a condition for societal prosperity and affluence has been the influential message conveyed by mainstream urban economists to politicians and policy-makers over the last two decades or so. And their message has been heard globally.

This chapter aims to challenge urban economists' utterly elitist conception of the technology-based economy, arguing that this conception offers a political justification for the large income and wage inequalities and the consequent wealth polarization that exist within and among cities in present-day techno-capitalist economies. In doing so, we continue subverting the common understanding of the capitalist economy in an age of techno-monopoly. In order to go beyond a merely ethical stance towards the rights and the status of service workers in contemporary techno-monopoly capitalism, this chapter will delve into an analysis of the role of human labour in the generation of economic value in technology-based economies. In doing so, the chapter offers an expansive, pluralistic understanding of "knowledge labour" in the urban field, which also includes purportedly low-skill service workers. The purpose of the proposed approach is to overcome the conventional distinction between manual and knowledge workers, between low-skill and high-skill workers, which in our view is at the origin of today's social inequalities and human labour's exploitative conditions.

LABOUR AS SOURCE OF ECONOMIC VALUE

This chapter is concerned with the role of human labour in the generation of modes of economic value extraction that are grounded in the social fabric of cities and urban spaces at a time of advanced technology-based transformation of their economies and societies, within the context of what we define as "techno-monopoly capitalism". Human labour is the source of economic value creation and extraction in a capitalist society. Each of the founders of modern political economy, such as the physiocrats, Adam Smith and David Ricardo, as well as their main critic, Karl Marx, formulated their own understanding of the so-called "labour theory of value" (Pitts 2021; Roll 2002). While the physiocrats looked at the materiality of labour in the agriculture sector, Smith, Ricardo and Marx focused their attention on the manufacturing industry as a crucial sector of the emerging capitalist economy. Marx moved forward in the debate, by calling attention to the analysis of "abstract labour" founded on the production of exchange values that are characteristic of a capitalist society, rather than of merely "concrete labour" associated with particular activities and the production of use values. Smith, Ricardo and Marx had in common the fact of viewing labour as the determinant of the value of a commodity in a capitalist economy. Marx explicitly linked the labour theory of value to capitalist exploitation, which occurs through the extraction of a surplus value and its monetary realization in the form of profit (Roll 2002).

The recent technology-based transformation of contemporary economies has re-enlivened discussions over labour-based theorizations of value in heterodox economic thinking, after a long dominance of subjective, market-based interpretations of value centred on the marginal utility of a good or service for consumers, advocated by mainstream economists. Since the early 2000s, the rise of web 2.0 based on user-generated content and digital interfaces and the subsequent platformization of techno-capitalism have deepened the crisis of standard measurements of labour value, as capitalist production has increasingly come to rely on socialized mechanisms of value creation. These mechanisms are largely external to the capitalist firm and its research and development divisions. The fact that the line between production and consumption is increasingly blurred in today's business practice is now common wisdom in management studies as well as in sociological analyses of contemporary capitalism (Kornberger 2010; Ritzer, Dean & Jurgenson 2012). The evidence shows that the entanglement of production with consumption has now become an important source of innovation in the capitalist system. Recent research in business studies, for instance, has found that online user-generated content has positive effects on both the initiation and completion of product-development activities (Ho-Dac 2020).

The idea that the production of economic value exceeds the conventional sphere of the capitalist firm and its value chains is now well accepted. The advent of the so-called "platform revolution" has further extended the extra-firm creation and extraction of economic value, as platform business multiplies mechanisms of value production through the network effects it generates. It does so mainly by reducing the friction and barriers between producers and consumers, or through other mechanisms that create "sources of excess value", as platform companies are known for generating more value than they capture (Parker, Van Alstyne & Choudary 2016). This excess of value is symptomatic of the larger difficulties in measuring the value of things in today's capitalist world and, more particularly, in commensuration of economic value with calculable measurements not only of human labour as such, but of human activity more broadly understood. In the digital sphere, the creation and capture of economic value exceed the conventional labour process in production. Through online platforms, in particular, technology corporations allocate underpaid or unpaid tasks to the users of their services, employing the data obtained from the interaction with users to the production of artificial intelligence and machine learning operations (Casilli & Posada 2019).

In the next section of this chapter, we will revisit contemporary debates about the crisis of the conventionally firm-centred labour theory of value. These debates will then lead us to discuss current forms of labour exploitation in techno-monopoly capitalism. Along with other low-paid frontline workers, gig workers, which will be analysed in the third section of this chapter, are a living proof of the expanding and qualitatively changing conditions of exploitation of labour power in contemporary techno-capitalism.

THE QUANDARIES OF VALUE MEASURABILITY

In recent times, two main lines of heterodox economic thinking have interrogated the problem of value measurement in contemporary techno-capitalism. On the one hand, the post-Marxist strand of so-called "autonomist" thought (also known as *operaismo*: for a brief introduction to this body of thought, see Nigro 2018) has put forth a radical thesis about the crisis of the measurability of value based on labour in post-Fordist capitalist economies. On the other hand, the work of Mariana Mazzucato – the economist known for her "entrepreneurial state" thesis (see also Chapter 2) – has raised important questions regarding the distinction between value creation and extraction in contemporary capitalism.

"Autonomist" theorists have reinterpreted Karl Marx's visionary concept of the "general intellect", which he briefly exposed in his "Fragment on machines" as part of the *Grundrisse* manuscript, where he maintained that "knowledge has become a direct force of production" (Marx 1973: 706). Karl Marx believed that the value of knowledge is embodied in what he defined as "constant capital", which comprises fixed assets such as machinery and other physical means of production that can be considered "dead labour" (Harvey 2018). Autonomist theorists have amended Marx's idea of the general intellect by emphasizing the knowledge value of living labour (Virno 1996). According to these scholars, along with the dead labour embodied in machines and other commodities, labourers' performative actions and linguistic faculties incessantly nourish the general intellect, particularly in their relationships of collaboration with other workers, as it can be seen more clearly in post-Fordist settings of collaborative production. In this perspective, single-work operations alone are insufficient to measure the socially necessary labour time – the source of value in Marx's thought – to produce goods and services in contemporary knowledge-based capitalist societies (Marazzi 2008).

"How can you measure the value of an idea, an image, or a relationship?", ask Michael Hardt and Antonio Negri in their theorization of the emergence of "immaterial labour" in post-Fordist societies (Hardt & Negri 2009: 270). Immaterial labour has been a key concept in the Marxist autonomist strand of thinking, especially in the 1990s and the 2000s. Interestingly, the notion of immaterial labour is not confined by these authors to a particular set of high-skill workers, such as the "symbolic analysts" (Reich 1992), the "knowledge workers" (Bell 1976; Drucker 1969), or the members of "the creative class" (Florida 2012) identified by mainstream interpreters of the "knowledge turn" in capitalist economies.

Management consultant Peter Drucker was probably the first author to neatly anticipate the rise of knowledge work, in the late 1960s, heralding the advent of an economic order in which – as he put it later – "knowledge, not labour or raw material or capital, is the key resource" (Drucker 1994: 53). Economic analysts such as Drucker and Robert Reich have looked at knowledge supplanting traditional economic units as the main source of economic value generation, including labour and capital. But their writings also interestingly disclose the deeply political and even geopolitical nature of the value creation process with regard to different segments of labour in the technology-based economy (Moisio 2018a). Writing in the early 1990s, Reich (1992), in particular, anticipated that the rise of the global technology-based economy would result in deepening social divisions between high-skill professionals (what he calls "symbolic analysts") and low-skill workers (what he calls routine production workers and in-person service workers). In his view, these divisions emanate from the capacities of different segments of the labour force to generate economic value in the global economy. Accordingly, Reich believes that this new divide leads to the fragmentation of nations, as "those citizens best positioned to thrive in the world market are tempted to slip the bonds of national allegiance, and by so doing disengage themselves from their less favoured fellows" (Reich 1992: 3).

For their part, since the 1990s, Marxist autonomist authors have highlighted the emergence of affective and cognitive labour in the post-Fordist economy and its unexplored potential for radical politics (Virno & Hardt 1996). In doing so, these authors have not opposed knowledge to labour and capital, but have interpreted the advent of "cognitive capitalism" (Moulier Boutang 2011) as a qualitatively advanced articulation of the capitalist rationality of value creation and extraction. Their usage of the notion of immaterial *labour* is indicative of this approach. For them, the distinctive trait of immaterial labour is the fact of "involving a series of activities that are not normally recognised as 'work'" and are customarily associated with work in creative industries (Lazzarato 1996: 132). In putting forward this notion, these authors emphasize the fact that immaterial labour should not only be associated with conventionally understood high-skill workers, as many of the mainstream authors believe. In his seminal book *The Age of Discontinuity* published in 1969, Peter Drucker explicitly opposed knowledge workers to manual workers, writing that "the new industries differ from the traditional 'modern' industry in that they will employ predominantly knowledge workers rather than manual workers" (Drucker 1969: 37).

On the contrary, as Lazzarato underlines, present-day immaterial labour tends to comprise manual work too, as this latter "is increasingly coming to involve procedures that could be defined as 'intellectual' and the new communications technologies increasingly require subjectivities that are rich in knowledge" (Lazzarato 1996: 133). As we have anticipated, this expansive and inclusive understanding of immaterial labour is crucial to the goal of this chapter, which will bring to the fore the knowledge value of labour in the platform economy and of service workers in general. In doing so, the chapter aims to challenge the commonly held assumptions that are behind today's job polarization and related wage inequalities between high-skilled knowledge workers performing non-routine cognitive tasks and the supposedly lesser-skilled workers performing routinized tasks (Goos & Manning 2003).

The second line of thinking on the theory of value that is worth engaging with here is represented by the work of Mariana Mazzucato, a leading exponent in the field of the economics of innovation. After having published a highly successful book titled *The Entrepreneurial State* (Mazzucato 2013) in which she demanded attention on the overlooked state contribution to the rise of the highly celebrated technology-intensive commodities and related districts in the US (see Chapter 1), Mazzucato wrote a more theoretically informed book published with the eloquent title *The Value of Everything: Making and Taking in the Global Economy* (Mazzucato 2018).

In the *Value of Everything* Mazzucato begins her analysis by lamenting that interrogations over the value of what we consume have disappeared from public and scholarly debates alike. In her opinion, the main culprit for this obliteration is mainstream neoclassical economics, which has long conflated values with the fluctuating prices on the market. As a result, mainstream neoclassical economics is no longer concerned with the substantive questions that animated classical economic inquiry, namely the sources of economic value creation. Management studies, for their part, are – according to Mazzucato – more eager to deal with these issues. However, their analyses grapple with economic value measurement, concentrating on issues such as shareholder value and capital market valuation from a perspective of accounting and business finance, while avoiding an interrogation of the foundations of the value-creating process.

According to Mazzucato, to disentangle the long-debated "enigma of value" (Napoleoni 1998) and its specificity in today's technology-based capitalism, "we need to examine where value comes from in the first place" (Mazzucato 2018: 62). This implies asking the following key question: "What exactly is it that is being extracted?" Mazzucato herself answers this question by distinguishing between "value creation" and "value extraction" as follows:

> By "value creation" I mean the ways in which different types of resources (human, physical and intangible) are established and interact to produce new goods and services. By "value extraction" I mean activities focused on moving around existing resources and outputs and gaining disproportionately from the ensuing trade. (Mazzucato 2018: 16)

Mazzucato's definition is relevant to the discussion here on the value of human labour in the current conjuncture of techno-monopoly capitalism and the urban field. In her book, Mazzucato explicitly applies her propositions and theoretical formulations to the variety of economic forms that are dominating contemporary capitalist economies: sharing economy, platform economy, experience economy and the like. These economic forms are characterized, in her view, by the fact of "moving around existing resources and outputs, and gaining disproportionately from the ensuing trade", rather than "producing new goods and services" (*ibid*.: 16). Evoking David Ricardo's conception of rent extraction associated with the rise of an unproductive class of rentiers (see also Christophers 2022), Mazzucato argues that the latter are unproductive "takers" (rentiers) of economic value being created by the "makers" of the global economy. Hence, the unproductive takers of the platform economy represent a parasitic economic power that is evocative of the forced appropriation of surplus products imposed by feudal lords on producers to satisfy their unproductive consumption (Mazzucato 2018: 54).

Mazzucato's thesis resonates with ongoing debates in the public sphere about the parasitic tendencies of the high-tech giants that have taken the lead in contemporary capitalism, giving rise to a new era of so-called "techno-feudalism" (Dean 2020; Kotkin 2020; Varoufakis 2023). The emphasis that this author along with a growing number of commentators on the academic left place on the predatory nature of platform capitalism functions as a powerful force of social criticism directed towards tech giants' monopolistic practices of economic value extraction. However, Mazzucato's representation of the contemporary economy as polarized between takers and makers requires a critical appraisement. The main question here is the following: is Mazzucato's association of value creation with "producing" and of value extraction with "moving around" tenable at a time of supply chain capitalism? In the social sciences, since the 1980s a growing number of authors have exposed how the logistical fix brought on by supply chain capitalism has radically transformed the geographies of circulation, production and consumption, turning logistics into a key value-adding activity in all economic sectors (Coe & Yeung 2015; Danyluk 2018; Mezzadra & Neilson 2019). From a logistical perspective, the fixity and motion of capital accumulation are interdependent and at the same time contradictory processes in the global circulation of capital, as critical theorists in geography and sociology have long argued (Brenner 1998; Harvey 1985b). Proponents of the "logistical approach" in particular argue that the property control of the infrastructures that allow the dialectics of fixity and motion in contemporary extractivist capitalism – from data storage to conventional logistical infrastructures, such as ports and supply value chains – is at the centre of present-day rent extraction and the current conditions of labour exploitation in capitalist economies (Arboleda & Purcell 2021).

Expanding on the latter proposition, this chapter looks more closely at the defining characteristics of labour exploitation in the logistics-led, consumption-based urban economy and particularly in the platform economy. In doing so, the chapter aims to shed light on the overlooked dimension of cognitive and affective extraction in this form of human labour that is customarily represented as merely manual labour, thus implicitly justifying its devaluation (low wages and precarious employment) in the contemporary economy. In this vein, it is argued that property relations impinge not only on the access to corporate-owned digital platforms but also on the platform-mediated control and subsumption of the knowledge value and relational abilities embodied in the urban labour force at large. In today's techno-monopoly capitalism, the urban labour force can be seen as a collective body functioning as a repository of the circulation of knowledge, relationalities and capacities to cooperate that traverse urban space. However, the fact that mainstream theorists of contemporary techno-capitalism, who are highly influential among policy-makers and the mass media, assign knowledge value only to a restricted class of high-skill workers has the effect of devaluing workers in the platform economy. This same process of devaluation has arguably affected other service sectors, including the essential frontline workers that the Covid-19 pandemic has brought to the fore of public debates in recent years.

EXPLOITING LABOUR POWER IN TECHNO-CAPITALISM

Within the contemporary scenario of techno-monopoly capitalism, the exploitation of labour power can be seen through two lenses. A classic lens in critical economic thinking looks at the differential dynamics of surplus value extraction from human labour. In his critique of political economy, Karl Marx famously theorized the extraction of surplus value from the labour process as a key driver of capital accumulation. According to Marx, capitalists pursue the extraction of surplus value in two ways. On the one hand, "absolute surplus value" is obtained through the prolongation of the working day beyond the labour time necessary to the existence of the worker, or by increasing the intensification of labour. On the other hand, "relative surplus value" is obtained by reducing the cost of labour power through the increased productivity of sectors that produce the means of subsistence for the workers; or, it is obtained by reducing the individual value of certain commodities through technical improvements, thus stimulating inter-firm competition in the same economic sector (Marx 2004: ch. 16).

In his work, David Harvey has pointed to the continued exploitation of labour power, as it was described and conceptualized by Marx, across the different stages of capitalist history. According to Harvey, recent decades have seen even the recrudescence of labour exploitation in the capitalist economy, as what he terms "the neoliberal counterrevolution" has pursued more vulnerable workforces through the relentless expansion of globalization (Harvey 2018). In the last decade, the advent of "platform capitalism" (Srnicek 2017) and its monopolization by a handful of technology corporations, or what we call here "techno-monopoly capitalism", has even exacerbated this trend. The main manifestation of techno-monopoly capitalism has been the rise of the platform economy in the urban field, an on-demand economy that relies on formally freelance, underpaid and highly casualized workers. The resulting phenomenon of gig workers shows how classic forms of surplus value extraction have resurged in techno-monopoly capitalism. In this form of capitalism, the reduction of the cost of labour and the instrumentalization of technological innovations for surveillance and control purposes are defining features of the labour process.

Despite the evident exploitative conditions, in the early stages of the rise of the platform economy, the corporate rhetoric openly sought to persuade the wider public that working for app-based platforms should be seen as a kind of post-work experience, guaranteeing higher autonomy and flexibility to workers and an enjoyable time at work. This was the positive and even progressive image of the platform economy in its early stages. In an interview published in November 2015, when the digital food delivery industry was in its infancy, the CEO of a leading company in this key sector of the platform economy told *Business Insider* that he delivered food himself daily for the first ten months of the company's history and that even after the company's success he was still occasionally doing it on the weekends: "I do it for fitness and because it's fun", he said (Edwards 2015). This kind of post-work rhetoric on fun jobs in happy cities has never totally vanished, but it has had to come to terms with an increasingly widespread contestation of the actual materiality of gig work. Controversies around gig work began in late 2015 when protests of underpaid couriers erupted for the first time in London and shortly after in other cities in many national contexts. In December 2015, *The Guardian* published its first article highlighting the harsh working conditions in this economic sector (Stern 2015). In subsequent years, labour activists' protests and heated debates over the contractual and pay conditions of gig workers have spread worldwide. However, working conditions have not changed significantly, as hyper-precarious working arrangements persist in most countries.

Despite all the criticism, about one decade after their appearance, technology companies in the platform economy continue to rely on the existence of a reserve of low-wage labour that is typically excluded from permanent work contracts of wage labour and is recruited as "independent contractors" and hence as formal entrepreneurs. The availability of a flexible workforce deceptively recruited as "entrepreneurs" is enabled by two mechanisms, one cultural and one legal. On the one hand, as we have seen from the interview with William Shu, contemporary public discourse reproduces the allure of flexibility, a defining feature of post-Fordist economies and neoliberal societies since the 1990s (Sennett 1998). The appeal of labour flexibility lies in the fact that it offers a response to people's aspirations for greater autonomy and a better balance between work and private life. In this context, the standard contracts of wage labourers become to signify the purported rigidity and top-down nature of the past economic forms.

However, research on the platform economy has shown that through various techniques of algorithmic management of the labour process (such as constant updates to the worker-facing app, unnegotiated changes of workers' payment systems, platform-based rating and reputation systems, etc.), technology companies can enforce subtle and often invisible forms of workforce surveillance and control (Rani & Furrer 2021; Shapiro 2017; Wood *et al.* 2019). Autonomy and flexibility, therefore, end up being an illusion or – even worse – a deceptive story that hides a rather crude reality of workers' exploitation, precariousness and physical unsafety.

The cultural construction of flexibility as an aspiration that quickly turns into a societal imperative and even a nightmare, particularly for young people, racialized communities and immigrants, could not be effective without being accompanied and legitimized by the succession of legal acts and procedures enacted by state authorities over the past three decades in a growing number of countries across the world. The state-led pursuit of flexible regimes of labour market (de)regulation dates back to the 1980s, at a time in which the pro-market restructuring of national political economies became the priority for governments globally, committed to waging a "war" against inflation in the late 1970s (McCormack 2012). In reality, the labour market (de)regulations were the response to the workers' struggles of the second half of the 1970s, which demanded wage rises following price increases (Hung & Thompson 2016). The subsequent strategy of the neoliberal Schumpeterian competition state (see Chapter 1) consisted in the generalization of short-term contracts and the restructuring of the social Keynesian state along workfare lines (Jessop 1993).

Contemporary dynamics of labour exploitation, therefore, do not happen in a vacuum but take shape within a politico-economic context that has been prepared by the intervention of the state over a long time. This has significant similarities with what Karl Polanyi identified as the two paradoxes of the state-led capitalist transformation of European economies in the nineteenth century: the first being that "the invention of labour saving machinery had not diminished but actually increased the uses of human labour"; the second being that "the introduction of free markets, far from doing away with the need for control, regulation, and intervention, enormously increased their range" (Polanyi 2001: 147).

Increased use (and exploitation) of labour and all kinds of planned deregulation of the market economy can also be found in today's techno-monopoly capitalism, as we have seen. At the same time, the defining feature of today's techno-capitalism is the fact of bringing together long-standing forms of surplus value extraction with novel dynamics of economic value capture that are characteristic of platform economies in the urban field. This chapter contends that, in order to understand the contemporary dynamics of economic value capture, we need to throw light on the societal roots of economic value generation and capture in techno-monopoly capitalism. In this kind of capitalism, it becomes increasingly apparent that economic value generation arises from the productive interaction of digital technologies, human labour, the corporatized state and the rich social ecologies of the urban field, rather than from purportedly "innovative" and "bold" business activity carried out within the boundaries of the capitalist firm or of a network of firms.

However, before engaging in the analysis of these dynamics, a clarification is needed about the nature of value extraction in contemporary techno-monopoly capitalism: is today's value extractivism a new manifestation of rentierism, in the form of techno-feudalism, or should it be understood as an intensification of the capitalist logic of surplus value extraction in the context of post-Fordist cognitive capitalism?

The blurring of rent and profit

The previous section pointed out that the dynamics of surplus value extraction through the direct exploitation of labour power allowed by the new technologies exemplify the long-term continuities within the capitalist mode of production. At the same time, we have anticipated that the exploitation of labour power in today's techno-monopoly capitalism is revelatory of the societal roots of economic value generation. This means that technology corporations seek to capture economic value that is socially produced within what we define as the urban field through a productive hybridization of algorithmic technology and human labour. In other words, the coming together of digital technology and the labour force is the most important prerequisite for both the generation and extraction of economic value.

Economists who have emerged as public intellectuals scrutinizing the role of technology corporations in contemporary societies, such as Mariana Mazzucato and Shoshana Zuboff, along with a large number of scholars specializing in the critical study of digital technology companies and their market power, view this capture of economic value as a novel type of rentierism

(Christophers 2022) in what they define as "the taking economy" (Calo & Rosenblat 2017; Mazzucato 2018; Zuboff 2019) or as "techno-feudalism" (Dean 2020; Kotkin 2020; Varoufakis 2023). Zuboff (2019) has importantly argued that as part of their business activities related to data gathering on individual behaviours, technology companies are also seeking to modify the actions of people in such a manner that maximizes the monetization of what she defines as "behaviour surplus", obtained from corporate prediction of consumers' choices.

In the previous section, we have underlined the limits of theorizations of the technology-based economy centred on the dichotomy between "makers" and "takers" of economic value. At the same time, the merit of these discussions lies in the fact of having aroused renewed interest in the theorization of rent and rentierism brought on by the advent of techno-monopoly capitalism, led by predatory "Big Tech" corporations. Therefore, it is worth looking back at key theorizations of rent extraction in economic thinking.

The founders of classical political economy, such as the aforementioned Adam Smith, David Ricardo and Karl Marx, used the term "rent" to refer to forms of value creation that – contrary to those based on profit – were not beneficial to societies per se, as they did not imply the increase of productivity, but only corresponded to the "price for the use of land", as in Adam Smith's foundational definition (Smith 1977: 205). In the 1970s, the Marxist theory of rent was revived by Ernst Mandel, the Marxist economist known for his theory of long waves of capitalist development. In his conceptualization of late capitalism, Mandel individuated the existence of "technological rents" conceived as "surplus-profits derived from a monopolisation of technical progress", which he understood as the outcome of monopoly practices adopted by multinational corporations (Mandel 1975: 192). As we will see, Mandel's theorization is evocative of contemporary debates about the relationship between rent extraction and the market power of technology companies.

In recent years, the heightened financialization of the global economy has sparked renewed interest in the theorization of rent, which has been observed as a socially pervasive force, no longer conceived as a merely degenerative phenomenon (Mazzucato 2018). Indeed, in conventional understandings of financialized capitalism (see, for example, Strange 2016), rent has been customarily seen in opposition to profit, as a force that has to be distinguished from "real capital". This latter is concerned with investment in the production process, as in the traditional Marxist sense, while rent is supposed to be distinct from the goods-producing "real economy" (Lapavitsas 2013). However, other scholars of contemporary financialization point out that finance today is not somehow suspended above the real economy, but it actively contributes to its transformation (Durand 2017). In this conception, financial and productive activities are closely related to each other, and evidence shows that a great deal of financial activity supports production (Krippner 2012).

However, the resurgence of rent extraction within the socialized mechanisms of production in today's techno-monopoly capitalism does not have to do only with the weak or strong linkages of finance with production. Rather, this has to do more fundamentally with the fact that profit-making has morphed into a form of rentierist practice, highlighting what autonomist Marxists have defined as the "becoming-rent of profit" as a distinguishing characteristic of "cognitive capitalism" (Vercellone 2010). It is important to ask what this particular sentence means in the context of techno-monopoly capitalism.

We can respond to this question with the following proposition: the distinguishing trait of techno-monopoly capitalism is not the existence of "technological rents" identified by Ernst Mandel. As we have seen, today's techno-monopoly capitalism no longer bases its power on the "monopolization of technical progress" that characterized technocratic monopoly capitalism at the time of Mandel's writing, during the postwar decades (see also Baran & Sweezy 1966). On the contrary, as we said in Chapter 1, compared with the centralized technocratic systems of the Fordist era, algorithmic technology is ubiquitous, small-scale and decentralized. This characterization of today's technological paradigm is illustrative of how what Hardt and Negri have defined as the "metropolis" has become a central site – rather than the capitalist firm as such – for the extraction and capture of economic value within cognitive-affective capitalism (Hardt & Negri 2009).

The power of today's techno-monopoly capitalism lies, therefore, in its ability to extract economic value through a combination of the direct exploitation of the workforce with the indirect exploitation of the use-value of labour power in the urban field (Rossi 2019). In doing so, technology corporations not only extract surplus value through appropriation of labour time. In algorithmic techno-monopoly capitalism, the extraction of value also occurs indirectly, through the incorporation of the knowledge value that is embodied in the urbanized labour force, as algorithmic technologies are learning machines that continuously improve their performances through interaction with consumers and labourers. The control of the urban field and its human logistics – as a reservoir of entrepreneurship, labour, human capital and forms of life – becomes crucial to techno-monopoly capitalism, particularly through what we have defined as the corporatized state.

We have already touched on the intermeshing of production and consumption in contemporary technology-based economies. For their part, interactions between algorithms and labour happen both "behind the scenes" and at the frontline of economic activity. On the one hand, behind the scenes of search engines, apps and smart devices are workers paid with miserable salaries to clean data and oversee algorithms (Jones 2021). On the other hand, frontline service workers, such as those in the platform economy, incessantly apply and renew the human knowledge fixated on the algorithmic machinery of digital apps. The latter knowledge is fundamental in any efforts to change the behaviours of the populace for the further extraction of value.

Even the relationship of labourers to algorithmic management is not as straightforward as one might think, presupposing infallible technology-controlled techniques of surveillance of gig workers (Ferrari & Graham 2021). Research on digitally-based food delivery systems shows that workers do not passively follow the algorithmic management instructions but can combine a variety of adaptive behaviours that comprise compliance, relief, flexible response and resistance (Anwar & Graham 2020; Wu *et al.* 2023). Social scientists define human ways of dealing with external entities as "coping strategies", a term introduced by social psychologists investigating the ways in which humans respond to stress and other aversive situations (Carver, Scheier & Weintraub 1989). The notion of "coping strategies", however, is criticized by feminist authors who see it as a kind of imposed knowledge that risks shifting responsibility for economic insecurity from government to individuals and marginalized groups (Hall 2022).

Whatever significance we attribute to workers' agency, the human-made nature of platform-economy industries such as the food delivery service goes beyond the coping strategies and adaptive behaviours of labourers. In an ethnographic study conducted by one of the authors of this book with food delivery couriers in Turin in 2017 (Rossi 2019), gig workers who took the lead in the protest against their exploitative work conditions reclaimed their fundamental contribution to economic value creation, portraying themselves as a kind of human logistics that cannot be replaced by automated machines and self-generating algorithms. As an experienced courier and labour activist said:

> In this sector, companies cannot work without human bodies that rapidly move across the city, without human brains that know how to deal with restaurants and customers and how to cope with all unforeseen events like bad weather conditions, traffic jams, a broken bike and other accidental dysfunctions during the delivery process. And my feeling has always been that algorithms are constantly improving, as they learn from our own knowledge and labour as humans.   (Interview quoted in Rossi 2019)

This comment is illustrative of how today's technology-based urban economies, like the food delivery sector, are the result of the interrelation of living labour and the fixed capital of machinery incorporated into the company's algorithms (Tola & Rossi 2019). Living labour in this frontline service is not just physical but is also cognitive, relational and affective, in particular, as it requires engagement with the social and environmental constituents of the urban field (customers, restaurants, weather events, traffic conditions, etc.).

In this context, far from being crystallized into an immutable technology, the service delivery process is continuously renewed through the interactions of the technological device with its human logistics (the worker-bike complex) and the surrounding human-environmental fabric of the urban field. In this sense it can be argued that algorithmic technology, human labour and the governmentalized urban field are today's new "triple helix" (Etzkowitz 2008) in economic value creation and extraction. This means that techno-capitalism extracts value from the complex assemblage of human labour, personal data and social behaviours that underpins the production of ideas, images, codes and performances at its foundational stage (the scientific endeavour behind the creation of an algorithm and its applications) (Pasquinelli & Joler 2021). At the same time, the capitalist extraction of value happens through the continuous valorization of human labour in both its physical work and affective engagements with the social fabric of the urban field. The social fabric of the urban field, therefore, becomes productive of economic value: a "social factory", using the classic terminology of *operaismo*, where labour becomes diffused, decentred and "the whole society is placed at the disposal of profit" (Negri 1989: 79; a genealogy of the concept of social factory is in Thoburn 2003: ch. 4).

In today's technological reconfiguration of cognitive-affective capitalism, a handful of corporate giants have acquired a de facto monopoly position over the capture of economic value that is co-created through the interaction triangle of algorithmic technology, human labour and the urban field. The discrepancy between the socio-environmental roots of economic value creation, in which undervalued labourers play a key role as "human logistics" of the consumption-based urban economy, and the corporate seizure of this economic value has become a highly contentious issue in contemporary societies.

THE CONTESTED CONTROL OF THE URBAN FIELD

This chapter has elaborated on the idea that today's techno-monopoly capitalism is the continuation and intensification of a form of cognitive-affective capitalism in which the private firm is no longer the exclusive site for economic value creation. Using the terminology of Michael Hardt and Antonio Negri, the company's outside environment is crucial to the generation of economic value in this form of cognitive-affective capitalism, particularly in what is defined here as the "urban field", as well as in what Hardt and Negri define as "the metropolis". This latter is defined by them as "the site of biopolitical production ... the space of the common, of people living together, sharing resources, communicating, exchanging goods and ideas" (Hardt & Negri 2009: 250). It is in this context, as this book aims to show, that technology corporations strive to monopolize the extraction of economic value through their control of the urban field, as an unrivalled reservoir of entrepreneurship, labour, human capital and forms of life, and they do so with the support of the corporatized state.

Hardt and Negri's definition of the "metropolis" resonates with debates in mainstream urban economics on the social determinants of the urban economy. In the standard language of urban economists, this means that capitalist innovation relies on a wide range of agglomeration-driven interactions (knowledge spillovers, face-to-face engagements, labour pooling, incremental innovation, etc.), which take place within an increasingly polymorphic business environment (Rosenthal & Strange 2004; Storper & Venables 2004). The socio-relational thickness of urban environments explains why today's technology corporations are so eager to become part of innovation-oriented business ecosystems in the urban field.

Unlike traditional technology corporations that customarily located their headquarters in suburban environments (e.g. IBM), today's dominant technology corporations opt for headquarters in city-central areas, even though this locational choice in some contexts can raise public controversies. After a highly publicized competition that involved many candidate cities across the country, in November 2018 Amazon announced the decision to locate its second headquarters in a densely populated area of the Queens borough in New York City, as well as in Arlington, Virginia, in Washington DC's wider metropolitan area. The decision was initially supported by a complacent city government in New York City. Mayor Di Blasio offered Amazon nearly $3 billion in incentives, in exchange for the new 25,000 jobs in the high-tech sector promised by 2030. Despite the possible "hidden costs" of winning Amazon's new headquarters already highlighted by some commentators (Steinmetz 2017), by actively supporting Amazon's so-called "HQ2 project" the city government expected to give a boost to New York City's growing reputation as an emerging global tech city (Rossi & Di Bella 2017; Zukin 2020).

However, in the following months, Amazon's project became increasingly controversial. Neighbourhood activists, labour unions, urban planners and city councillors drew attention to the likely negative impact of the proposed headquarters on the city's socio-ecological metabolism, in terms of pressure on the housing market (increase in house prices and consequent intensifying of gentrification processes) and on urban infrastructure (increased numbers of public service users of sewers, public transport, etc.). In response to the harsh social contestation, Amazon eventually cancelled its plans, deciding to keep only its other second headquarters in Arlington, Virginia. However, Amazon did not totally renounce a physical presence in New York City. Less than a year after the unexpected turn of events that led to its retreat, the e-commerce giant signed a lease for a much smaller office space in the protected enclave of Hudson Yards, Manhattan's new luxury mega-project (Morris, 2019), benefitting from huge tax breaks (Capps 2019). Hudson Yards is among many other examples of what the historian Quinn Slobodian has defined as the "zones" of global capitalism at a time of rising economic nationalism: state-sponsored investment spaces freed from ordinary forms of regulation (Slobodian 2023).

The story of Amazon's failed attempt to establish its second headquarters in New York City is illustrative of the contested control of the urban field as a site for economic value creation and extraction and particularly of the possibilities for a grassroots resistance to the appropriation of urban space by capitalist companies such as Amazon. At the same time, the fact that Amazon has ended up creating its own office space, albeit in much reduced size, in Hudson Yards shows the stubbornness of tech giants and their political capacities. The supportive role of the corporatized state enables technology corporations to reach their goals, although with diminished ambitions in this case, in spite of social contestation and criticism in the wider public.

Getting back to the previous parallel discussion of Hardt and Negri's definition of the "metropolis" and urban economists' view of the social determinants of the urban economy, it is worth noting how Hardt and Negri's thinking converges with that of urban economists, but at the same time it conflicts with them when it comes to evaluating the political implications of their respective analyses. The intention of mainstream urban economists is to confirm the legitimate power of the capitalist firms to appropriate the economic value generated outside the conventional boundaries of business activity and, in doing so, to redesign urban social welfare at the service of the "high-skill" professional elites employed by these firms. On the other hand, Hardt and Negri intend to demonstrate the relative autonomy of economic value creation in contemporary capitalism and the fact that its seizure by corporate actors – accepted and endorsed by the corporatized state – can be politically and socially contested. From this perspective, what is interesting for them is the fact that "economists are recognizing the increasing importance of factors external to capital because in fact, to reverse the conventional economic formulation, capital is increasingly external to the productive process and the generation of wealth" (Hardt & Negri 2009: 141).

What does this "conflicting convergence" between post-Marxist radical thinking and mainstream urban economists (such as Richard Florida, Edward Glaeser, Enrico Moretti) as well as management gurus (such as Robert Reich,

Peter Drucker and more recent advocates of the existing knowledge economy) imply for the determination of value in contemporary capitalism? The response here has to do with the value that we assign to human labour in contemporary societies, beyond the conventional distinction between manual labour and knowledge work. This distinction is at the heart of the division of labour in a capitalist economy and, above anything else, is instrumental in the reproduction of social inequalities and labour exploitation in contemporary techno-monopoly capitalism.

CONCLUSION

The contemporary governance of capitalist development has been premised on the assumption that wage inequalities in existing societies are dependent on what labour economists have long defined as "skill-biased technical change". According to this theory, the ascendancy of information and communications technologies as the techno-economic paradigm of our society with the invention of microprocessors since the early 1970s (see Chapter 1) has deepened disparities among workers in terms of the skills they can offer to the production process and the earnings they consequently gain from their employment (Violante 2008). The dominant view holds that workers' earnings in a market economy depend fundamentally on their productivity, which corresponds to the value they produce through their labour. And in turn – so the theory goes – workers' productivity depends on their capabilities and the practical skills that enable them to accomplish more or less difficult tasks. The so-called "skill premium", in the final analysis, determines their demand and therefore their price on the labour market (Autor 2014).

This view, however, not only bypasses the problem of value measurability in the context of algorithmic capitalism, but it also ignores other factors behind the rise in wage inequalities in the last decades, such as policy choices adopted by national governments and other governmental entities in the first instance (Mishel, Schmitt & Shierholz 2014). In a book published in 1988, Harrison and Bluestone offered a different understanding of low-wage job creation in the US (Harrison & Bluestone 1988). In their analysis, the growth of low-paying jobs was due to the profit squeeze suffered by corporations with the economic downturn of the 1970s and the consequent restructuring process that led them to increasingly rely on part-time temporary workers and the adoption of more or less explicit anti-union policies. The "supply-side" policy embraced by Ronald Reagan in the US, Margaret Thatcher in the UK and a growing number of national governments in the following years simply supported corporate interests and their low-wage policies. The combination of corporate strategies and government policy led to the devaluation of working-class labour and the growing wage gaps that we observe today.

Moreover, in more recent times, economic historian Robert Gordon has questioned the commonly held assumption that the information technology boom of the last few decades has led to a higher increase in labour productivity, compared with previous techno-economic paradigms (Gordon 2016). Finally, even if we accept the current techno-economic paradigm, the dominant view overlooks the contribution of human labour that is conventionally viewed as "low-skill" – such as the service workers analysed in this chapter – to the incessant renewing of algorithm-based machinery in today's techno-capitalism, as well as their relational skills and the cognitive value in the socio-interactional process of service delivery.

Even so, despite the evident contradictions of the skill-biased technological change thesis and the widely debated problem of wage inequalities in recent years, national and local governments continue to prioritize the attraction of both technology corporations and high-skilled/high-paid workers and professionals at the city level. The attraction of technology companies and "high-skill workers" is supposed to boost technology-based urban and national development. Its economic growth effects are believed to trickle down to the working classes, particularly in the service sector at the city level, through the mechanism of what urban and labour economists call "human capital externalities" (Moretti 2012). However, the resulting picture is rather different, as the grassroots mobilization in New York on Amazon's second headquarters project has highlighted: the sudden influx of several thousands of high-skilled/high-paid workers associated with the arrival of a monopolist technology corporation such as Amazon would lead to heightened pressure on local infrastructures and especially to a rapid increase in the cost of living (housing and subsistence goods and services). This would not only affect the majority of urban residents who earn wages significantly lower compared to the high-skilled/high-paid workers attracted by Amazon's arrival, but would irremediably subject the entire urban field to the control of techno-monopoly capitalism.

The next chapter will therefore explore how the creation and attraction of "human capital" has become the priority of today's governmentality of the urban field, at the service of techno-monopoly capitalism, threatening to erase the heterogeneity of urban societies.

CHAPTER 4

HUMAN CAPITAL

INTRODUCTION

The previous chapter has shown how the capitalist imperative on cities that dictates to attract an elite of high-skilled workers as a way to boost their economies ends up devaluing the majority of workers who are supposed to be low-skilled according to conventional parameters of labour-value measurement. This conventional view stems from the so-called "skill-biased technical change" thesis, an economic theory that has become commonsensical in mainstream analyses of the impact of the information technology "revolution" on labour and the economy. This view is premised on the assumption that the influx of highly skilled workers is crucial to a local economy and therefore also to local labour markets. Accordingly, the increase of highly paid knowledge workers is thought to be functional to the development of the consumption-based service economy.

The emphasis that is placed today on the measurement of knowledge and skills as an alleged parameter for the productivity of labour is derived from the economic theory of human capital, which traces its origins back to the late 1950s and the early 1960s, when it was first proposed by the Chicago School economists. Since then, human capital has become one of the most influential concepts in economics and the wider social sciences concerned with education, learning and more generally with the investigation of knowledge-based societies, such as sociology, pedagogy and management studies. Simultaneously, the human capital approach has become highly influential in policy-making in both the Global North and the Global South. However, compared with policy ideas and recipes commonly associated with neoliberalism and its more distinctive economic policies (such as monetarism, tax cuts and tariff rebates, labour flexibility, privatization of state-owned enterprises, attraction of foreign direct investment, export-led growth), the theory of human capital has not received equal attention from a critical standpoint in urban studies, human geography and cognate fields.

This chapter, therefore, aims to explore in more depth the trajectory of human capital theory and its political and intellectual reception since the Second World War years up to now, as its influence has been decisive in the transitioning to today's techno-monopoly capitalism. Since the mid-1990s, with the consolidation of technology-based economies, the theory of human capital has become even more central to explanations of economic growth and technological change in mainstream economics, particularly within the framework of the so-called "endogenous growth theory", also known as new growth theory. To illustrate such a perspective, Paul Romer (1990) offers an influential take on what creates economic growth in technology-driven capitalism. Romer highlights the economic value of knowledge as an investment asset in generating economic growth and prosperity. In such a view, human capital is located at the centre of both economic and political success, thus expanding the propositions of early proponents of human capital theory.

In recent years, the latest generation of human capital theorizations has inspired the proposal in different geographical contexts (in the Americas, in sub-Saharan Africa and East Asia most particularly) of entrepreneurial projects aiming to create from scratch new cities that are portrayed as havens for business and human capital, variously named "charter cities", "talent cities" or "startup cities". According to their proponents, these new cities would be modelled on existing, economically thriving city-states and special economic zones, particularly in East Asia, such as Hong Kong, Singapore and Shenzhen. The implementation of this idea, which has been somnolent for quite some time, is now being revived across the globe by new city projects launched by ambitious startups and adventurous tech entrepreneurs such as Elon Musk, as well as by the government-sponsored creation of science cities and innovation districts.

After having delineated the long trajectory of human capital theory and its economic and social impact on the urban field, this chapter will therefore focus on entrepreneurial projects of "new cities" and discuss their implications for the urban condition and the evolution of techno-monopoly capitalism, particularly from the viewpoint of the established modes of living and economic value extraction.

THE RISE AND RISE OF HUMAN CAPITAL THEORY

What would impress anyone concerned with the history of the notion of human capital theory is its resilience and continuous renewal as a theory and policy practice over more than six decades. The notion of human capital originally appeared in academic journals in the late 1950s. Since then it has witnessed a slow but constant popularization in policy circles and in the media. The popularization and even trivialization of the idea of human capital has reached its peak in the last 15 years with its adoption by prominent international organizations such as the United Nations, the World Bank, the EU and the OECD, among others. As a result, human capital has become a policy panacea that penetrates most of the policy sectors of the corporatized state.

Human capital theory thus started its trajectory as an academic topic. Scholars affiliated with the Economics Department of the University of Chicago – forming what is commonly defined as the Chicago School of Economics – have played a leading role in the ascendant phases of human capital theory. The Chicago School of Economics is generally known for its substantial contribution to the spread of free-market ideas and more specifically to the macroeconomic theory of the variation of money supply as a fiscal policy (the so-called monetarist theory). The Chicago School's economic recipes were highly influential on national governments and central banks at the time of the economic and monetary turbulence of the 1970s and the 1980s, particularly during the "great inflation" crisis that hit the world economy in those years.

The work of Milton Friedman is representative of the most influential strand of free-market thinking and monetarist theory in the Chicago School of Economics. Marxist-inspired critics of neoliberal economics have customarily concentrated their attention on the role of Milton Friedman as a theorist of monetarism and advocate for market-oriented fiscal policies, who directly advised or inspired conservative and authoritarian government leaders such as Ronald Reagan and Augusto Pinochet on their neoliberal economic strategies in the 1970s and 1980s (Harvey 2005; Peck 2010; van Horn & Mirowski 2009). In his more disseminative work, particularly in the treatise *Capitalism and Freedom* (Friedman 1962), Milton Friedman grounded his economic ideas in a general understanding that views society "as a collection of individuals each unequally endowed with personal capacities and with material wealth", as Marxist economist Paul Baran pointed out in a review of Friedman's book (Baran 1963: 591). A chapter of *Capitalism and Freedom* titled 'The role of government in education' is the reprint of a book chapter that Friedman published in 1955, in which he made the case for school vouchers, based on the idea that governments should fund rather than administer schools (Friedman 1955). In subsequent years, Friedman's ideas on education have inspired market-oriented programmes in public education in the US, such as the so-called "charter schools", as well as in other countries across the world, including Chile and Sweden.

The rise of the theory of human capital, therefore, has to be understood against this ideological backdrop dating back to the postwar decades. The embrace of human capital theory by different key figures of the Chicago School of Economics in the aftermath of the Second World War is illustrative of neoclassical economists' willingness to broaden the scope of standard economic analysis, beyond the conventional realm of economics. In doing so, the theory of human capital has opened the way to the penetration of mainstream economics and its policy recommendations into the vast universe of social life and human behaviour, which were traditionally prerogative of other human and social sciences, such as sociology, psychology, anthropology and human geography. In this way, the theory of human capital has offered scientific justification for the integration of the economy with the social and the spatial spheres in present-day neoliberal economies and societies.

The early stages of human capital theory

The first academic article that explicitly grappled with the notion of human capital was authored by Jacob Mincer in 1958, with the title "Investment in human capital and personal income distribution" (Mincer 1958). The article was published by *The Journal of Political Economy*, a leading journal in economics linked to the Economics Department of the University of Chicago, of which Jacob Mincer was an eminent representative throughout his career. It is noticeable that many of the influential texts focusing on human capital have been published in this same journal, also in the 1990s, when the human capital approach took centre stage in the dominant economic governmentality.

Mincer's (1958) article laid the foundations for successive theorizations of human capital. The article stressed the role of "rational choice" as a key driver behind "individual investments" in what at that time the author already termed as "human capital", although still not offering an extensive definition of this term. Mincer put forward an argument that became a classic theme in the theory of human capital. Individuals are rational agents who invest in human capital on the basis of the subjective calculation of how "the time spent in training constitutes a postponement of earnings to a later age" and how this calculation "implies higher annual pay in occupations that require more training" (Mincer 1958: 301).

In an article published three years later, titled "Investment in human capital", Theodore Schultz – another key representative of the Chicago School of Economics – acknowledged Jacob Mincer's article as a "pioneer paper" and refined the understanding of human capital by associating this notion with "knowledge and skills", a definition that has become commonly accepted in subsequent years. In doing so, Schultz for the first time put forward the idea that the major implication of human capital theory for economic theory was that human labour represented a new form of capital: "laborers have become capitalists not from a diffusion of the ownership of corporation stocks . . . but from the acquisition of knowledge and skill that have economic value" (Schultz 1961: 3).

As both Mincer and Schultz had remained vague about the institutions accommodating what they defined as "investments in human capital", their colleague Gary Becker – another eminent economist of the Chicago School and in subsequent years a proponent of behavioural economics – drew attention to the wide range of activities instrumental in the accumulation of human capital, investigating "their effects on earnings", such as "schooling, on-the-job training, medical care, migration, and searching for information about prices and incomes" (Becker 1964: 11). This formulation was bound to exert an enduring influence on the literature dealing with human capital policy in economics and the other social science disciplines concerned with learning, education and schooling.

From this short overview of early propositions of human capital theory, it is clear that numerous leading Chicago School economists were simultaneously working – even though they authored their texts as single authors, as it was the norm at that time – on a joint intellectual project that centred on the notion of human capital, not only at the scale of the individual but also at that of political communities. This project later took the form of a larger paradigm shift in economic research, as economists started venturing into the analysis of human behaviour through micro-economic lenses. As we said, Gary Becker has been a leading proponent of the behaviourist turn in economics.

What links these foundational treatments of human capital together is their usage of the term "capital", in line with the neoclassical tradition in economics, which conceives assets – including intangible assets such as skills and knowledge that form human capital – as a claim on future income. This understanding of capital leaves aside classical definitions of capital as a factor of production, as well as the Marxian association of capital with the ownership of the means of production.

Chicago economists' rethinking of labour as capital captured the attention of Michel Foucault in the late 1970s. In his widely debated lectures on neoliberalism, Foucault identifies human capital as a distinguishing trait of "American neoliberalism", as he calls it (Foucault 2008). In particular, Foucault argues that the success of human capital theory lies in the fact that it promises a more active role to labour in the capitalist process of economic value creation, compared with conventional economic theories in both classical political economy and modern economics that tend to objectify human labour as a mere factor of production along with capital and land (Foucault 2008). As we will demonstrate later, this is a crucial observation in the context of local and national urban policies as these have unfolded since the 1990s, in particular.

As a conclusion, Foucault (2008) makes the important claim that this shift in the conceptualization of human labour will lead to a changing meaning of the *Homo economicus* from a partner of exchange to an entrepreneurial subject. In the following years, Foucault's emphasis on the innovative character of human capital theory from a neoliberal standpoint has attracted the criticism of some commentators on the academic left, who have interpreted his appraisal of the significance of human capital theory as an apology of neoliberal ideas (Zamora & Behrent 2016) – an attempt to escape sovereignty as a mode of power. However, critics of Foucault's position on neoliberalism do not consider the fact that his lectures were only a first draft and were published posthumously. This means that it is likely that in a later re-elaboration Foucault would have spelled out his critical approach more explicitly. Be that as it may, one cannot deny that Foucault was prescient in understanding that the entrepreneurialization of society was bound to become a distinctive trait of neoliberal societies and that the theory of human capital was pivotal in the pursuit of this political and societal project.

At the same time, it is true that Foucault's analysis did not illuminate other problems in the early formulations of human capital theory, as they were proposed by the Chicago School economists. The consideration of the class-based structuring of the educational system in capitalist societies was a notable weakness in human capital literature. The problem of inequalities was substantially ignored by the mainstream economists, who presupposed that investments in educational institutions alone are capable of increasing the entrepreneurial abilities of workers, professionals and entrepreneurs, regardless of their social backgrounds. Writing a few years earlier than Foucault, Marxist economists Samuel Bowles and Herbert Gintis offered a compelling critique of human capital, objecting that in its standard theorizations workers were abstracted from the realities of their social lifeworlds and were treated like machines that can increase value and productivity thanks to their better training in allegedly impersonal institutions (Bowles & Gintis 1975). According to Bowles and Gintis, human capital theory prevents an understanding of how in present-day capitalist societies the main function of schools and of the wider educational system is not the social emancipation of deserving individuals, as the conventional wisdom holds, but is the legitimation of the unequal relations of class, place, gender and race in the name of the abstract notion of meritocracy (Bowles & Gintis 1976).

Redefining the role of the state

In the decades after the Second World War, human capital theory acted as the driver behind state-driven educational investments. In developing countries, especially in Latin America, educational investments aimed at forming new political and intellectual elites at a time of sustained economic modernization, as it was defined in those years. The Alliance for Progress in Latin America was announced by US President Kennedy in 1961 as a response to fears of communism and social revolution in what was regarded by Western leaders as "the most dangerous area in the world" (Rabe 1999).

In this context, the adoption of human capital theory in the economics programmes of Latin American universities was instrumental in the international circulation of US-derived individualistic conceptions of modernization and economic growth. A few years after the launch of the US-backed Alliance for Progress initiative, many Latin American countries – starting with Brazil in 1964 – underwent authoritarian drifts in their political systems. The new authoritarian regimes adopted growth-driven agendas for economic reform and, in some cases – such as Chile after the 1973 *coup d'état* – openly embraced a free-market ideology. Under the Pinochet dictatorship, Chile became a laboratory for the importation of neoliberalism in Latin America (Harvey 2005; Sigmund 1983). During the 1960s, the Chicago School of Economics established an active collaboration with the private Catholic University in Chile, training a new generation of economists that later served the Pinochet government (Burnett 2023).

In the postwar years, a key role in the operationalization of human capital theory was played by Theodore Schultz, at that time serving as head of the Department of Economics at the University of Chicago. Along with the theorization of human capital, Schultz was known for his work recommending the "modernization" of what he called "traditional agriculture" in developing countries (Schultz 1964). Drawing on Milton Friedman's concept of stationary equilibrium, Theodore Schultz contended that the stationary stock in the means of production prevented traditional agriculture from modernizing in "underdeveloped" countries. According to Schultz, the improvement of the means of production had to include not only material factors, which commonly attracted the attention of experts and policy-makers, but also the skills and capabilities of the farmers. These latter – as human capital theory stated – would be increased by investment in education and would be conducive to the increased productivity of agriculture. Schultz, therefore, brought a proto-neoliberal conception of human capital into the field of development economics and the agricultural sector more specifically, emphasizing the ability of farmers to adopt new techniques of production and thus to innovate the agricultural sector (Schultz 1981). In doing so, Schultz offered a market-based alternative to the structuralist approach to economic development, centred on ideas of import substituting industrialization, unequal exchange and technological cooperation, which was prevalent at that time in key institutions such as the UN Economic Commission for Latin America (known as

ECLA in English and as CEPAL in Spanish and Portuguese) (Medina 2011; Sikkink 1997).

In their work on agriculture and the developing countries more generally, Schultz and his Chicago School fellows attempted to shift the attention of scholars and policy-makers from the structural conditions of economic dependency between centre and periphery to the empirical observation of markets and individual decision-making processes. Schultz and his colleagues did not dismiss the role of the state as such, but pushed towards its drastic reworking. The state was no longer viewed as a democratically accountable institution charged with the redistribution of income, land or capital, as the prevailing approach to economic development policy held at that time. The state was now reconceived as an entrepreneurial entity committed to investing in the skills of individual actors and their capacity to adapt to constantly changing circumstances in a dynamic global economy (Burnett 2023).

When it appeared in the 1960s, Schultz's view attracted much criticism (e.g. Dandelar 1966) and apparently remained at the margin of policy practice and of key institutions concerned with economic development such as the CEPAL in Latin America. However, the market-oriented approach to economic development and governance became predominant in the 1980s and the 1990s, not only because of the direct influence of the so-called "Chicago Boys" (i.e. Latin American economists trained at Chicago and other economics departments in the US) on national governments, but also as a consequence of the wider paradigm shift in the development policies pursued by leading institutions such as the International Monetary Fund (IMF) and the World Bank, known as "Washington Consensus" (Sikkink 1997). In this context, far from "retreating" from the scene, as a straightforward narrative of globalization has put it for quite some time, particularly in the early stages of the global era (Ohmae 1995; Strange 2009), the state becomes committed to integrating the economic with the social through citizen-individuals. In this process, the state incentivizes individuals to realize their lives in entrepreneurial form through the assignment of new kinds of self-governing capacities, duties and responsibilities (Raco & Imrie 2000).

The first wave of human capital theory, therefore, played a distinctive role in the international ascendancy of neoliberalism. In particular, its trajectory shows how neoliberalism should not be conceived only as a set of macroeconomic policies that coalesce around goals of privatization, commodification and austerity, but has to be viewed as a larger "human-centred" project of societal governmentality. In this sense, as Wendy Brown has pointed out, neoliberal governmentality "produces subjects, forms of citizenship and behaviour, and a new organisation of the social" (Brown 2003: 37). The resulting reinvention of the economy in late liberal societies is founded on the entrepreneurialization of society and individual conduct, a principle that is at the heart of human capital theory, as early proponents of human capital theory demanded an investment in education and schooling as a way of nurturing the entrepreneurial ability of individuals as market actors. Michel Foucault presciently signalled the key role played by human capital theory in the early stages of neoliberalism in his lectures of the late 1970s. In the ensuing years, the urban field would become the testing ground for this project aimed at asserting entrepreneurial living as the dominant form of being-in-the-world in late liberal societies.

Human capital's new clothes: endogenous growth theory

As we have seen in the previous chapter, since the late 1960s, management gurus and social forecasters such as Peter Drucker and Daniel Bell announced the imminent knowledge-driven transformation of capitalist societies. The following years confirmed their forecasts, exposing how the post-industrial society they had prefigured found strong empirical evidence in economic and social indicators relating to the job market and the contribution of economic sectors to the gross domestic product, particularly in more prosperous capitalist economies. The transition to a post-industrial society, however, was not as smooth and peaceful as futurists and social forecasters such as Drucker and Bell had predicted.

Following in the wake of the economic turmoil of the second half of the 1970s and the early 1980s, governments in the Western world staged a war against the labour unions, seeking to drastically reduce their power in society. The economic justification for this war was to put an end to the prices-wages spiral that was allegedly behind both the great inflation of the late 1970s and the early 1980s, and the falling rates of profits. During 1984–85, Margaret Thatcher – the UK's Prime Minister and an iconic figure of neoliberalism in the 1980s – engaged in a harsh and prolonged confrontation with the miners' movement, which ended with a historic defeat of the workers. As a highly mediatized affair, the defeat of the miners' movement in the UK had a symbolic significance that went largely beyond the confines of Britain and Western Europe. Not only was the era of industrial capitalism over, but with it the Keynesian "collective" social compact that seemingly brought together the interests of both capital and labour in the name of national coherence lost legitimacy in the eyes of the ruling elite.

The abrupt end of manufacturing-centred capitalism and the dismantling of Keynesian social welfare gave way to the accelerated rise of the technology-based economy as the dominant form of capitalist societies. The restructuring of the welfare state also involved the education system, which had been at the centre of human capital theorists' attention. The acceleration in the post-industrial transformation of capitalist economies and societies and the neoliberal turn in economic and social policy instigated a revival of interest in human capital theorizations. In the second half of the 1980s, a new wave of economic scholarship dealing with the externalities of human capital started to inundate academic journals, under the banner of the so-called "endogenous growth theory", or new growth theory as it is known more popularly.

The work of the Chicago economist Robert Lucas on technological change and human capital and that of his former PhD student Paul Romer on market incentives, externalities and knowledge spillovers have been major sources of inspiration for this influential wave of scholarship. Lucas's theoretical model incorporated knowledge obtained through "learning by doing" and not just through schooling, identifying a linearity in the accumulation of the "individual's human capital". In his view, human capital can act as an "engine of growth" thanks to the increasing returns of knowledge functioning as an investment asset (Lucas 1988). The idea of the increasing returns of investment in knowledge was bound to become a distinctive characteristic of endogenous growth theory during the early stages of techno-capitalism. This idea was further developed by Paul Romer, who emphasized the role of market incentives in endogenous technological change, which results in his view from "intentional investment decisions made by profit-maximising agents" in research and development activities (Romer 1990: S71). In these approaches, human capital and knowledge as its concrete materialization became a potentially infinite source of growth. In policy circles, the widely shared understanding of the investment potential of knowledge has been a fundamental discursive element during the rise of the techno-capitalist economy as the dominant societal and spatial formation.

Both Lucas and Romer postulated knowledge as a "non-rival good" that endogenously generates spillovers among firms competing in the same market, thus allegedly avoiding concentration of market power in one company. The subsequent phenomenon of tech giants acting as de facto monopolist agents in their economic sectors, however, has revealed how it is illusory to rely on the self-adjusting mechanisms of market regulation in a context of advanced techno-capitalism. Even more substantially, at the heart of Romer's endogenous growth proposal there appears to be a subtle marketization of knowledge, which ceases to be a free good provided by the state through universal education and becomes a target of individual appropriation and remuneration. Far from vanishing, the state's new role is, therefore, to support and legitimize the market-based constitution and regulation of knowledge (Herrera 2006).

Despite the increasingly contradictory evidence about its assumptions and theses, endogenous growth theory has remained highly influential in academia and public policy alike over the last three decades or so. While the first wave of human capital theory led by Jacob Mincer, Theodore Schultz and Gary Becker remained somewhat peripheric in policy-making, the new growth theory proposed by Robert Lucas and Paul Romer has become unrivalled in terms of hegemony over public policy and society at large for a long time now, reaching the most diverse fields such as demography, the educational system and science, trade, market dynamics, entrepreneurship and – most importantly here – cities (Warsh 2007). This expansion of influence has taken place concomitantly with knowledge becoming the organizing principle of capitalist economies and societies in a technology-shaped world.

As we will see, the contribution of human capital theory to the political construction of the urban field in techno-capitalism is derived essentially from the latest tide of human capital-derived theorizations of endogenous technological change. In his article on the mechanics of economic development, Robert Lucas ends with an evocation of the work of urbanist Jane Jacobs on the economy of cities (Jacobs 1969). In Chapter 2, we mentioned mainstream urban economists' fascination with the work of Jane Jacobs. For his part, Lucas links Jacobs' emphasis on the economic value intrinsic in the geographical proximity of people and a diverse set of industries in cities to his conceptualization of "external human capital", which he considers an engine of growth in economic development.

This revisited Jacobsian approach has become typical in new urban narratives, *á la* Richard Florida (2012), built on the assumption that social diversity fosters innovation in cities, as well as in the work of urban economists investigating what they call the micro-foundations of urban agglomeration economies, such as the impact of urban specialization and diversity on firm location and relocation (Duranton & Puga 2001). At the same time, the Jacobsian revival has been reflected in sociological and political celebrations of urban variety and diversity, the eroticism of city life and the "open city" put forward by liberal theorists such as Iris Marion Young (1990) and Richard Sennett (2018a).

In the current techno-monopoly era, these conceptions are aligned with the new urban ideology of mobility and anonymity nurtured by algorithmic technologies that allow encounters with strangers, particularly in urban environments, through GPS-enabled apps for sex and dating to sharing economy platforms that facilitate the peer-to-peer exchange of services (Koch & Miles 2021). The burgeoning phenomenon of the so-called "digital nomads" (McElroy 2020) – typically, "high-skill" young professionals working solely in an online environment who move from one city to another in search of life experiences – and other temporary populations that inhabit the contemporary "short-term city" (Brollo & Celata 2023) is illustrative of the rise of a kind of open, fluid, anonymous urbanism that is believed to offer unprecedented possibilities for leisure, work-life balance and freedom (Tsipursky 2023).

URBAN ECONOMICS MEETS HUMAN CAPITAL THEORY

As has been noted, the endogenous growth theory and Lucas's enthusiastic rediscovery of Jane Jacobs persuaded a growing number of economists to get back to the then dormant field of urban economics in the 1990s (Peck 2016). The newly coined concept of "Jacobs externalities" (Glaeser *et al.* 1992; van der Panne 2004), which postulates the value of agglomeration economies associated with the coexistence of complementary firms forming a trans-sectoral business ecosystem – rather than firms in the same field, as in Alfred Marshall's industrial districts or in Michael Porter's business clusters – have inspired a new wave of literature on urban growth and creative economies.

The rediscovery of urban economics coincided with the revitalization of urban economies, after two decades of urban decline from the mid-1970s to the mid-1990s, which resulted in the revamping of urban real-estate markets and the housing bubble that persisted until the financial crash of 2008 and resumed in the 2010s with the new boom brought on by the digitalization of housing markets. Despite her original intentions, Jane Jacobs' idea of urban diversity has provided a decisive contribution to the new culture of neighbourhood distinctiveness that has become a tool of economic elites to drive up real-estate values and effectively force out the neighbourhood "characters" (Zukin 2010). Aptly combined with Jacobs' idea of urban diversity, human capital theory has provided justification on the micro-economic level for the new wave of urban revival experienced in capitalist societies since the late 1990s. As such, it has become an important constituent of the urban field in the age of techno-monopoly.

Along with Edward Glaeser and his coauthors (Glaeser *et al.* 1992; Glaeser 1999; Glaeser & Saiz 2004), labour economist Enrico Moretti has been a leading importer of human capital theory into the field of urban and regional economics and, indirectly, into that of urban policy. His conceptualization of the "human capital externalities in cities" has extended the beneficial effects of human capital endowments from individual life chances and firm-centred investment – at the centre of human capital theory in economics and the social sciences, as we have seen – to the economy of cities. As he puts it in a foundational essay in the urban economics literature on human capital: "We observe that cities with a well-educated labor force tend to have better amenities, better institutions, better infrastructure, a more modern industry structure, and more technologically advanced firms than cities with a less-educated labor force" (Moretti 2004: 2246).

In his work, Moretti particularly emphasizes the positive externalities of human capital attraction at the urban level. According to Moretti, the multiplier effects of human capital attraction are reflected in a wide range of economic, social and political domains that altogether contribute to the improvement of social well-being ("better amenities" and "better infrastructure"), to technological advancement ("more technologically advanced firms") and even to the attainment of a stronger democracy, as it is assumed that people with better education tend to make more informed decisions as voters and citizens ("better institutions").

While Moretti has enthusiastically endorsed human capital theory at the urban level, subsequent developments have exposed the cumulative negative effects related to the influx of highly skilled and high-paid workers on urban societies in terms of income disparities and larger social inequalities and their reverberations on the urban fabric, such as unequal access to housing, subsistence goods and essential public services.

The effects of the attraction of highly skilled and highly paid workers and professionals on housing prices are widely debated in contemporary urban affairs. The attractiveness of urban centres for high-skilled professionals and workers has increased with the growing urbanization of technology companies since the 2010s. During this decade, technology companies no longer concentrated only in suburban technology districts such as Silicon Valley and the Research Triangle in the US, but started to cluster around startup tech ecosystems in urban and metropolitan centres across the world, such as New York, San Francisco, Berlin, London, Shenzhen, Singapore, Nairobi and Cape Town. This shift in the geographies of venture capital has made a decisive contribution to the overheating of real-estate prices in cities and surrounding urban areas.

In his original essay on human capital externalities in cities, Moretti observed that "land prices are positively correlated with human capital stocks" (*ibid.*: 2281), seeing this increase in land values merely as a "positive externality". Importantly, Moretti here associates the economic potential of human capital with the purportedly "positive" developments of land rents and thus of the exchange values of the real-estate sector more generally. This coupling of what Henri Lefebvre and David Harvey defined as the secondary and tertiary circuits of capital (real estate/built environment and research/development, respectively) is a notable feature in the agglomeration-centred urban economics.

Moretti's original academic essay on human capital externalities in cities was published in 2004, at the peak of the housing bubble in the US that only a couple of years later burst, causing the financial crash of 2007–08 and the "great contraction" of 2009. In the years of the housing bubble, the US government stimulated the economy's increasing dependence on consumer spending and real-estate speculation through property tax cuts and mortgage tax deductions as well as diminished costs of money borrowing, while the manufacturing industry was abandoned to its pre-existing declining path (Brenner 2012). This policy paved the way to "private Keynesianism" as a dominant model of social reproduction, based on the financialization of the economy as well as on rising household indebtedness functional to the usage of housing as an investment asset rather than as a use-value (Crouch 2009).

Mainstream economists played an active role in justifying this economic model on scientific bases. The revitalized fields of urban and labour economics took the lead in the new economic discourse centred on the seductive rhetoric of a "people-centred" – rather than corporate-centred – economic path (Florida 2012), which found its roots in the human capital theorizations of the past decades and of the 1990s in particular. The departing point in economists' theories of human capital was in fact the idea that traditional economic scholarship had overlooked "human resources" as a key determinant of economic growth and development. Economists thus became concerned "with activities that influence future monetary and psychic income by increasing the resources in people" (Becker 1964: 11). These activities were defined by them as "investments in human capital", as we have seen (*ibid.*).

Human capital, therefore, became the new orthodoxy in a wide set of applied fields of mainstream economics: labour economics, urban and regional economics, new economic geography and international trade, development economics (see, e.g. Stiglitz & Greenwald 2014) and business management studies since the late 1990s. Business management theories are particularly important to mention in this context. We therefore suggest that business management theorizing has taken up the question of human capital and played an essential role in ordering, reproducing and transforming capitalist social formations in the age of putative global knowledge economy (Jessop 2004; Moisio 2018a). Since the 1990s, management theorists have drawn attention to the pivotal role of geographical concentration of human capital, hence highlighting the role of urban development in contemporary inter-spatial competition.

The political force of business management theories can be illustrated, for instance, through the work of Michael Porter, an influential business strategy theorist and professor at Harvard Business School. His work in the 1990s ultimately highlights the growing prominence of innovation, learning and human capital for the purposes of firms in such a manner that facilitates the production of nation-states but also of cities and regions as innovation-driven economic territories. Porter's work has been particularly alluring for local and national states that are trying "to move away from dependence on cheap labour and natural resources", as he put it (Porter 1998a: xxviii). Since the late 1980s, Porter's work has been embraced by many state and city governments, as well as agencies and political institutions such as the OECD, IMF, EU and World Trade Organization, and it has been arguably important in reframing the nature of territorial competition.

One of the logical consequences of this theory is that all competitive nations should host and attract a reasonable amount of expensive labour. Their expensive jobs are an embodiment of skills that are needed to bring into existence "clusters". In this manner, the theory of human capital takes the form of geographical micro-spaces where firms produce high economic value – with the necessary support from local and national governments. Cluster therefore refers to "a geographic concentration of competing and cooperating companies, suppliers, service providers, and associated institutions", and often includes governmental or other institutions such as universities (Porter 1998b: 78). Because the "basis of competition has shifted more and more to the creation and assimilation of knowledge", Porter (2008: 171) continues, "the role of the nation has grown". The pivotal question in Porter's conceptualization of national competitiveness is how to increase productivity. He singles out various factors of national competitiveness, and lists diverse infrastructure issues such as housing stock, health care, cultural institutions, transportation systems, as well as resources such as a nation's human capital resources and the availability of investment capital.

The proposed firm-centred view of competitiveness based on business clusters by Porter is only qualitatively different from the people-centred view of human capital theories *á la* Romer and Lucas – Porter's contemporaries. Their differences are hence primarily conceptual, given that they all highlight the theory of agglomeration and are premised on utterly market-oriented prescriptions. In Porter's (1998a) popular diamond model, human capital is discussed as an important dimension in the context of "factor conditions". Here, Porter discusses "advanced" and "basic" factors as well as "specialized" and "generalized" factors in generating competitive advantage. The advanced factors of production include skilled labour, knowledge, capital and infrastructure. All the factor conditions boil down to the question of skills and human capital, which Porter associates with innovative professionals such as computer scientists and engineers. In such a perspective, the unskilled and cheap labour can be obtained by all companies and cannot hence constitute competitive advantage.

Even though Porter's work has often been associated with the scale of the national state, his work also highlights the role of what we term as the urban field in the generation of economic value in the technology-based economy. Indeed, one may consider the 2001-founded Institute for Strategy and Competitiveness as a continuum of development at the Harvard Business School, which in the 1980s had already begun to organize symposiums to promote particular strategic business planning approaches to urban governments.

Porter argues how "the enduring competitive advantages in a global economy lie increasingly in local things – knowledge, relationships, and motivation – that distant rivals cannot match" (Porter 1998b: 78). It is a quality of "advanced nations" in particular to be capable of enhancing value production in local milieux. In his related work on the competitive advantage of the inner city, Porter (1995a, 1997) discusses human capital/skills explicitly as a pivotal factor in the generation of competitive advantage and what he calls the "rise of the urban entrepreneur" (Porter 1995b). In this context, his theory takes the form of a critique of the then purportedly social and redistribution-based governmental programmes that sought to solve the problems of inner cities through non-market means. According to Porter, the applied social approach had inadvertently undermined the creation of economically viable companies in inner-city areas. Porter's idea is that the revitalization of inner-city areas should take place through the power of market forces and real income generation; more generation of wealth and less redistribution (Porter 1995a).

In his writings on the competitiveness of inner-city areas, Porter brings the theory of national competitiveness and business clusters to the local scale and seeks to "identify the inner city's competitive advantages and the ways inner city businesses can forge connections with the surrounding urban and regional economies" (Porter 1995a: 57). Here, Porter places the issue of human capital (human resources in his terminology) at the centre and combines this with his firm-centred view on social development (for a critique, see Blakely & Small 1996). Even though Porter (1995a) has a somewhat negative view on the skills of the inner-city residents in some cities, he argues that, over time, successful job creation will trigger a self-reinforcing process that raises skill and wage levels. In his view, this would partly solve the potential mismatch between the needs of knowledge-intensive firms for highly skilled professionals and the available labour pool in the inner city.

Human capital and the housing crisis

In 2001, the OECD officially adopted the term human capital as a driving concept of its economic and societal development rationale, along with that of social capital derived from sociological scholarship (CERI/OECD 2001). In 2017, the World Economic Forum published its first "Global human capital report", in which human capital is defined as "the knowledge and skills people possess that enable them to create value in the global economic system" (Samans *et al.* 2017), but also going beyond them, as in Richard Florida's theory of the creative class.

For his part, Enrico Moretti remained more loyal to human capital theorizations and reproposed them from a new economic geography perspective in his bestseller book *The New Geography of Jobs* (Moretti 2012). The book appeared in 2012, when there was still vivid memory of the great recession of 2009 but at a time when the US economy had started to grow again, particularly in technologically booming urban areas (see Chapter 1). In the book, however, the positive correlation between human capital stocks and increasing land values disappears from Moretti's analysis, probably not because this was no longer the case at the time of writing, but because in the meantime the overheating of housing markets had become a highly contentious issue in US society and elsewhere. In short, the contradiction between the exchange values and use values of housing had become more and more salient in the most "vibrant" cities in the global technology-based economy, hence adding another dimension to the socially polarizing effects of such an economy (see Storper & Scott 2009) increasingly in the hands of monopoly capital at the time of his writing.

After the crisis of the late 2000s, constantly inflating housing prices in economically thriving cities and the consequent lack of affordable housing were at the centre of heated debates. According to economists such as Enrico Moretti and Edward Glaeser, but also to the conventional wisdom in powerful news media outlets such as the *New York Times*, Bloomberg and *The Economist* (e.g. Clark 2017), the solution to the housing crisis in cities that are "rich in human capital" is to build more housing and to relax housing regulations, such as the existing zoning codes in the US. In one of many articles discussing the housing crisis in California, eloquently titled "Build Build Build Build Build Build Build Build Build Build Build Build Build Build", the economics reporter specializing in housing and real estate at the *New York Times* wrote in February 2020: "It's true that the state is addressing facets of the mess, with efforts on rent control, subsidised housing and homelessness. But the hardest remedy to implement, it turns out, is the most obvious: Build more housing" (Dougherty 2020). This view is not limited to academics and mass media outlets but is now supported by the "pro-housing" movement self-designated as "YIMBY" ("yes in my backyard"). The YIMBY movement, which is composed mainly of high-skill millennials, opposes what it considers the NIMBY (not in my backyard) phenomenon of longtime residents that stand in the way of new housing development in cities with unaffordable housing markets in the US and Canada (Pearson & Schuetz 2022; Tretter & Heyman 2022).

The commonly held assumption in the pro-housing development stance is that relaxation in housing regulations would enable more construction, ensure higher density of the urban environment and will thus tackle the affordability problem in an effective manner, attracting new human capital and potential entrepreneurs. We saw in Chapter 1 that economists Edward Glaeser and Kristina Tobio identified the "Southern tolerance for new construction" (Glaeser & Tobio 2008) as a decisive factor behind the economic ascendancy of the Sun Belt in the US. However, the effect of policies that seek to create new capacity for residential development can be very different. For instance, empirical evidence shows that recent upzoning efforts in Chicago, aimed at increasing density in some urban areas, have had the effect of increasing prices of existing housing units (Freemark 2020).

The conflict between the highly skilled and highly paid newcomers and local residents became a hot issue in the early 2010s in the US. This conflict was brought to the fore of public debates, perhaps for the first time, by local residents in San Francisco, who took to the street to protest against the shuttle buses employed by technology companies to transfer their employees from San Francisco to Silicon Valley on a daily basis. The so-called "Google buses" or "tech buses" were viewed by local residents as symbols of gentrification and displacement (Rossi 2017). Interviewed by *Time* magazine, which asked for a solution to the housing affordability crisis highlighted by the Google buses protests, Moretti did not hesitate to join the "build more housing" front contending that "by constraining the amount of new housing, San Francisco has essentially pushed up the price of housing" (Steinmetz 2014: 32).

In regions and states such as California with a high population density, new building activity is limited by land use regulations that were obtained by the environmentalist movements in the previous decades. Land use regulations and other types of regulatory constraints are likely to become increasingly more pressing in the years to come with the exacerbation of the global environmental crisis. According to the UN Environment Programme, the building and construction sector currently accounts for around 37 per cent of energy and process-related CO_2 emissions (UNEP 2023). In some countries, recent years have seen novel experiments with sustainable housing. For instance, in 2022 the municipality of Skelleftea, a city in the north of Sweden, announced the construction of sustainable wooden, high-rise buildings that make use of solar panels and are designed to distribute surplus energy to nearby buildings (Horton 2022). However, zero-emission buildings are still a rarity and are likely to remain so in the foreseeable future. Therefore, the drastic reduction in new building activity remains the best solution from an environmental viewpoint, along with a reinvigorated public intervention in the regulation of housing markets. Moreover, and very importantly here as we will see in the remainder of this chapter, critics of policies aimed at the relaxation of housing regulations point out that rather than the supposed restraints to the supply of housing highlighted by economists and the mainstream media, it is the changing geography of labour demand and skills that should be viewed as a key factor behind the housing affordability crisis (Rodríguez-Pose & Storper 2020). This controversy epitomizes one of the ways in which human capital and urban space are brought together as a political question.

Supply-based explanations of the housing crisis, advocated by pro-human capital economists such as Moretti and the mainstream media, draw a veil over the responsibilities of the state in the regulation of market distortions and the alleviation of social inequalities. Housing crises are not new, of course, having historically afflicted capitalist cities in one form or another. The ambitious public housing programmes pursued by many Western governments after the Second World War tried to mitigate this social problem at that time. With the neoliberal turn in economic and social policy in the 1980s, the combined effect of the retreat of the state from universalist social welfare, the state's "regulated deregulation" of the construction sector and real-estate markets through tax breaks, financialization and other business-minded policies, as well as the polarizing effects of the information technology "revolution" on wealth, income and jobs have led to the current housing affordability crisis, which is unprecedented in terms of global reach (Wetzstein 2017).

Today's impact of the housing affordability crisis goes beyond the housing sector, having contributed in a substantial manner to the erosion of the sense of community in contemporary societies, fomenting social resentment, populist anger and anti-urban sentiments, particularly in those places and communities that have remained at the margins of contemporary technology-based urban transformations. The case of San Francisco is just the most visible of several urban stories of displacement affecting longtime residents, caused by the influx of high-paid workers linked to the expansion of the technology economy and, particularly in global cities, to the growth of high-paying jobs in the financial sector (Godechot 2012).

Since the second half of the 2010s, the rapid growth of the so-called "sharing economy" of short-term rentals (Airbnb and similar platforms) has further aggravated the housing affordability crisis in a growing number of cities, particularly in regions of the global periphery that have witnessed the intensification of international tourism inflows. Moreover, the so-called "populist explosion" that erupted at the national level in different key countries across the world in the second half of the 2010s – such as India, Brazil, US, UK – is largely the result of phenomena of socio-spatial polarization that originate from the expanding divide between winning and losing places. Housing policy can certainly alleviate the problem of affordable housing shortage, as it happened in the decades after the Second World War. However, the larger problem of socio-spatial polarization that affects contemporary capitalist economies in the age of techno-monopoly requires an in-depth interrogation of the human capital orthodoxy that has driven economic policy in the last four decades.

THE HUMAN CAPITAL DYSTOPIA IS YET TO COME

Rather than critically reappraising the societal effects of mainstream human capital theory in terms of social inequalities and economic polarization, the governmentality of urban development in the age of techno-monopoly tends to become entirely forged by the theory of human capital, which treats knowledge as an essential component of firms' strategic assets and people as primary sites for investment. A key role in this regard has been played by Paul Romer. He has been an active proponent of new growth theory – or endogenous growth theory, as it is more technically known – along with his former PhD supervisor Robert Lucas. In his 1990 article in particular, as we have seen in this chapter, Romer theorized that knowledge understood as an investment asset can function as a driver of long-term economic growth. This is due in his view largely to the ways in which ideas, understood as "non-rival goods", are able to circulate and spread between firms through dynamics of information spillovers, thus guaranteeing market competition (Romer 1990).

In 2009, Paul Romer gave a TED talk (https://youtu.be/mSHBma0Ithk) in which he presented to the wider public a new idea for long-term economic growth. The idea was presented with a new catchphrase: "charter cities". The notion of charter cities is evocative of the charter schools that were originally theorized by Milton Friedman with his proposal of school vouchers in the mid-1950s, as we have seen. In short, charter schools are publicly funded institutions that operate independently, like a private business, and are subject to fewer rules than state schools.

The charter cities movement (see https://chartercitiesinstitute.org/) imports this concept into the proposal for privately run city-states. In his talk, Romer outlined the economic rationale behind the charter cities proposal: in developing countries, human capital is constrained by lack of market incentives for firms to compete in functional markets and for families to realize their human potential. Taking up the model of economically prosperous cities with special administrative status such as Hong Kong – a "fantasy island" for charter city proponents (Ebner & Peck 2022) – or designated as special economic zones such as Shenzhen in China's region of Guangdong, Romer contended that people and leaders need efficient rules in order to get their projects done smoothly. According to Romer, this goal can be obtained by creating new cities from scratch endowed with business-sensitive legal and governance systems. In Romer's view, the negotiation and approval of new city projects would be facilitated by the contribution of democratic foreign states (citing Canada and Western European countries) acting as guarantors of each project. On this point, Romer reassured the audience, saying that the charter cities strategy would not be a way to reintroduce colonialism in the world, because colonial power was based on coercion and discretion, while the charter city project stems from an agreement involving different interested parties. Romer in his talk and subsequent interventions repeatedly pointed to Africa as an ideal laboratory for the charter cities model, as this continent is rich with "uninhabited land" – as he put it – even along its coasts. According to Romer, thanks to rationally defined rules and legal systems, charter cities would find themselves freed from crime and would be hospitable places for skilled immigrants looking for a satisfactory education system and a dynamic labour market.

After launching his idea, Romer became involved in the project of creating a new city in Honduras. In 2011, the government of Honduras even amended the state constitution by including the possibility to build new special development zones. As Romer described it at that time, the project was conceived as a government-led process in which a new governor would have been appointed by the Honduras government. Afterwards, the governor's second appointment would have been handled by a "board of trustees" formed by "highly reputable people" from across the world entitled to designate a new governor. After these initial stages, Romer added, the populace of the charter city would vote for the local government, including the governor. The project of instituting a charter city in Honduras, however, was short-lived and never succeeded. In 2012, Romer withdrew from the project, stepping down from his collaboration with the Honduran government due to the lack of transparency in the charter city process. Only one year later, in 2013, the project officially ended, as it was declared unconstitutional by the Honduras Supreme Court. Since then other tentative projects for new cities – also defined as "startup cities" or "talent cities" – aimed at attracting ambitious entrepreneurs and talented people willing to invest in the technology sector have been proposed in several countries, including Nigeria, Zambia and, most recently, in Tanzania (Pilling 2023).

In Tanzania, the e-commerce firm Wasoko – presented on the company website as "one of the fast-growing companies in Africa" – has taken the lead in a public-private partnership with the national government, which aims at creating a novel startup cluster called "Silicon Zanzibar". The newly created ecosystem would compete with existing tech hubs in key cities and metropolitan centres in Africa, such as those of Nairobi (the so-called "Silicon Savannah") and Cape Town (known as "Silicon Cape") (Pollio 2020). The stated aim of the project is to diversify the economy of Zanzibar, beyond the tourist sector on which the island mostly depends, even though the feasibility of the project remains uncertain at the moment (Mitchell 2023).

The idea of creating new cities from scratch is becoming increasingly linked to the pursuit of a novel tech-driven urban era freed from the constraints of democratic political systems. Elon Musk – the tech magnate known for provocative inventions as well as for being the richest person in the world – has recently made public through a report published by the *Wall Street Journal* (Grind *et al.* 2023) his project of creating a new town in Texas, in the urban area of Austin, where different legal entities controlled by Musk have purchased about 3,500 acres. The new town – called Snailbrook – would host the employees of two of Musk's companies located in the Austin area: Space X, which specializes in spacecraft manufacturing, and The Boring

Company, specializing in infrastructure and tunnel construction services. Both companies are iconic enterprises founded and owned by Elon Musk, closely connected to his project of planning a futuristic city that would free the population of cars and related carbon emissions. Snailbrook pledges to provide its new inhabitants with below-market-rate homes. In Musk's intentions, this would prevent quarrels over affordable housing between different income types in the residential population, like those that sparked the "Google buses" protests in San Francisco in the 2010s.

Snailbrook is not the first new town projected by Musk. In 2021, the tech multibillionaire announced through Twitter – the social media platform he bought one year later – his plan to create the "city of Starbase" in Texas, in seaside Boca Chica, about 350 miles from the Austin area, where already 1,600 employees work in SpaceX. The incentives offered by the governor of Texas in 2014 to move the company's establishments in Boca Chica clearly prompted Elon Musk's decision. But probably more than the financial incentives, the fact that, as Musk publicly confessed, "Texas has the right amount of rules and regulations", has been the decisive factor behind his move from California to Texas (Lowry 2022).

Rampant technology companies are not alone in planning new startup cities, as in the case of Wasoko in Zanzibar, or entirely new towns and cities, as in the case of Elon Musk in Texas or in that of singer and entrepreneur Akon in Senegal (www.akoncity.com). Futuristic cities and towns, in particular, are designed for hosting technology hubs, providing workers with liveable conditions in terms of environment and housing costs that existing cities cannot offer to them, according to their proponents. In December 2021, the Norwegian government announced a significant expansion of Oslo Science City, an existing research district of limited size at the moment (https://osloc iencecity.no/en/). The newly expanded science city is expected to accommodate 150,000 scientists, students and entrepreneurs that will have "new spaces to live, work and share knowledge", as the Danish architectural firm that has developed the project reports (Geschwindt 2021).

Viewed together, charter cities, startup cities, futuristic towns, as well as government-designed innovation districts elicit different kinds of emotions and intellectual postures from the critical observer. Charter cities and futuristic towns are intimately associated with neoliberal conceptions of a deeply individualistic, homogeneous society governed by the pure logic of free-market capitalism. Innovation districts planned by governments in liberal democracies are more benign representations of the attempt to recreate urban societies in a way in which entrepreneurial living becomes the norm rather than only one of the many social articulations of human living (Kayanan 2021). Despite their differences, all of these projects aim for a kind of socially cleansed urban environment in which any possibility of conflict, disorder and heterogeneity of life forms would be erased and pre-emptively repressed by law (Smith 2001). Ironically, these projects become more visible at a time when the tech-dominated era of global capitalism, or what we call here "techno-monopoly capitalism", seems to have come to a standstill, due to the increasingly more challenging macroeconomic conditions at the global level epitomized by the wave of massive layoffs in the tech industry and the sudden collapse of Silicon Valley Bank in 2022–23.

CONCLUSION

As we have seen in this chapter and Chapter 3, the distinction between high-skill and low-skill jobs has enormous discursive power in the context of contemporary urbanism in the age of techno-monopoly. Its impact is also significant at a wider level, as it plays a productive role in the shaping of economic, education and immigration policies of nation-states across geographical contexts. In fact, the entire human capital approach to national economic development, which is typical today in the corporatized states, is fundamentally premised on this distinction, which generalizes an urban logic of social competition and entrepreneurialization of human living.

In the trajectory that has led to the current configuration of techno-monopoly capitalism, the theory and operationalization of human capital have acted as key sources for the mutual reinforcement between the urban field, technology capital and the state. The creation of human capital is instrumental in the economization of knowledge as an investment asset and of the individual as a site for this investment. This process of economic value creation and extraction is believed to offer increasing returns thanks to knowledge's supposedly intrinsic tendency to spill over across firms and different economic agents that are part of the city's technology-based business ecosystem.

The state is an active agent in the economization of knowledge, prioritizing the urban field as a space where knowledge can be created and accumulated in a techno-capitalist economy: put differently, where knowledge becomes quite literally "knowledge capital". Through the urban field, therefore, the state attempts to harness the full potential of human life as a source of knowledge creation, multiplying its effects on the wide range of economic sectors that form the city's technology-based business ecosystem. The most ambitious or even reckless tech entrepreneurs, in this context, seek to constitute themselves as novel "startup states" (Moisio & Rossi 2020), in order to redefine rules and legal systems according to their corporate interests.

Today's growing fear in contemporary society about a revival of fascism or pseudo-fascist projects is largely the result of the subversiveness of the most powerful economic elites, such as the technology corporations trying to change the legality of economic activity or even to create a new legal order from scratch, as we have seen here and in Chapter 1. The return of the urban state in contemporary capitalism therefore takes different but largely complementary forms, either that of the legitimate state that seeks to harness the potential of urban life, so as to expand its economic base and strengthen national competitiveness, or that of the technology corporation that attempts to reconstruct the capitalist state on an autonomous basis, in order to get rid of the constraints of liberal democracies in terms of environmental regulations and labour laws: a corporatized state in its extreme.

CHAPTER 5

STARTUPS

INTRODUCTION

This book builds on the argument that the urban field provides today's techno-monopoly capitalism, as it has been defined here, with key sites for economic value generation: namely, labour, human capital, startups and forms of life. The third of these sites is, therefore, technology startup companies, a particular form of early-stage entrepreneurship that has come to dominate the business ecosystems of a growing number of cities and urban areas across the world after the advent of the information technology era.

This chapter shows how the urban startup economy should be primarily understood as an utterly speculative process aimed at creating and manipulating the market value of startup companies. Indeed, in our register, the startup economy is one of the key constituents of the urban field in the age of techno-monopoly capitalism. The basic idea is to demonstrate that the actual appearance of the startup economy as a capitalist formation effectively conceals its essence. In such a view, the startup economy appears as an ecosystem comprising high-skill labour and firms, digital technologies and dense urban environments expected to function as innovation machines. This appearance has been consolidated also by mainstream scholarship on startup economies and startup urban ecosystems. We, in turn, go on to argue that to understand the essence of this economy one needs to examine the ways in which the speculative process of valuation, the contributions by the state, and social polarization, actually constitute the startup economy.

In a mainstream scholarly view, the techno-capitalist economy signals the increasing significance of knowledge and innovation in the generation of profits. In such a view, the techno-capitalist economy is characterized by a strong legacy of what one may call a novelty tradition. This is a perspective that draws either explicitly or implicitly from Marshallian economics and underlines the role of agglomeration economies in creating economic value through a combination of knowledge spillovers resulting from spatial proximity, scale economies allowing input sharing among firms, and dynamics of labour pooling associated with urbanization or more generally with industrial concentrations (Rosenthal & Strange 2004). Such a lens to the contemporary economy highlights processes by which all kinds of technological novelties transform both the economy and society and provide fertile grounds for entrepreneurial subjects and firms to generate economic growth (see, e.g. Romer 1990). This research tradition hence customarily reduces the analysis of the technology-based economy to economic value creation and, at best, to the study of policies that contribute to value creation.

The above-mentioned economistic approach has the capacity to both depoliticize the technology-based economy as a societal phenomenon and instrumentalize certain forms of knowledge and human capital as potential in the creation of economic value in monetized form. Given the current pervasiveness of techno-capitalism not only as a mainstream scholarly abstraction but also as a policy panacea, the technology-based economy has become a central concern in the political agendas of nation-states and cities across the globe over the past few decades (Moisio 2018a; Pollio & Rossi 2023; Zukin 2020).

The techno-capitalist economy is not, however, a monolith but is constantly undergoing qualitative changes. In fact, the recent rise of startup economies and related interactions, human behaviours, skills and habits, represent the latest phase in this process. In this chapter we present a critical analysis of the ways in which the startup economy and the urban field are co-constituted in a context of techno-monopoly capitalism. We go on to argue that the urban field plays out as a key enabler of the startup economy and, conversely, that the startup economy is also one of the productive forces of the urban field as it unfolds in the present historical conjuncture.

We develop three arguments in particular. First, contemporary scholarship is dominated by "elitist" approaches that highlight the role of urban space as an innovation machine that enables and fosters the creativity of startup entrepreneurs. This kind of perspective reduces the urban economic value generation process of the startup economy to one segment of the population and their human capital (see also Chapters 3 and 4) and represents a kind of skill-based symbolic violence. This notion refers to the ways in which urban governmentality reduces the happiness, success and competitiveness of urban environments to specific "creative" or technologically capable/innovative segments of urban population. In so doing, this form of governing marginalizes the other segments of the urban population and hierarchizes urban development. Second, we argue that there is a discrepancy between the way the world of startup service firms appears in urban space and the way such an economy really is in the fundamental processes of market valuation of startup companies. Through a case study of a food courier company, Wolt, one of the most "successful" startups in the history of Finland, we seek to demonstrate that market valuation processes of startups are less about the actual business activities and more about the internal logics in the market valuation process itself. Third, we suggest that the "potential" of the urban field in terms of value extraction is an important factor in the market valuation process of startups and that the state contributes to the valuation process of the startup economy in many if implicit ways.

THE WORLD OF STARTUPS

As argued above, the startup economy has emerged as one of the ruling ideas in the advanced capitalist world over the past few years. In this sense, the startup economy has to be viewed not just as an economic form that is typical of contemporary techno-capitalism, but as an ideology instigated by specific fractions of monopoly capital and associated elites. As such, it can be argued that the startup economy is about ruling ideas as "ideal expression of the dominant material relations" (Marx & Engels 1998: 67).

Arguably, the startup ideology characterizes the latest phase of techno-capitalist expansion, as well as the latest developments in both entrepreneurial urbanism and state territorial restructuring (McNeill 2017; Moisio & Tarvainen 2023). Its origins are rooted in the Californian ideology of technological enthusiasm combined with libertarian individualism that began to rise in the 1970s and took form in the 1990s, based on the belief that information technologies empower the individual, enhance personal freedom and radically reduce the power of state bureaucracy (Barbrook & Cameron 1996). Californian ideology was part of an increasingly larger sensitivity in American society, bound to become common wisdom within the space of a few years. Accordingly, small-scale, decentralized technology was perceived as a more embracing concept and activity compared with the technocratic industrial systems that had been predominant in the postwar decades (Hughes 1989).

As an economic imaginary, the startup economy underlines how capitalism is increasingly based on immaterial forms of production. This production process has involved the commodification of knowledge, affects, visual images, to mention but a few, and it manifests itself in a range of spheres, from the production of spectacles, digital games, digitalized learning environments, to the service sector and beyond.

The paradigmatic actors in the world of Western startups are tech giants such as Amazon, Apple, eBay, Google, Meta, Microsoft and PayPal, the digital platform-based service network providers such as Lyft, DoorDash, Airbnb and Uber, as well as other powerful companies such as Tesla. To be more precise, these are former startups, a sort of iconic manifestation of the Californian startup model. These companies nonetheless play a role model function across geographical contexts. Growing fast is the key word here. These firms form the canon of the startup world in the Western hemisphere, however, not only because of their rapid growth but also because these companies can be understood as peculiar personifications of heroic startup human figures. The startup economy is premised on utterly entrepreneurial language that articulates the virtues and potentials of highly speculative risk-taking entrepreneurship.

Business magazines endlessly highlight how startup entrepreneurs are innovative, creative, disruptive, fearless, eager to break rules and challenge conventional ways of doing business, as well as being ready to fail and especially to "fail better" (Daub 2020). A venture capitalist and startup entrepreneur Paul Graham (2010) argues that a set of traits ranging from determination to naughtiness characterize startup entrepreneurs. They wear hoodies and sneakers in business meetings and have a purportedly relaxed attitude in their office space – if compared to executives in more established firms. Accordingly, the startup economy is constituted by high-skill innovative entrepreneurs – the creative class of digitalization – as a "cosmopolitan" and "diverse" paradise in its making (Noble & Roberts 2019; Shearmur 2007). The historian Jill Lepore (2014) aptly parodies the deep logics of the Californian model of startups and the ways in which these logics are premised on the (false) idea of disruptive innovation:

> The logic of disruptive innovation is the logic of the startup: establish a team of innovators, set a whiteboard under a blue sky, and never ask them to make a profit, because there needs to be a wall of separation between the people whose job is to come up with the best, smartest, and most creative and important ideas and the people whose job is to make money by selling stuff … The upstarts who work at startups don't often stay at any one place for very long. (Three out of four startups fail. More than nine out of ten never earn a return.) They work a year here, a few months there – zany hours everywhere. They wear jeans and sneakers and ride scooters and share offices and sprawl on couches like Great Danes. Their coffee machines look like dollhouse-size factories … They are told that they should be reckless and ruthless.

Indeed, literature dealing with "Western" startup entrepreneurs is premised on and recycles the colonial storylines on individualistic heroes who conquer new worlds and frontiers. As Tarvainen (2022: 9) has showcased, the innovation literature systemically portrays Silicon Valley as "the new 'Wild West' where the 'high-tech cowboys' and 'computer cowboys' live on the edge of technology and 'lone pioneers' ride into the 'western sun'". The contemporary visions for space colonization, as spread by the world's wealthiest persons and the leading entrepreneurs of the startup economy such as Jeff Bezos and Elon Musk, perfectly embody the culture of the technology startup economy as constant conquering and searching of frontiers by creatives equipped with unique human capital. As we will see in the remainder of this chapter, the ambition to create charter cities, also called "startup cities", in supposedly "uninhabited land" (see Chapter 4) is one of the most evident spatial manifestations of the colonial imaginary ingrained in startup ideology.

STARTUP ECONOMY AS A CONSTITUENT OF THE URBAN FIELD

Why think of the startup economy with the concept of the urban field? An obvious answer is that urban space has always been a key frontier of the startup economy, due to the intrinsic colonial imaginary of the latter, as we wrote earlier. In startup imaginaries, urban space hence appears as a relentlessly expanding site within which economic value can be generated and extracted in a potentially unlimited fashion. It appears either as a test site within which innovations emerge or as a consumerist marketplace that provides the necessary demand for the production of commodities and services. It is a site closely associated with the idea of the scalability of business; that is, with the presupposition of startup firms' inherent capacity to grow to meet increasing demand, as we said in Chapter 1.

It is important to note that the startup economy has developed concomitantly with a mainstream economic scholarship that emphasizes the endogenous dynamics of urban environments, leading the city to act as an "innovation machine" (Florida, Adler & Mellander 2017). As we have discussed in Chapter 4, at its root – starting with the work of Robert Lucas on human capital (Lucas 1988) – this economic scholarship draws inspiration from Jane Jacobs' conception of face-to-face urbanism (Jacobs 1961) and her understanding of the economy of cities as a dynamic combination of specialization and variety (Jacobs 1969). We argue that this kind of scholarship has not only contributed to the consolidation of startup entrepreneurship as an urban phenomenon but also effectively conceals the very essence of the techno-capitalist economy. In this mainstream view, the city is believed to act as an innovation machine thanks to the unique condensation of human capital in the economically thriving urban agglomerations and metropolitan areas (Florida 2012; Glaeser 2011). Influential urban economists and public commentators have hence formed a peculiar choir, which praises the intrinsic virtues of urbanism in the technology-based economy. Simultaneously, this choir effectively emphasizes the role of one segment of population in the constitution of the startup economy: the creatives whose human capital is customarily understood as constituting the startup city in the first place.

In the startup imaginaries, urban space acts a magnet for venture capital flows (Florida & King 2016) thanks to its functioning as an "ecosystem" that brings together technology enthusiasm, capital, creativity and a variety of communities of practice with their animating fantasies (Rossi & Di Bella 2017). Urban environments thus enable rather than hinder the individual to leverage their human capital as an "entrepreneur of themself". The capability of these startup entrepreneurs to commodify digital formats and contents – a kind of copyright economy based on the internet – as successful businesses, and the associated shift from "mere technology" to "content" is therefore almost invariably associated with the urban field. Accordingly, the new, economically profitable ideas arise from a cooperative and culturally and socially rich urban fabric. In these imaginaries, dynamic and lively urban environments are said to contribute fundamentally to the production of a new generation of innovative entrepreneurs (cf. Scott 2014). In the startup imaginaries, urban space hence both produces and hosts the "entrepreneurs of themselves" (Bröckling 2015). In short, the startup economy entails a relentless invention of entrepreneurial forms of life drawing on daily practices of cooperation in the city/metropolis understood as a "social factory" (Negri 2018).

Startup economies are customarily constructed upon the normalcy of city life. In these economies, the urban realm appears not as an empty space to be filled by investors, but as a socially rich and economically productive space within which the potential of life in its multiple forms can be harnessed to economic purposes. As production is seen in the startup economy to take place in social relationships (this is typical within the context of technocapitalism more broadly), the generation of relational subjectivity becomes vital, not just the possession of entrepreneurial knowledge per se. Here, the urban field marks a social space in which skilled startup entrepreneurs become involved in collaborative activities related to co-creation, co-option and enriching interaction, to name but a few, and produce economic value both through and in these interactions.

When it comes to the spatial forms, the city of startups is conceived as a densely populated urban environment. However, the real, dense entrepreneurial city "is made of flesh, not concrete" (Glaeser, cit. in Smith 2012), as one "celebrity urbanologist" (Peck 2016) revealingly puts it. In such an economic imaginary, "urban density provides the clearest path from poverty to prosperity" (Glaeser 2011: 1). Dense urban spaces are desirable, for they enable face-to-face interaction of people who cherish the sociability of a city and love new ideas that have economic potential. According to Glaeser (cit.

in Jenkins 2015), "what globalisation and new technologies do is radically increase the returns to being smart. We are a social species that gets smarter by being around other smart people, and that's why cities thrive".

Startup economic imaginaries are predicated upon a seamless connection between work in urban space and outside-work urban life, thus making the boundary between working time and non-working time largely obsolete. Its protagonists are aspiring happy-city entrepreneurs who mix ideas of common good, collaboration and sharing with the ambition of embodying the ability to create value through the pursuit of a truly people-centred economy (Cohen & Muñoz 2016; Glaeser 2011). In this capacity, the imaginaries of the startup economy bring together and meld the risk-taking economic subject with an urban communitarian figure who is inspired by an ethos of collaboration (Cohen & Muñoz 2015).

With regard to generating value, the startup economy blurs the boundaries between the workplace and the place of living and produces a particular segment of the population – the creative innovators and risk-takers – as the economic-political ideal. More importantly, their capacities and ethics are articulated as if the startup subjects resided in the affective micro-fabrics of the urban field. In other words, the urban field is understood as if it brought them pleasure both at work and outside of it – reconnecting the spheres of production, social reproduction and leisure. In the imaginaries of the startup economy, the constitution and maintenance of labour power is thus ultimately an urban question.

The urban fabric is understood by the startup economy boosters in particular as providing the necessary backdrop to rework the ways in which the startup populace understands their role as "constant innovators" for whom the boundary between work and non-work becomes increasingly blurred. It is for this reason that intensive urban space, in all its qualitative aspects, appears in the imaginaries of the startup economy as a crucial constitutive element.

In the startup economy imaginaries, the urban field appears as a vast open-plan office, a post-political laboratory for social interaction, a community-making platform, or a test bed in which the creativity of entrepreneurs is no longer restrained by old capitalists and state bureaucracy (Moisio & Rossi 2020). The urban field is thus built into the startup economic imaginaries with a strong libertarian tone. Quite paradoxically, the appeal of startup urban ecosystems across political parties also stems from their seemingly apolitical and post-statist nature. In the academic literature, too, the startup economy is often articulated as if it were less statist than the late-Keynesian forms of knowledge-based economization. In such a view, the technopoles of the 1980s and the 1990s are "more" state-orchestrated or statist in nature than the recent startup urban economies (Bunnell 2002; see, however, Pollio 2020 and Zhang 2023 on the development in other geographical contexts).

Given the close connections between the startup economy and libertarian ideology – which has been traditionally at the core of the Silicon Valley startup culture – it does not come as a revelation that one fundamental premise behind the urban foundations of the startup economy is the critique of the purportedly "political" nature of the nation-state. The above-mentioned startup imaginaries, premised on ideas of urban density and social collaboration in "happy cities" (Montgomery 2013), operate in tandem with an imaginary that contrasts with dysfunctional nationalism, purportedly rigid party politics, clientelism and seemingly functional and post-statist cities (see e.g. Barber 2013). In so doing, the latter imaginary combines economic productivity with the idea of a new post-national urban age.

In the libertarian startup imaginaries, the state represents nothing but a harmful collective form of political intervention. The urban imaginaries of the startup economy hence draw either implicitly or explicitly on reasoning according to which nation-states are not meaningful economic regions. In such a perspective, an analysis of the rise and fall of economic wealth should start with the economies of cities rather than states (Jacobs 1984). As Andrew Jonas has pointed out, this conception "fetishises the city as a productive entity in itself capable of generating wealth", where "the city is seen to possess organismic qualities and generate forces akin to the laws of nature" (Jonas 1986: 131). Jane Jacobs' conception would later become popular among globalization boosters, innovation gurus and scholars of "connectography" (Khanna 2016), who customarily argue that cities and city networks are more functional than territorial states in the global economy (Ohmae 1993) or that global governance should be increasingly based on cities rather than nation-states (Barber 2013).

This kind of spatial reasoning has been furthered also by Paul Romer, an influential growth theorist and successful entrepreneur who initiated the idea of "charter cities" as one possible solution to generate growth in challenging political contexts beyond the advanced capitalist states (see Chapter 4). The urban startup economy imaginaries range from libertarian floating communities as startup cities (Quirk & Friedman 2017) and charter cities to more conventional urban development projects. Regarding the latter, many of the local governments across geographical contexts have launched economic development strategies geared around the idea of urban ecosystems consisting of digital platforms, human capital, open data and venture capital.

An analysis of the recent urban growth strategies discloses a notable shift from both the Fordist and immediately post-Fordist management of urban economies, when the capitalist valorization of urban settings targeted conditions of obsolescence and devalued property in the built environment (Weber 2002). In those contexts, state intervention was intended to provide assistance to private investors through urban renewal programmes, as well as, more recently, through fiscal enclaves such as Business Improvement

Districts and special economic zones. Those fiscal expansionary policies – relying either on public expenditure or tax cuts – allowed the state to impose its sovereign prerogatives through situational procedures and norms granting entrepreneurial freedom to foreign and domestic investors (Ong 2006).

Conventional wisdom tends to portray startup economies in the technology sector as self-propulsive, city-centred phenomena. So far, academic scholarship – albeit still scarce and embryonic on this topic – has substantially seconded this idea (Florida & King 2016; Florida & Mellander 2016), while critical scholars have only drawn attention to the role of local governments and the real-estate industry in the rise of technology-oriented business ecosystems (McNeill 2016; Rossi & Di Bella 2017). Overall, existing scholarship has left issues such as state regulative practices, state restructuring, state bureaucracy and policy-making largely unexplored, providing an understanding of the urban realm as an entity somehow spontaneously generating high-tech entrepreneurship and economic value (see, however, e.g. Pollio 2020). City-centric conceptions of the startup economy have emerged in conjunction with a rapidly expanding knowledge industry, which tailors all sorts of startup city rankings, mappings and indices. These rankings produce cities discursively as actually existing startup "ecosystems" and economic territories that are involved in a purportedly fierce global inter-spatial competition (Moisio 2018a, 2019).

As we have noted above, the constitutive ideas of the startup economy are often comprehended as arising from a cooperative and socio-culturally rich urban fabric rather than from the governmental processes of the territorial state. However, as Dierwechter (2018) has argued, the role of the state in politically reconstructing an ideal of the good society has returned to prominence in the seemingly post-political contemporary context, characterized by the "animating fantasies" (Dean 2009) of smartness, creativity, ecosystemic innovation and place attachment (Rossi & Di Bella 2017). In a similar vein, we believe that it is analytically problematic to conceptualize the startup economy as a merely post-national, post-statist, city-centric and firm-based economic world. Certainly, the late-Keynesian interventions of the state differ from the recent economic interventions of the state. Neither do we deny the role of cities as "self-promoting islands of entrepreneurship" (Amin & Malmberg 1992: 413) or as effective "ecosystems" within which firms with a "symbolic knowledge base" (Asheim, Coenen & Vang 2007) are nurtured and developed. However, we make an analytic distinction between the urban field as a site of economic value creation, providing fertile ground for startup businesses and for the valuation of startup companies; and the new socio-spatial dialectic – what we characterize as the cross-fertilization between the state-orchestrated entrepreneurialization of the urban field and the strategic urbanization of the nation-state.

EXTRACTING ECONOMIC VALUE THROUGH THE URBAN FIELD

Startup economies are concerned with both the generation and extraction of economic value. Several scholars have examined the extractive dimensions of this economic formation. They have for instance scrutinized the ways in which data on individual behaviour has become one of the key constituents of profit-making in the contemporary tech-driven urban startup economies. Zuboff (2019) scrutinizes datafication/digitalization and demonstrates how Big Tech companies such as Google are effectively tracking actions of individuals and selling that data to different kinds of economic actors. Zuboff hence demonstrates how personal information is gathered by tech companies and how this data has been used by other firms operating on digital platforms not only to predict the behaviour of individuals in the future but also to manipulate their actions in such a way that ensures capital accumulation and profit-making.

In a similar vein, Wark (2019) examines how the ordinary life of human beings, based on sharing thoughts and feelings with each other and having connections to other people (what can be defined as the urban commonwealth: Hardt & Negri 2009), is being increasingly commodified in the age of techno-monopoly capitalism by a ruling class that "owns the vector along which information is gathered and used" (Wark 2019: 3). Both Zuboff and Wark hence underline some of the ways in which the extraction of economic value occurs through the urban field.

The internet bubble of the 1990s materialized in the form of mushrooming internet startup companies, some developing and selling the technology to provide internet access. Other companies, in turn, used the internet to provide services. This process disclosed some of the ways in which the tech industry became increasingly urban at the level of not only business strategies but also in the sense of local and national state governments seeking to satisfy the Big Tech companies (Zukin 2020). Ever since, the privatization of the commons, as an important constituent of the urban field in techno-monopoly capitalism, has been a notable feature in startup economies.

We argue in the ensuing paragraphs that in addition to the privatization of the urban commons, the nucleus of the startup world is the business valuation process itself: an attempt to increase the market value of a startup through rounds of investments (equity capital/venture capital), through the associated expansion (both geographically and with regards to products and services), and through powerful narratives regarding the potentially lucrative nature of the selected business model. Valuation in the startup world hence represents one of the key features of the startup economy and in so doing fundamentally constitutes its essence as a social and political object. Often, the valuation process is constructed around or at least closely connected to the founder of the company who interacts with investors, policy-makers and consultants as "value professionals".

Our analysis of the Finnish startup company Wolt – which we present in the next section – seeks to bring another dimension to the scholarly debate on the extraction of economic value through the urban field: the business valuation process of startup companies. This is important given the capacity of techno-capitalism to effectively separate phenomena, and in so doing to conceal some significant dimensions of economic formations. As a capitalist social formation, the urban startup economy is based on separating different kinds of producers of economic value, highlighting the role of high-skill human capital, in particular. Simultaneously, the urban startup economy separates the mundane business activities of startup companies from the hidden but equally real appearance of such an economy, namely the business valuation of startups. Valuation, as we understand it, represents a way of extracting the economic value in the urban startup economy through highly speculative practices.

The cheerleaders of the startup economy customarily highlight that startups seek to develop new products and services under extreme uncertainty (Ries 2011). The key potential in this allegedly risky and uncertain economy is that some of the products and services are scalable in such a manner that lays foundations not only for high revenues but also for high business valuations. The rise of platform businesses and their algorithmically mediated gig economies have, however, proved also that the new digital innovations often need cheap and precarious labour-relations in order to become scalable (Gebrial 2022; Srnineck 2017). This cheapness, as Gebrial (2022) argues in her studies on the expansions of Uber, is often founded on earlier phases of the colonial production of precarious migrant and informal labour. As such, the "processes of racialisation have been crucial at every stage of the platform economy's rise to dominance, and therefore constitutes a key organizing principle of platform capitalism" (Gebrial 2022: 1).

Success in scaling business nonetheless becomes both a strategy to generate profits and, even more importantly, a basis for the growth of companies for the sake of business valuation. Over the past decades, trying to get big rapidly became the ideal, leading to a kind of unicorn hype. In other words, scalability enables developing a given company towards unicorn status. The unicorn status – a highly symbolic category of startup companies constantly listed and reported by such prestigious magazines as *Fortune* and the *Wall Street Journal* – refers explicitly to a privately held startup with market valuation of US$1 billion or more. There can indeed be "successful" unicorns that have not been able to generate profits through their basic business operations. More generally, the valuation process and the creation of surplus value do not necessarily have any meaningful connection to each other in the startup economy. The future-speculative nature of the startup economy is hence embodied in the fact that the business value of startups is primarily based on other things than earnings. For most startups, their value rests on future potential.

The future-oriented valuation game of the startups is essentially based on the availability of investment money. This nature of the startup economy became increasingly visible in 2022 after a peculiar epoch that was characterized by very cheap money. During the past 10–15 years, the growth of technology companies, based on the cheap money granted by the low-interest rate policy pursued by central banks, in turn, was materialized as generation of new jobs, both expensive and cheap ones. In the startup valuation game, jobs are in fact needed for both practical and symbolic reasons. Regarding the latter, the new jobs are needed to demonstrate that the companies will to grow in both operational and geographical terms. The demonstrated will to grow is, again, a fundament to attract new cheap loans. The spiral of growth, and the related manipulation of expectations, have hence in the startup economy knitted together labour and finance in a peculiar manner.

Arguably, without the flexible coming together of cheap money and the generation of high-skill jobs, the extreme market valuations of tech firms ranging from food delivery companies to "innovative" car dealers would not have been possible over the past decade. The fact that the interest rates rose significantly since 2022 – resulting from multiple crises – disclosed the extreme nature of the startup platform economy as a business valuation game closely premised on the growth of companies that are often operating in cities and through the urban field.

Since 2022, as interest rates have gone up, the rapidly expanding technology companies have taken a reverse gear and have laid off massive numbers of their high-skill employees. As such, the employees of these companies are now experiencing the flip side of extreme business valuations and the associated aggressive strategies to boost market share. In 2023, previous startup technology companies forcefully cut their workforce. Not only startups but also established technology companies and even the most powerful tech giants were involved in this process of downsizing. To illustrate, Salesforce, a tech company that bought the office communications tool Slack for €26 billion, cut 8,000 people in 2023. Amazon, in turn, laid off 18,000 office workers. At around the same time, the stock market valuation of Amazon went down by nearly a trillion dollars (Streidfeld 2023). The recent rounds of layoffs, as well as the volatility of valuations, effectively disclose the "workings of capitalism", and the "operative spaces" within which these workings unfold, to use the language of Mezzadra and Neilson (2019).

A significant dimension of the business valuation process of startups pertains to the value-adding interaction between startup entrepreneurs, investors and other value professionals such as consultants and state authorities. This is the future-oriented field of business interaction whereby the actual valuation process of startup companies takes shape. A startup company is valued as worth something precisely in funding rounds within which venture capital is targeted to meet the needs of emergent firms, particularly in the high-tech sector. Startup investing has indeed become a unique branch in the world of capital. Not surprisingly, venture capital has expanded significantly in the age of techno-capitalism – both geographically and in terms of the number of venture capital firms. Simultaneously, of course, venture capital has been absolutely central in constituting the startup economy in the first place. Therefore, cause and effect.

The startup valuation business is premised on and structured around money-capital-related terms such as bootstrapping, business angels, equity finance and private equity. It is a form of business specialized in making or coordinating investments in companies, and in turning the fictionalized expectations and envisioned futures of startups into manageable forms as risk-laden potentials. In this process, the role of investment capital and investors is pivotal. In addition to possible investments by founders, startups seek to raise additional investment at different stages to lay foundations for future growth. This is how startups come together with private equity.

Venture capital searches for high returns. Representatives of venture capital hence usually invest in startups that have set up ambitious development milestones that articulate high growth potential in the short run and the long run as well. The leading Finnish newspaper interviews investors who are seeking to fund future unicorns and reports in a respectful tone how:

> Finding unicorns and breeding them is a skill. Lifeline [the company] has been a key early-stage investor in, for example, Supercell and Wolt ... Most of the investors are institutional, i.e. various pension companies and foundations. The remaining investors are typically asset management companies of wealthy families or individuals ... When reviewing business ideas, one of the key selection criteria ... is an assessment of whether any of the company's founders are capable of being involved in the company's management, even if the company grows really large.
> (Raeste 2023)

Venture capitalists negotiate with startups and in so doing select targets of investments. They gather data on the performance of startups and circulate such information. In cases where the startup company is meeting the milestones of growth, investors assign a higher value. Consultancies also play a crucial role here. These consultancies act as business valuation specialists providing estimates on the business value of startups, especially with little or no revenue and with uncertain futures. These companies also do due diligence checks on behalf of the investors.

Indeed, the job of assigning a valuation is particularly tricky in the context of startups. All the stages of business valuation of startups are highly speculative. Their valuation hence differs greatly from publicly listed mature businesses with steady earnings and revenues, as well as with other solid assets that can be valued according to the principles of mainstream business valuation manuals. In fact, a startup company's actual value is often connected to the cognitive capital (a mix of intellectual, affective and emotional elements) it embodies, and other intangible factors. Given the ambiguity of estimating the worth of startups, metrics such as cost-to-duplicate and stage valuation, as well as analysis of revenue multiples, and business forecasts are used in the valuating practices. All metrics indeed underline the speculative nature of calculating the worth of startups. This is irrespective of the fact that startup companies may also produce novel commodities and novel services, develop technologies, as well tailor effective ways of doing things.

Given the many opportunities to develop businesses on digital platforms – which mainly rest on the existing technologies, big data and algorithms – the startup valuation process has fundamentally marked the service economy in the age of techno-monopoly capitalism. Moreover, given the potential of urban digital environments for the geographical scaling operations, the characteristically urban internet-based service businesses have mushroomed over the past years and formed a significant cadre within the world of startups. Again, these urban-based companies customarily seek to expand their operations rapidly, generate profits if possible, and then leave the startup phase with a smooth exit strategy. In any case, the business valuation of urban startups discloses one of the ways in which techno-capitalism "hits the ground" (Mezzadra & Neilson 2019) on the urban field.

THE CORPORATIZED STATE IN THE STARTUP WORLD

The startup economy is essentially premised on libertarian tenets that highlight the post-statist nature of such an economy. However, the operations and valuations of the startup economy cannot be separated from the social and political conditions within which they are situated. In fact, it is impossible to envision startup economies outside flows of economic value through the state – both the local and the national. The corporatized state is an important player in the generation of economic value in the startup economy. Governments manipulate the playing field of startups, build regulative environments that seek to satisfy the operation of startups and create innovation complexes as discursive, organizational and physical spaces. The corporatized state also encourages and nurtures the startup culture. This is understandable given that local and national governments are fundamentally dependent on capital accumulation. Across geographical contexts, the startup economy hence embodies the potentiality of returns in the form of tax revenue and more.

The role of the state in startup economies has been recognized by critical analysts. Silicon Valley, customarily understood as the epicentre of the startup economy, would not have been possible without the investments from the military-industrial complex closely associated with the state (O'Mara 2020). As Weiss (2014) argues, American security and military interests have been driving the technology-development and venture investment since the inception of the Valley. For instance, the success of Palantir (and its valuation in the stock market) – a startup founded by well-known startup guru Peter Thiel – has been fundamentally based on the fact that it received massive early investments from CIA funds to develop its products. The products of Palantir enable effective monitoring and surveillance of large populations through specific algorithms, and in so doing the firm provides the state agencies with a notable resource to control populations in the name of national security. A true libertarian believer might consider the actual outcomes of this and many other similar startup companies as a terrible state-centred nightmare.

Contra neoliberal narratives, the state has always been a significant actor in the startup economy and in the associated creation of economic value. Mariana Mazzucato (2013), a suspicious economist and pundit in the eyes of libertarian startup boosters, has put forward the influential notion of the entrepreneurial state, which emphasizes the vital contribution that public policy has made with technology investment since the late 1980s in "innovative" regions and sectors such as Silicon Valley and the biotechnology industry in the US. Through this concept, Mazzucato challenges dominant political narratives on the advent of an economy of innovations. In such a dominant view, "business is accepted as the innovative force, while the state is cast as the inertial one – necessary for the 'basics', but too large and heavy to be the dynamic engine" (*ibid*.: 1).

Mazzucato (2013) argues that the entrepreneurial state is a key player in the value creation mechanism. Governments create economic value rather than merely interfere with firms in their innovative attempts. Put briefly, the entrepreneurial state creates economic value through government interventions. In addition, the entrepreneurial state has not only acted as a direct value creator, but also played a key role as an investor. Mazzucato (2013) highlights that the state has funded both basic and applied research that have contributed enormously to bringing about some of the well-known knowledge-intensive commercialized products ranging from smartphones to pharmaceutical products. Indeed, the state has not only taken the role of an investor, but it has also taken the role of a high-risk-taking venture capitalist: the state has played a greater role than venture capital funds in investing in vulnerable early-stage firms – many of which fail and disappear (*ibid.*: 47–9).

Libertarian, firm-centred and anti-state reverberations notwithstanding, the startup economy has become an accumulation strategy also among local and national state governments (Zukin 2020). As such, the startup economy brings together the high technology sector, venture capitalists, early-stage entrepreneurs, universities, consultancies, international organizations and funding bodies, tech enthusiasts, and nation-state and local state administrations, and is embodied spatially in learning regions, technology parks, special economic zones, innovative milieus/complexes, clusters, business incubators, business accelerators and all kinds of ecosystems of innovations. Despite the ideological construction of its operations, the startup economy is not a clearly delineated hegemonic project in Gramscian terms (Moisio & Rossi 2020). We rather conceptualize it as an intrinsically combinatorial project that has more clearly emerged in the post-2008 conjuncture of capitalist restructuring, bringing together people, government, firms, technologies, organizations and governmental technologies in the name of economic growth, development and national success. It is no surprise, then, that the startup economy still possesses a particular aura of progress across geographical contexts. This has become highly salient in the context of cities.

In the ensuing pages we develop our arguments through the illustrative evidence provided by one case study, drawing on direct observation in Finland, as well as on mass media sources and official documentation. We examine the startup unicorn Wolt, often considered one of the national champion startups in Finland – together with a handful of mobile game developers. This case is among the many that motivate one to rethink the entanglement of urban space, state action and value extraction as it unfolds today in techno-monopoly capitalism. Moreover, this case underscores that in the contemporary extraction of value the different forms of the urban field play equally important roles.

THE STORY OF WOLT AS AN URBAN STARTUP COMPANY

Finnish food delivery startup Wolt announced in November 2021 that it had been acquired by the US food delivery company DoorDash (one of the largest food and retail delivery platforms in the world) in an all-stock transition of €7 billion. To date, this economic transaction is still one of the largest startup deals in Europe. According to the press release by DoorDash Inc., "Both companies share a mission to build a global platform for local commerce that connects consumers with the best of their community, drives incremental revenue for merchants, and provides meaningful earning opportunities for millions of Dashers and couriers around the world." (Cision 2021). Moreover, Tony Xu (2021), CEO of DoorDash, highlights how "DoorDash and Wolt share a vision to build a global platform for local commerce that empowers the communities we operate in". In so doing, Xu draws attention to "shared value", an increasingly salient business discourse that quite revealingly characterizes the ways in which the contemporary technology-based economies are often understood as being connected to the local social fabric. Accordingly, "the competitiveness of a company and the health of the communities around it are closely intertwined. A business needs a successful community, not only to create demand for its products but also to provide critical public assets and a supportive environment" (Porter & Kramer 2011: 6).

Wolt was founded in 2014 by a few young Finnish startup boosters who had their background in the Aalto University (a state-orchestrated university of innovations) and Slush, one of the largest startup events globally. When Wolt was acquired by DoorDash, the firm had raised investment capital of around €600 million from investors such as Mark Zuckerberg's ICONIQ Capital, Tiger Global, Israel's 83North and London-based Highland Europe. It is a significant amount of capital given that Wolt raised its first pre-seed round of investment in 2014 (of around €400,000). All this money poured into a firm that was not able to generate profits through its basic operations as a food delivery platform. In 2022, Wolt Enterprises made an operating loss of approximately €422 million. In 2021, the operating loss was approximately €192 million. In its annual report published in 2023, Wolt estimates that it will continue to make losses in the future (Niemi 2023).

The development of Wolt as a success story and the related rise of the market value of the firm has been based on several rounds of investments (Series A in 2016), which have brought together global venture capital and institutional investors. A company called EQT Ventures – which makes equity investments in startups in Europe and the US – reports how the exit valuation of Wolt when it was sold to DoorDash represents an approximate 200 times uplift compared to the initial investment they made to the company in 2016. For EQT Ventures, one of the most important aspects of Wolt as a successful startup was the engagement of owners, investors and delivery couriers with the company and its business model. Accordingly, "Wolt's obsession with stakeholders' experience and success, not just their own, has been their winning strategy. They have continued to orchestrate this three-party dance, ever-deepening the features and streamlining the process for all involved, which has given them superb unit economics along the way" (Jörnow 2021).

Moreover, one of the seed investors (Inventure) argues that Wolt has "taken better care of its drivers by always paying more than minimum wage and has never been included in the negative press coverage its competitors receive" (Billing 2021).

From a narrow perspective, the valuation of startup unicorns seems to be very logical. Accordingly, given that the recent historical conjuncture has been characterized by low interest rates and stocks already traded at very rich valuations, it is only logical that investment money pours into equity investor funds, which then invest into the most "promising" startups. Consequently, market valuations of some of these startups become extremely high. End of story. In the context of the Wolt case, one, however, immediately recognizes that, as an innovative and aggressively expanding service delivery platform company, there is something inherently urban in startups and their valuation. We argue below that the extraction of value in the context of Wolt and similar companies is indeed connected to complex urban processes that touch upon the urban field and what Hardt and Negri (2009) have conceptualized as "the metropolis" in cognitive and affective capitalism. As such, both the creation and extraction of value in the context of startups is an urban process par excellence, and the ways in which the urban field plays out in these processes merit more scholarly attention.

Many technology firms that operate in services brand themselves as if their business operations were based on cities. DoorDash, for instance, brands the firm as one that operates in more than 7,000 cities in North America, Australia and Japan. As such, the business potential that these companies both articulate and embody is essentially premised on the process of urbanization. As such, their business potential is constituted through the urban field, which, in turn, is transformed into the potential increase in shareholder value (Xu 2021). Hardt and Negri, however, argue that access to the reserve of social relations embedded in it is the basis of production in the metropolis at large, "and the results of production are in turn newly inscribed in the metropolis, reconstituting and transforming it" (Hardt & Negri 2009: 250). This is the reason why in the startup economy the space of economic production and the space of the city as a constantly produced "commonwealth" overlap (*ibid*.: 251) and bring together different types of social subjectivities. The market valuation of startups such as Wolt and other similar cases inescapably signals how capital captures the value of the urban field in a broad sense.

In the context of urban startups, value is extracted from the urban field and capital is realized in the money form, but not solely as land rent. We suggest that the market valuation of Wolt, among the many other similar success stories, signals how the objectified and monetized value of the firm is produced through finance capital, which abstracts and represents cities as huge market potential that ensures the future success of firms. The "potentiality" of the urban field is embodied in the market valuation process itself, and hence plays out in money form as an abstraction. At the same time, this abstracted potential of the urban field rests on the increasingly polarized nature of cities as social spaces.

The value of the urban field derives from the social space that can be harnessed through/with qualified workers who constitute the "high-level cultural-cognitive workers" (Scott 2017: 122), or what Robert Reich defined in the early 1990s as the "symbolic analysts" of the service- and information-driven economy (Reich 1992). Similarly, the abstracted value of the urban field is linked to the upper tier of the labour force through its expected effective demand. But the abstracted value potential of the urban field is also inherently connected to the reserve of low-wage labour that is typically excluded from permanent work contracts of wage labour and enticed to work as entrepreneurs, recruited as "independent contractors". From a critical perspective, their status as independent contractors potentially confuses their identity as workers in the highly polarized urban platform economy – hence structuring their further subordination and restricting their capacity to practise a politics of subjectivity. This aspect alone epitomizes one of the ways in which social relations in the age of techno-monopoly capitalism, and their mediation in the urban field, can be judged in terms of their objective consequences.

The flexibility and responsibility of an entrepreneur characterizes the low-wage servile class in cities and larger urban environments in today's techno-monopoly capitalism. Simultaneously, the existence of this entrepreneurial reserve of living labour is also based on the legislative power of the state, which has in the Finnish context allowed service firms such as Wolt to treat couriers as entrepreneurs and not employees. In 2021, two years after the government began inspecting the status of workers in the platform economy, Wolt continued treating couriers as entrepreneurs, despite objections from the Regional State Administrative Agency for Southern Finland and from the Finnish Labour Council. In November 2021, the Regional State Administrative Agency for Southern Finland, which acts as the occupational safety and health authority in Finland, decided that food couriers should be employed by Wolt and should not be treated as independent entrepreneurs. Wolt has appealed the decision to the Administrative Court; the court decided in early 2024 that the couriers should be treated as entrepreneurs rather than employees of Wolt. This process alone discloses some of the basic dynamics of the urban platform economy in contemporary techno-monopoly capitalism. Indeed, treating couriers as entrepreneurs seems to be at the core of Wolt's business model: the business risks mentioned in the 2023 report of the Wolt Board of Directors relate fundamentally to the employment status of food couriers. In particular, Wolt mentions various official investigations against the company and legal proceedings concerning the employment relationships of food couriers as risks to its business. (Niemi 2023).

The legal fight that Wolt set over couriers' employment status is also a political contention over the value of the urban field. Indeed, this latter aspect of the urban field and related identities is arguably crucial in the market valuation of Wolt and similar types of firms, and it is based on the increasingly visible social polarization of cities in the techno-capitalist economy. The socially polarized urban field consists of the skilled workforce and low-wage service workers whose role in the purportedly innovative "startup urbanism" is to satisfy the "in-person" needs of the former, and whose urban professional identity is constructed and represented as couriers, drivers, etc. (Dashers, Wolters, etc. being docile entrepreneurial subjects with ambition to work hard even with low wages). As such, the economic potentiality of the urban field in terms of market valuation of startup companies operating in the platform economy lies in the fact that the existence of a low-wage labour reserve (as a service class) is also connected to the expected demand by all kinds of professionals and creatives whose purportedly high-skill occupations are believed to nurture the city as a value-creating innovation machine. In short, the contemporary economization of the "metropolis" (Hardt & Negri 2009) is fundamentally based on the social polarization of the urban field, and it could not function without these divisions.

The above-mentioned divisions and associated social relations are also lived and experienced by food couriers. *Helsingin Sanomat* reported in September 2023 that food couriers were protesting in Turku, Finland. Couriers argued that the reason was that the platform company Wolt had unilaterally weakened delivery terms. The changes were made after DoorDash became the owner and when a significant technological update to the courier digital application changed the reward model of the firm. It is worth quoting the experiences of the couriers at length:

> With around 3,000 Wolt orders, Emmanuel is so fed up with the new contract terms that he plans to stop working as a food courier. Even a man who works more than 90-hour weeks says that he used to earn between three and four thousand euros gross per month, whereas now he earns about 1,500 euros with the same hours. It doesn't even leave money for food, he says. According to him, everything changed after a message suddenly popped up on the app earlier this year stating, "your updated contract will go into effect on February 27, 2023" ... Wolt drivers have organised protests in August and not accepted gigs due to changes in conditions. However, they cannot go on strike because they are not actually employed by Wolt. According to the couriers interviewed

by *Helsingin Sanomat*, the protests have had no effect. According to them, the company has indicated that there will be enough new couriers ... Emmanuel, says that many others have come to the same decision as he intends – to stop working for Wolt. However, many acquaintances with an immigrant background have become unemployed due to, for example, lack of language skills or education. Wolt says that new people are always coming. They hire more people to replace those who have left and send us messages telling us that there are new arrivals. It feels like a threat.

(Paajanen 2023)

The implicit role of the state in the valuation process

Capital has been an engine of abstraction in the context of Wolt's market valuation. However, the case also indicates how the capitalist abstraction, as well as the process of monetizing the startups (even though some of these are not yet making a profit), rest ultimately on the urban field but need state intervention of the corporatized state to become possible as a profit-generating formation.

The state has figured prominently in the production of the startup economy and the associated set of social relations and divisions. Both the national state and the local states in the Helsinki city-region have been eager to support developments premised on developing cities as "living laboratories for rapid prototyping and testing innovations" (Cohen, Almirall & Chesbrough 2016: 6). As such, the state has increasingly taken the role of an enabler of open innovation rather than a bureaucratic constraint of innovations.

From this perspective, state intervention paves the way to the market valuation of startups, which is grounded in representing and hence abstracting the product and productivity of the urban field with its fragmented social life and associating social life as hidden potential with the future performance of a particular economic sector through metrics, indicators, etc. (abstracting, again). In this manner, financialization and related market valuations of startups should not be understood as self-generated activities; they need support from the state in different forms, visible and invisible. Nor are they only parasitic activities (which they, of course, also are). Rather, this form of financialization is also about the production of social relations in urban spaces, so constituting the materiality of the city as division of labour and related social identities. As such, the market valuation of Wolt can be understood as both immaterial and material production of the value of the urban field.

The market potential of the urban field as proximity, density, human capital, labour reserve and as a space of effective demand and consumption plays a significant role in the contemporary valuation of some technology startup companies, the economic importance of which is openly highlighted by both local and national governments across different geographical contexts. Indeed, the abstracted value of startups and their often astonishing market valuations reveal the normative power of techno-monopoly capitalism to represent startups as societal exemplars that should be nurtured and pampered politically.

Representations of startup unicorns as "exemplars" reveal one of the ways in which techno-capitalism is constructed not only as an economic model but also as an ideal form of political organization. Indeed, Wolt and a handful of other technology startups have some time been discussed in the Finnish mass media as "national" success stories, which the nation desperately needs in order to cope with the harsh global competition. This all began in Finland some years ago when startups in the gaming industry grew very quickly, received international recognition and were praised by state authorities as representing the future of the Finnish economic growth model. Indeed, the role model status of these companies has been articulated by state authorities in terms of their capacity to produce tax revenue, rather than in terms of the content of their products.

As noted above, the interests of the state towards startups also stem from their potential to generate tax revenue. Indeed, the state government has to focus on "guaranteeing and safeguarding a 'healthy' accumulation process upon which it depends" (Offe & Ronge 1982: 250) simply because the power and legitimacy of a given state's management is dependent on the generation of economic value through fresh growth models. Both nurturing and capturing the potential economic value of urban startups thus need to be understood as a contemporary effort to maintain the power of the territorial state. In that sense, the power of the state and the socio-political construction of the urban field in terms of market potential for technology firms are integrated and co-constituted processes. This is one interesting feature of the corporatized state.

In many respects, the strategies of the Finnish current and past governments have explicitly articulated how the growth-oriented and globally significant startups should in the future form an important basis for the national economy and for the associated tax revenue. As such, the Wolt case effectively demonstrated for the Finnish state authorities that startups are also lucrative from the perspective of the state's coffers: the acquisition of Wolt by DoorDash was estimated to secure nearly €600 million of tax revenue. This is one of the reasons why, after the announcement of the deal, the founders of Wolt were invited by the government to celebrate the corporate acquisition together. In the televised meeting, the minister responsible for economic development not only expressed deep satisfaction of the government on the deal, but also declared that the state should refrain from developing policies and regulation that cause "harm" to the further development of startups. To illustrate the effectiveness of this latter principle, in 2022 the government stepped back from launching an exit tax. This would have been taxation of the increase in the value of a person's assets when moving abroad from Finland. The model would aim to prevent, for example, capital gains from the sale of investment assets, such as shares, from not being taxed due to emigration (Matinen 2020). The government decided to not proceed with this tax after the Ministry of Finance stated that such a tax would harm the attractiveness of the state in the eyes of foreign startup entrepreneurs. According to the highest executive in the Ministry of Finance, "the new taxes would bring little revenue to the state, but they have been interpreted by startups as hostile actions" (Muhonen 2022).

In many ways, the state was the political community that not only claimed a kind of political ownership in the market valuation of Wolt, but also articulated the political importance of startup unicorns in the overall societal development of Finland as a nation-state (see also Programme of Prime Minister Sanna Marin's Government 2019). This has been the case irrespective of the fact that the transaction was carried out as a stock exchange transaction (so that in the transaction the owners of Wolt received DoorDash stocks), and that the DoorDash stock has dropped from $206 to $77 since the announcement of the deal (indicating less tax revenue for the state) (Finnish National Broadcasting Company YLE 2022).

In the context of the startup economy, the state has played many "latent" roles over the past years. The Wolt case, for instance, does not directly touch upon the construction of built environments (tech parks, innovation districts, etc.) or other physical elements of entrepreneurial "tech ecosystems" within which novel startups are "incubated". This case rather discloses the operation of the cultural power of the state, which articulates startups and related cultural features such as risk-taking, entrepreneurship and "global" mindset as fundamentally positive political markers that secure economic growth. This cultural power of the state resonates with the rhetoric of lobbyist and economic players such as the Finnish Venture Capital Association and is embodied, for instance, in the actions of Business Finland, a government organization for innovation funding. But this cultural power of the state also characterizes the contemporary construction of the urban field. It has hence enabled the production of what Hardt and Negri (2000: 327) conceptualize as "smooth space" on which capital's subsumption power relies. Here, the state mediates and in fact co-constitutes capital's "plane of immanence" (*ibid.*) rather than obstructs or disturbs its operations.

The case of Wolt is, of course, inherently connected to what is customarily labelled as platform economy. Digital platforms and their operations, in turn, are constituent of the urban field as a post-political space for startups and other urban entrepreneurs. It is important to notice that the state has figured prominently in the formation of the urban field also in the Finnish case (Moisio & Rossi 2020), so contributing to the emergence and operations of Wolt and other similar types of startups. One may argue that Wolt is a clear manifestation of the state-orchestrated discourse of startup economy-making, a process that has become evident over the past years. In other words, if the platform economy is understood beyond mere technology within cities, the state has played both direct and indirect roles. In education policies, this role has manifested itself in higher education; for example, in the founding of Aalto University as a sort of national yet "global" university of nurturing innovations, as well as in the increasingly visible ethos of entrepreneurship in the school curricula (Moisio & Kangas 2016). As such, the economization of the urban field has been associated with a kind of human capital-centred approach to the governance of the startup capitalist state.

The developments mentioned above are among the many that disclose "deep state" strategies (Lofgren 2016) around the economy of innovations, a phenomenon that has become salient over the past decades. At the same time, labour policies of the state illustrate more indirect actions that have enabled the constitution of the urban field as low-wage entrepreneurial labour reserve. The entrepreneurialization of the low-wage labour force has taken place concomitantly with the launch of experimental border policies such as startup visas, which seek to attract the purportedly footloose global talent. The programme of Prime Minister Sanna Marin articulates explicitly how:

> Finland needs active work-based immigration. The Government aims to increase work-based immigration of experts. The assigned priorities of work-based immigration concern sectors suffering from labour shortages, and the specialists, students and researchers who are essential for leading and growing fields of research, development and innovation. A wide-ranging action programme will be compiled to attain this target.
> (Programme of Prime Minister Sanna Marin's Government 2019: 147)

These forms of regulation by the state, which ultimately touch upon the largest cities, have been coupled with public investments into innovation ecosystems, often funded together with local governments. These examples alone speak directly to the fact that the state has been a value creator in the sense suggested by Mazzucato (2013), but also, albeit more implicitly, a producer of the urban field – its division of labour and social relations. In such an indirect producer role, the state figures prominently as a political and cultural facilitator of the techno-capitalist economy and as a contributor to the market valuation process. As such, the nation-state has become a powerful force not only in urban governance but also in the urban economy, albeit in many indirect forms (Ward & Jonas 2004), hence facilitating the "strategic urbanisation of the state" (Moisio & Rossi 2020).

CONCLUSION

In this chapter, we have highlighted the generative force of the startup economy in constructing and representing the market potential of the urban field. As such, our arguments resonate with Lazzarato's (2004) claim that post-Fordist capitalism is not only a mode of production but a production of a world. This latter dimension underlines that the production of the urban field in the age of techno-monopoly and the different segments of the populace employed in the myriad of activities of such an economy form a peculiar political-economic constellation. Indeed, the startup economy that appears in the figure of a food delivery courier resonates with the contemporary debate on the social polarization of major cities. As Savage (2021) discusses in detail, major cities have become not only the fundamental spatial locus for capital accumulation, but also drivers of inequality. In this context, it is important to ask whether the polarization of cities in the age of the startup economy is a mere result of the operation of such an economy, or whether the social polarization of major cities should be understood as a necessary condition of the operation of this economy in the first place. With an analysis of Wolt, we have demonstrated how the startup economy not only produces social polarization but is rather founded on social divisions in cities and larger urban environments. In this process, the corporatized state plays a significantly constitutive role.

The urban startup economy is also productive of entrepreneurial subjectivity. Understanding the startup economy as a generative force of the urban field, closely associated with the market valuation of startup companies, is for us a way to discuss the urban field in such a manner that overcomes the binary between productive capitalism (the so-called "makers" of economic value) and parasitic/speculative financial capitalism that is based on fictitious capital and the related predatory practices by investors (the "takers" of economic value). In short, we have sought to highlight some of the ways in which the startup economy embodies the contemporary urbanization of capital and the role of the state in this process.

In spite of its seeming algorithmic basis, the urban startup economy rests on living labour, human capital and forms of life. It is hence important to examine the ways in which techno-capitalism not only rests on and constitutes the urban field, but also how it works through different segments of early-stage entrepreneurship, labour, human capital and forms of life. As a capitalist social formation, the urban startup economy has the capacity to separate intellectual work from manual labour, as well as to objectify human capital and commodify forms of life.

One of the messages of our analysis is that the urban startup economy should be examined also from the perspective of the subordinated segments of the populace: those workers who are employed as devalued human capital in the startup economy under poor conditions and with low salaries, or those low-income urban communities whose more attractive forms of life are sold in the global marketplace of mass tourism as lifestyles. Low-skill workers and low-income city dwellers are often silenced in the mainstream urban economic approaches, which tend to portray cities as innovation machines. Indeed, the dominant discourses of the urban economy are fundamentally premised on a sharp distinction between the high-skill and low-skill jobs, between good and bad forms of life, and the value-creating forms of human capital and city living that these economies are in search of. This distinction has a notable constitutive function in the dominant urban economy form, as it values and devalues different segments of labour, human capital and life unevenly and positions these segments dissimilarly in the processes of value generation and extraction. This same distinction also has the capacity to devalue and naturalize the purportedly low-skill service labour or those irregular forms of life that are not consonant with the mainstream narrative of city happiness.

By way of homogenizing high-skill labour or marketable forms of life as a collective subject, this very distinction in the urban economy also conceals the uncertain lives of some of the high-skilled "creative" workers – such as those working in the broad cultural/creative economy – or more meaningful forms of life. Homogenization, in turn, depoliticizes the divides within this segment of labour or within an urban populace as a whole. One of the consequences of such homogenization is that even if the same volatility and vulnerability characterizes many of the low- and high-skill jobs or different sectors of the urban populace, their common interests are not politically recognized, let alone represented. This phenomenon characterizes the urban economy, and the urban field that becomes constituted in the processes of such an economy.

CHAPTER 6

FORMS OF LIFE

INTRODUCTION

This chapter explores how place-specific forms of life have become a key site for economic value generation in today's techno-monopoly capitalism. It does so by investigating Naples' pathway to becoming a mass-tourism city and, more particularly, a laboratory for experiential tourism. We argue that the analysis of Naples effectively discloses some of the ways in which the so-called experience economy is constituted as a crucial component of the urban field and its economic value extraction processes in the age of techno-monopoly capitalism. In this particular instance, the urban field brings together technology monopoly capital through the operations of digital platforms, the corporatized state, social polarization and the commodification and monetization of urban symbols and forms of life.

The conceptualization of the experience economy originated with management theorists who were the first to explore in the late 1990s the marketization of human living and local forms of life in post-Fordist economies (Pine II & Gilmore 1998). The emergence of the experience economy, therefore, occurred well before the advent of corporate-owned digital platforms and online social networks, which have significantly contributed to the recent reconfiguring of the experience economy as a crucial component of the urban field in the age of techno-monopoly. Through the analysis of Naples, the chapter makes visible the recent economization of human living and place-specific forms of urban life, as well as the negative outcomes that this economization and the related urban regeneration brings about: a new housing shortage, displacement of longtime urban dwellers and the exploitation of living labour, to mention but a few. In doing so, we continue to examine the dynamics and contradictions of the urban field in the age of techno-monopoly and the role played by the contemporary corporatized state in the orchestration of urban economies that are designed to extract value from place-specific urban forms of life.

The previous three chapters in particular have looked at the way in which the urban field has become a key site for observing the transformations of startup entrepreneurship, labour and the invention as well as utilization of human capital and the related mechanisms of economic value creation and extraction in contemporary techno-monopoly capitalism. These mechanisms bring together old and new forms of valorization and exploitation of human activity, which now also involve place-specific forms of life, as this chapter will show, looking at mass tourism in Naples. The arrival of mass tourism was unexpected in this city, hit by an unprecedented waste crisis in the 2000s and continuous cycles of local crime and municipal debt emergencies. This is, therefore, an example of fast urban revival taking place in a context of long-term urban crisis periodically turning into forms of disaster urbanism (Rossi 2022). As this chapter will show, the disruptive advent of corporate-owned platforms, particularly those for short-term holiday rentals, has opened the way to a consumption-based urban revival that extracts economic value from Naples-specific forms of life, with the active support of the government-orchestrated machineries of the experience economy.

CONSTITUTING THE URBAN EXPERIENCE ECONOMY

The tourism sector is particularly illustrative of the complex role that the governmental state plays in the constitution of contemporary market economies, a role that is not always visible and active but is nonetheless crucial. The common wisdom believes that the state has only marginally contributed to the unprecedented growth in urban tourism that has been observed worldwide in recent years, as this growth is associated with the market expansion of this sector brought on by the advent of digital technologies, such as online platforms for short-term rentals such as Airbnb and Booking.com most notably. Recent scholarship examining the rapid expansion of mass tourism in the context of Southern Europe, however, has highlighted how the state has played an important role in the attraction of real-estate capital, favouring investment in infrastructures for tourist uses (Estevens *et al.* 2023). In so doing, the state has paved the way for the platform-driven massive development of urban tourism that we observe in this region and elsewhere, particularly in peripheral regions of the planet.

The role of pro-real estate public policy in contemporary capitalist economies is part of a larger structural tendency analysed in critical urban studies. As Samuel Stein has evidenced with reference to New York City, the power of landlords and real-estate developers comes to permeate every level of government (Stein 2019). While the state's structural involvement with the power acquired by the real-estate business in contemporary societies has received wide attention in urban scholarship and social activism alike, this chapter draws attention to the performative dimension of government agency in the touristic transformation of urban economies and societies in the European south, with particular reference to the example of Naples.

The trajectory of Naples becoming a mass-tourism city within the space of a decade has relied on what Giorgo Agamben has defined as the liturgical and ceremonial dimensions of societal government in contemporary democracies founded on the power of the public opinion and of the mass media in particular (Agamben 2011). With the rise of online social media, the pursuit of this dimension of societal government has become a central activity for government leaders and politicians (Dean 2017). As Giorgio Agamben writes, the power of media derives not only from the fact that "they enable the control and government of public opinion", but also from the fact that "they manage and dispense Glory, the acclamative and doxological aspect of power" (Agamben 2011: xii). According to Agamben, the acclamative dimension of power becomes "indiscernible from oikonomia and government" (*ibid.*). This means that acclamation and other ceremonial and almost liturgical exercises of power become inseparable from the effective management of the economy and, therefore, from the standpoint of this book, from the construction and maintenance of the urban field as a site dedicated to economic value generation through the extractive operations of capital.

The path of Naples becoming a mass-tourism city has been punctuated by iconic figures such as Sophia Loren and Diego Armando Maradona. These figures have been reified and used as "mythical objects" functioning as a "mode of signification", as Roland Barthes would have put it (Barthes 1973: 107), instrumental in the naturalization of market imperatives, such as the inevitability of mass tourism for Naples as a kind of disaster-hit city and permanently struggling economy. In contemporary urbanism, the grip of iconic figures used as "mythical objects" derives from the fact that they are evocative of place-specific forms of life, understood as an aggregate of socially embedded practices and habits (Jaeggi 2018). As an ensemble of practices and habits embedded in local society, forms of life are indicative of the essence of the urban field (its "authenticity") and the place that the urban field can occupy within the global arena of inter-city competition, at a time of "cognitive capitalism" nourished by emotions and affects (Hardt & Negri 2009; Moulier-Boutang 2011) and dominated by monopolist technology corporations, such as Airbnb in the case of tourism-driven urban revival.

Management theorists have been the first to observe how in post-industrial economies "experience" replaces the traditional primacy of more tangible and measurable entities, such as commodities, goods and services

(Pine II & Gilmore 1998). The experience economy originally took form with the development of theme parks, amusement sites and other spectacular urban spaces in the so-called "postmodern city" (Dear & Flusty 1998). The common characteristic of these experience-driven spaces was their physical detachment from society and their artificial recreation of atmospheres of leisure (Harvey 1989a). In getting rid of any distinction between the real and the virtual, between the authentic and the imagined, the advent of digital platforms has led to the reinvention of the experience economy in the age of techno-monopoly, which is now the driver behind the search for the "authenticity" of forms of life in "real cities". As we will see in the remainder of this chapter, in Naples the mobilization of iconic figures used as mythical objects such as Sophia Loren and Diego Armando Maradona serves as a re-signifier of local forms of life. This, in turn, ensures that the same life forms can be sold as lifestyles (Jaeggi 2018) in the global marketplace of mass tourism through the artifice of the experience economy in "authentic" urban places.

In the age of techno-monopoly, the platform-mediated experience economy finds an especially fertile ground in the context of cities that are located at the margin of the world economy, such those in the Global South, as well as those in the southern periphery of the Global North. The European south is illustrative of the latter, as its cities were more mildly touched by processes of gentrification during the previous decades, thus being able to retain place-specific forms of life to some extent. In more recent years, however, the supposed lack of economic alternatives, given the round of austerity measures that neoliberal states have imposed on their urban societies, has been offered by politico-economic elites as justification for the acceptance of a socially extractivist pattern of urban and economic development. This pattern tends to eliminate any possibility of resistance to the naturalization of market imperatives, such as the necessity of mass tourism for cities on the margins of the global economy. As we will see through the example of Naples, southern urban societies respond to these pressures through ambivalent forms of "neoliberalism from below" (Gago 2017) that reproduce forms of popular economies while absorbing the dominant logics of neoliberal societies.

NAPLES: BECOMING A MASS-TOURISM CITY

Today Naples is viewed as an emerging laboratory for experience co-creation in tourism (Buonincontri *et al*. 2017). Even though the city has been traditionally renowned for its cultural creativity (particularly in music, cinema, theatre), its tourist attractiveness is a recent phenomenon. After a positive decade in the 1990s, when a narrative of urban renaissance prevailed in the city's representations, the 2000s saw the deterioration of the city's image caused by the intensification of violence between criminal gangs and their high mediatization (the so-called Gomorrah phenomenon), as well as by the exacerbation of the environmental emergency brought on by a waste management crisis in its urban region. In the early 2010s, in concomitance with the sovereign debt crisis that hit Greece and other countries in Southern Europe, including Italy, an unprecedented municipal debt crisis started to affect Naples' local government, undermining its ability to deliver essential public services, such as transportation, social aid and infrastructure maintenance.

At the same time, over the 2010s, despite the persisting problems affecting its economy and government structures, the image of Naples improved again, thanks to different factors, including the apparent end of the waste management crisis and a more reassuring narrative of the city in cinema and literature, starting with Elena Ferrante's internationally acclaimed "Neapolitan novels". Since the mid-2010s, the city has become a popular destination within the new wave of global mass tourism instigated by the invention of digital platforms for short-term rentals. The advent of the short-term rental sector has favoured the arrival of mass tourism in a city where tourism was previously almost non-existent, despite its remarkable historical heritage and the beauty of its natural environment. In Naples, Airbnb-led short-term rental business has found a fertile ground for developing, given the traditionally informal character of the built environment in the city's historic areas (Lieto 2021). The informality of the urban fabric has favoured the expansion of a business activity that, like the other corporations that are at the centre of the current age of techno-monopoly, has always had an ambivalent relationship with legality, as we have seen in the first chapter of this book.

Despite the recent tourist boom, economic conditions and local infrastructure are far from being adequate in Naples, as a heavy municipal debt continues to impinge on the city's finances. Locally provided public services such as public transport, green spaces and childcare are below national standards, and the job market remains highly dysfunctional, with one of the highest unemployment rates nationally (about 30 per cent of the workforce, compared to the 11 per cent nationwide in Italy), particularly hitting young people and women. According to demographic projections based on Eurostat data, the city's metropolitan area, which has a population of about 3 million people, is estimated to lose nearly 700,000 residents in the coming decades, until 2100 (Fontana 2023). Population statistics show that over ten years – from 2014, the year in which airport passenger figures show a clear increase in tourism arrivals (see Wikipedia, n.d.), up to 2023 – the city has already lost about 6.5 per cent of its residents (see Tuttitalia, n.d.). While population decline is not due to tourism directly but to the city's weak economy and the related effects of austerity policies, it is clear that the advent of mass tourism not only failed to improve the economic situation of the city as a whole, but it produces new contradictions, particularly in the housing sector of the central urban areas, creating conditions for deurbanizing dynamics of population loss in historically densely inhabited areas (Rossi 2022). Housing in the city's historical neighbourhoods has become unaffordable to local residents, similarly to what happens in all contemporary cities that have witnessed rapid increases in tourism flows based on digital platforms in recent years.

Sophia Loren and the politics of the event

Despite the problems that a tourism-dependent economy can bring to society, in recent times local and national governments in Italy have actively supported the development of mass tourism as the engine to drive local economic regeneration, particularly in the southern regions of the country. In that sense, Italy has taken a new form as an entrepreneurial "tourist-experience state". The state-led orchestration of a novel hallmark event industry has been central to this project: cultural and commercial festivals have proliferated in cities and towns all across the country since the early 2010s. At the level of national policy, the cultural sector has formally allied with the tourism sector since 2013, when the responsibility for tourism policies was devolved to the Ministry for Cultural Heritage.

In Naples, a key turning point in the city's trajectory of the 2010s has been Dolce & Gabbana's three-day special event sponsored by the city government in July 2016. Domenico Dolce and Stefano Gabbana – the two Italian stylists owning Dolce & Gabbana, the internationally renowned fashion house – organized the event in Naples to celebrate their 30 years of activity. The choice of Naples was due to their attachment to the Italian south, Naples being the largest city in southern Italy. One of the two stylists is originally from Sicily and, therefore, despite their firm being headquartered in Milan, Sicily and the wider south of Italy have been adopted by Dolce & Gabbana as major sources of inspiration, or their "DNA" as they declared in an interview with an online magazine: "The secret of our success is in the investigation and celebration of our roots, our passion for Italian culture: the warmth, hospitality, importance of family, food and ritual, which lend integrity to our aesthetic" (Radaelli 2016).

The three-day fashion show saw the participation of actress Sophia Loren as a guest star. Denying rumours on the participation of other international celebrities such as Madonna, Monica Bellucci and Nicole Kidman, at the launch conference Dolce and Gabbana emphasized that Sophia Loren was the only guest of honour in the event. A long-standing collaborator of Dolce & Gabbana, Sophia Loren was chosen by the two stylists as the iconic figure of the event due to her Neapolitan descent and current popularity in Naples, despite a long absence from the city. The fact that her popularity was highly evocative of local forms of life played a key role in the selection of Sophia Loren as a guest star of the fashion show.

In the 1950s, in the early stages of her career, before embarking on an international career in the US, Sophia Loren became widely known to the public for her roles, among others, in musical and comedy films set in Naples, such as *Neapolitan Carousel, Poverty and Nobility, The Gold of Naples*. In particular, *The Gold of Naples* is now considered a classic of Italian neorealism, representing city life at a time when Italian society was returning to normal after the devastations of the Second World War and the harsh years of its aftermath. The latter was at the centre of war drama films in the first phase of Italian neorealism, such as *Rome Open City* (1945) and *Paisà* (1946), where living conditions in Rome and Naples were represented in terms of extreme deprivation. On the contrary, *The Gold of Naples* provides images of happy and frenetic life in Naples' popular districts, offering an almost "touristic vision" of the city, as film critic and cultural urban geographer Mark Shiel wrote in 2006, somehow anticipating subsequent developments of the city a few years later (Shiel 2006: 78).

In one of its episodes, Sophia Loren famously portrayed a pizza maker, serving fried pizza (or, *pizza fritta* as it is now internationally known) to passers-by in a busy, narrow street of Naples' old quarters. When the new wave of global tourism reached the city in the mid-2010s, the film scene became an iconic representation of Neapolitan city life and particularly of its street food culture. At this time, international media started adopting the "beloved pizza fritta", as the BBC put it (Hobart 2020), as a symbol of Naples' street culture and forms of life. In recent years, fast-food eateries serving pizza, mainly to tourists, have proliferated in the city's most popular historical districts, such as Decumani (the oldest part of the historic centre), Sanità and Quartieri Spagnoli (Spanish Quarters). It is customary that these eateries now use Sophia Loren acting in *The Gold of Naples* as their reference image in the storefronts.

As official proof of her iconic value to the city, during the Dolce & Gabbana event Sophia Loren received the title of honorary citizen from the mayor of Naples. The award was the way in which the mayor and the municipality publicized their sponsorship of Dolce & Gabbana's three-day event, which had been formalized by a city council deliberation. At that time, the mayor of Naples was Luigi de Magistris, an independent politician (and ex-public prosecutor by profession) who was elected for the first time in 2011, unexpectedly defeating favoured candidates of the mainstream political parties. In June 2016, Luigi de Magistris won another landslide victory in the local elections that designated him as mayor of Naples for a second term that lasted until 2021.

Figure 6.1 Sophia Loren's iconic picture in the storefront of a pizzeria in the Spanish Quarters, Naples
Source: Photo by Ugo Rossi.

The local elections of 2016 took place one month before the Dolce & Gabbana event. Inevitably, the organization of the event became part of the electoral campaign. In this sense, this event is an example of cultural and commercial festival explicitly used by city leaders as an "urban propaganda project" aimed at instigating civic boosterism (Boyle 1999). The local political context in which this "propaganda project" took shape deserves critical scrutiny. At the time of Dolce & Gabbana's event, Mayor de Magistris had embraced the politics of new municipalism that in the mid-2010s was gaining increasingly wide currency in Europe, particularly in austerity-hit Southern Europe (Russell 2019). One year after his re-election, de Magistris published a book titled *Naples as a Rebel City* (de Magistris 2017) in which he exposed his approach to municipalism founded on the mobilization of civic pride in a city vexed by social and environmental emergencies, a struggling economy and an oppressive public debt (Pinto, Recano & Rossi 2022).

The revitalization of civic pride was pursued by the mayor through informal partnerships with a diverse set of local and global actors, most notably with radical social movements and with corporate actors. On the one hand, in 2015 and 2016 the city council legitimized as "urban commons" several "freed" public buildings – most of them in the historical quarters of the city – that had been occupied by social movements and citizen groups in previous years. The recognition of the urban commons became a flagship policy of the city administration emphasizing the need for community involvement within the local government process. On the other hand, the mayor enticed external corporate actors willing to organize international events in Naples, in his effort to rebuild the reputation of the city. The process of image rebuilding had two key moments: first, in 2012 the hosting of the America's Cup – the renowned sailing trophy – in the bay of Naples; second, the three-day Dolce & Gabbana fashion show in 2016.

Both the America's Cup and the Dolce & Gabbana fashion show had a significant impact on the city's international ascendancy as an emerging destination for global tourism in the 2010s. In local debates, the America's Cup is customarily viewed as the departing point in Naples' path of city revival, while Dolce & Gabbana's event is associated with a more advanced stage in which the city consolidated its international ascendancy. In the space of the four years between the two events, the city rapidly changed its attractiveness rating, as testified by passenger figures of the local international airport, which steadily rose since 2014, with the highest growth between 2016 and 2017 when yearly arrivals increased 26.6 per cent (Wikipedia, n.d.).

The America's Cup and the Dolce & Gabbana fashion show not only happened at different moments of the urban revival's trajectory, but also represent different ways of engaging the social fabric of the city through a hallmark event. The America's Cup can be seen as a more conventional sports event, characterized by a physical separation of the race field from the urban fabric and its life forms. The America's Cup had a long-lasting impact on the urban fabric as it paved the way to the permanent pedestrianization of the most valuable part of Naples' sea promenade. The pedestrianized promenade was defined as *"lungomare liberato"*, or "freed promenade", by the city mayor, using a terminology that was evocative of the urban commons strategy in a rather different policy context. In subsequent years, the pedestrianized promenade has seen the proliferation of cafes, bars and restaurants, thus becoming a key area for consumption, attracting both locals and tourists. However, the event was experienced in a physically detached manner by the audience, as the public watched the sailing races from afar.

On the other hand, the Dolce & Gabbana show did not have an impact on the city in urban planning terms, but the way in which it was organized was intended to break down any line of separation between the city and the event in a truly ceremonial and liturgical fashion. This time, the social fabric of the city, particularly that of the most evocative area of the city in identity terms such as its densely populated historic centre, became a constitutive part of the event. Dolce & Gabbana's idea of organizing their shows as open-air events originates from an approach to fashion shows that gained ground in the 1990s, when the fashion show became a kind of hybrid performance art, with traditional commercial aspects of the clothing industry becoming secondary compared to the spectacle offered by the show arranged as a theatrical experience (Duggan 2001). This approach clearly resonates with the experience economy's way of engaging customers as a kind of theatrical performance, where the experience offered to them replaces the traditional primacy of material goods and services. The urban revival path pursued by many cities in the 2010s provided a new performing environment for this new type of experiential fashion shows. At that time, the technology-driven wave of mass tourism increasingly took the form of the experiential tourism model adopted by digital platforms such as Airbnb and popularized on an everyday basis by online social networks such as Instagram, Facebook and later TikTok.

The involvement of Sophia Loren as honorary guest of the Dolce & Gabbana event enabled the organizers to offer a stronger justification for the city council's sponsorship. On its second day, the event – which had about 500 invited participants – took place in the streets of Naples' historic core, the area known as Decumani, dating back to the Greek-Roman age, and particularly in a street known for the open-air market of local crafts of the famed Neapolitan nativity art. Unlike similar historic centres that have been gentrified in other Italian and European cities, Naples' historic core remains a densely populated, socially mixed area with a high presence of low-income residents, even though the massive influx of tourists is now endangering the presence of local urban dwellers. The event was presented with great excitement by local media and the city administration alike, particularly as a long-awaited celebration of Neapolitan culture, contributing to the ongoing renewal of Naples' image at an international level.

Despite all the acclamation, the fashion show raised some controversies, particularly due to the fact that the densely inhabited area of Decumani was made inaccessible to the public and that the municipality even declined to receive any monetary compensation from Dolce & Gabbana for the use of public space. In a public gathering, right-to-the-city activists wore T-shirts with the fake logo of Dolce & Gabbana turned into *Disagio & Gentrificazione* (or, distress & gentrification). In doing so, activists were questioning the urban marketing implications of the event at a time when urban tourism had suddenly shifted from being nearly non-existent to becoming increasingly pervasive. Local shopkeepers also lamented that their businesses suffered from the restrictions required by the event, as customers could not access their stores. Interviewed when the fashion show was passing through the historic core of Naples, Domenico Dolce avoided engaging the local debate, redirecting the attention on the social value of the fashion show: "Everything is so authentic here in this street of Naples, everything is real." he said to local media (La Repubblica Napoli 2016).

The effects of the Dolce & Gabbana fashion show on the city's trajectory of urban revival at a time of global techno-monopoly have been remarkable in terms of tourism attraction in the short run. As we have seen, airport passenger figures saw their highest increase in the aftermath of the event and continued to grow in the following years up to now, with the exception of the international slowdown of this sector in 2020–21 caused by the Covid-19 pandemic. However, the effects of the Dolce & Gabbana event have not only been on the quantitative side but also on the qualitative side, as it demonstrated all the potential of Naples as an emerging laboratory for experiential tourism, as we said.

Staging the open city

In the ensuing years, the boom of experiential tourism in Naples has intensified in the city's historic centre. The large area comprising the historic districts of the city, which was designated as a UNESCO World Heritage Site in 1995, has become a magnet for mass tourism. This area not only condenses the city's exceptional cultural heritage but also the place-specific forms of life for which Naples is internationally known. These forms of life have become especially attractive for tourists in search of "experiences". During the early stages of the Airbnb boom in the second half of the 2010s, the experiential tourist economy concentrated on the rediscovery of the so-called *bassi*: small (usually single-room) street-level properties serving as unhealthy, traditionally overcrowded homes with a lack of windows and no secure housing tenure. For instance, on Tripadvisor travellers can access the *"vascitour"* (Tripadvisor-1, n.d.) travel package that offers an "emotional tourism" experience in Naples based on three services: (1) overnight stay in "typical Neapolitan homes"; (2) social eating at a local family home; (3) tours organized by local residents.

Historically, these ground-floor homes have been associated with the harsh living conditions of low-income households in the city's historical quarters. In the 1930s, the fascist regime approved a bill that banned the use of *bassi* as homes, ordering the relocation of their dwellers in newly built social housing projects in the urban outskirts. A marble plaque prohibiting their use for housing purposes with the writing *"Municipio di Napoli-Terraneo non destinabile ad abitazione"* ("Municipality of Naples – street-level property unit not for housing") was placed above the entry of the *bassi*. Despite the prohibition by law, the *bassi* continued to exist in large numbers in the ensuing decades. Today, a mix of native and foreign residents (mainly immigrants of South Asian descent) live in the *bassi*, which remain densely inhabited by multi-generational families. Currently, however, a growing number of local people are evicted by landlords opting for the more lucrative market of short-term rentals for tourists, as the *bassi* meet today's growing demand for tiny apartments in international tourism.

Physical size alone does not suffice to explain today's interest in the *bassi* by the travel industry and real-estate businesses. It is therefore worth looking at their legacy as a dwelling practice in Naples to understand how these street-level dwellings have come to embody the idea of experiential tourism in authentic urban places. An accurate description of the *bassi* was provided in the late 1960s by journalist, communist and feminist activist, Rome-based Maria Antonietta Macciocchi. In 1968, Macciocchi spent a long time in Naples, having decided to centre her electoral campaign as a member of the parliament on the emancipation of the women living in the *bassi*. She reported about her experience of political campaigning in Naples' historical districts to French Marxist philosopher Louis Althusser through a mail correspondence that was published as a book. In her correspondence with Althusser, Macciocchi starts with a detailed description of the *bassi* and particularly of their physical structure:

> You ask me to explain what the *bassi* are: there is a whole body of literature on this topic, given that Naples has never changed its basic structure, which is that of a "pile of houses", as a German 19th-century poet described it. The *bassi* are a tangle of structures made up each of a single room, or cave. They open on to the ground floor, or, more precisely, the street, with divided wooden doors like stables. Since there are no windows, the doors also serve for ventilation, and for this reason they are almost always partially opened. (Macciocchi 1973: 90)

In her account of everyday life in the *bassi*, Macciocchi underlines how street-level living entails dwelling and socializing with neighbours in the same space, as well as working for making a living, as women customarily engage in domestic labour, understood not just as home care but also as work done for enterprises subcontracting the production process to domestic workers. Macciocchi here underlines that "the women of Naples always work and are the keystone of the family economic structure" (*ibid*.: 75), adding that "in all the travel diaries of the great foreigners who visited southern Italy, from Goethe to Dumas, it is hard to find even a passing reference to women's work" (ivi).

> In the *bassi* – which are house, workroom and shop all in one – space is so restricted that people are born and die there side by side; the toilet, with a flowered curtain around it, is right next to the stove and pans, and the floor is made of paving stones, exactly

the same ones you find in the streets . . . In order to make living conditions hygienic, the women of the popular quarters work incessantly, transforming the *bassi* with sweat and strain. In these miserable hovels, where daylight is a constant shadow, they continuously wash the paving stones and never stop laundering. This, in fact, is the mysterious explanation for all those mysterious lines of washing strung out across the alleys: it is to guarantee a continuous change of sheets and clothes, given the limited amount that they own. On the basis of statistics calculated in 1967 by some Catholic sociologists, 200,000 people live in some 50,000 *bassi*.

(*Ibid.*: 91)

Today's investment attractiveness of the *bassi* for the travel industry lies in the forms of life that these living spaces embody, as they bring together key functions of city living such as dwelling, working and socializing with neighbours. In this sense, the *bassi* are reminiscent of the kind of people-centred urbanism based on face-to-face contacts in a crowded sidewalk life originally theorized by Jane Jacobs (Jacobs 1961; see also Hill 1988). Jane Jacobs' socially dense urban way of life has been rediscovered and celebrated in much "urbanophile" and agglomeration-centred literature in recent years, including the new urban economics, from Richard Florida to Enrico Moretti, as we have seen in Chapter 4.

In a recent book on the ethics of urban dwelling, sociologist and urban theorist Richard Sennett has offered a reappraisal of Jane Jacobs' anticipatory view of the ideal of the "open city" that he advocates in his work. Sennett, in particular, argues that Jacobs' understanding of city life, which directly stemmed from her living experience of West Village in New York, exposes a kind of "neighbourliness without intimacy" that is characteristic of open urban societies. This means, as Sennett writes, that "although recognizing one another on the street, or chatting about prices in the shops or the latest outrage perpetrated by landlords, yet people kept their distance, seldom getting to know each other very deeply" (Sennett 2018b: 250).

For residents of West Village at the time of Jane Jacobs – characterized by a "block of townhouses which are plain and, to my eyes, depressed buildings", Sennett writes – the "quality of the built environment" was of relative importance, as local residents kept "nipping and tucking and adapting these structures to their ways of living" (Sennett 2018b: 257). Sennett's recounting of Jane Jacobs' West Village's way of living in the 1960s is evocative of the urban environment that Naples today offers to visitors in search of low-cost "urban authenticity".

Interestingly, in the book, Richard Sennett uses a photographic image of Naples in a section titled "Opening the city", containing pictures taken

141

from different cities across the world (Medellín, Naples, Mumbai, New York, among others). These pictures are intended to exemplify existing conditions or prefigure possibilities for an "open city", understood as an urban space that gets rid of social and physical boundaries and barriers, and hence represents a kind of urban inclusion. In the photo caption dedicated to Naples, Richard Sennett associates the openness of the city with the recent arrival of tourists: "In Naples, the presence of outsiders, in the form of tourists, brings life to a previously dead street" (Sennett 2018b, image 41).

Ironically, the picture used by Sennett portrays a key street of Naples' historical centre – the famous Spaccanapoli, or "Naples splitter", a landmark in the city's landscape as it physically divides its historical area into two parts – that has always been lively in terms of people, shops and other activities taking place there, independently from the "presence of tourists". Even though Sennett does not use the conventional terminology of urban regeneration, his Jacobsian idea of the "open city" reproduces the conventional logic of urban policy that targets supposedly lifeless spaces in order to provide justification for intervention, renewal, "regeneration" (Rossi & Vanolo 2013).

The representation of a densely populated place like Naples' historic centre as "lifeless" or declining is typical for conventional urban regeneration thinking, which is premised on the assumption that "there is no alternative" to urban regeneration understood as a competitive strategy of urban attractiveness. Richard Sennett's mistake, therefore, can be seen as a kind of Freudian slip. In the book, Sennett does not explicitly theorize the role of tourism for urban regeneration, but the mistaken visual evidence of his argument reveals an interiorization of the dominant logic of urban development at a time of techno-monopoly that uncritically associates mass tourism in economically struggling areas with a return to "life". In reality, this return to life is a synonym to activating the urban field for the extractive operations of capital.

The cult of Maradona

The rediscovery of the *bassi* for tourist purposes has been the departure point in the embrace of an experience co-creation model of urban revival in this city. In the ensuing years, a growing number of site-specific "experiences" have been added to the *bassi* as a symbolic site for Naples' experiential tourism.

Following the unexpected death of Diego Armando Maradona in November 2020, the city has seen the proliferation of murals and different sites of commemoration dedicated to this football legend. Maradona played in Naples for seven years in the 1980s, enabling the local football club to win the national league for the first time ever, followed by a second success. After a negative experience in Barcelona, Maradona immediately felt at home in Naples, with its deprived and at the same time bustling living environment that so closely resembled that of the popular neighbourhoods in Buenos Aires where he grew up. In the mass media, the image of Maradona's childhood spent in a slum of Buenos Aires was often compared with that of *scugnizzi* in Naples, the young children from low-income families who spend most of their time on the streets of Naples' historical districts.

The fact of having a social background similar to that of local people in Naples led Maradona to develop a close relationship, which became even symbiotic at times, with the city, which endured even after his departure. In 2017, Maradona received the title of honorary citizen from Luigi de Magistris, the mayor of Naples. After a short formal ceremony in the city hall, a public celebration organized by the football fans took place in Piazza Plebiscito, Naples' largest public square, gathering a large crowd of participants. Only three years later, however, Maradona passed away. The municipality immediately took the decision to rename the stadium and a local train station near the stadium as "Diego Armando Maradona". New murals and commemorative sites started to appear in different parts of the city. Most of the murals that are now revered by visitors date back to the late 1980s and have been

Figure 6.2 Maradona's commemorative site in the Spanish Quarters, Naples
Source: Photo by Ugo Rossi.

made and remade by local and international graffiti artists. The most famous is undoubtedly the mural in the Spanish Quarters, a key area in Naples' recent tourism boom (Tondo 2020). The mural was created by a local amateur artist in 1990 and repainted and partially revisited by an Argentine graffiti maker in 2017. After Maradona's death, the popularity of Maradona's mural in the Spanish Quarters has overcome that of a giant mural painted in 2017 by a local graffiti maker on the facade of a high-rise building in a housing project in San Giovanni a Teduccio, in the city's working-class outskirts. In other areas of the city, giant murals have been created in more recent times, such as most recently in Miracoli, another historical neighbourhood that is more overlooked in contemporary tourism routes.

Visiting the mural and the larger site commemorating Maradona in the Spanish Quarters has become a highly popular experience that attracts large crowds on a daily basis. The influx of tourists and local visitors reached its peak in 2023 when the local football club again won the national league after a 33-year-long abstinence. In April 2023, the municipality decided to recruit local volunteers to deal with the large influx of visitors in the narrow alleys of the Spanish Quarters. Having large crowds of people visiting the area is an novelty for this area. Despite their central location, the Spanish Quarters have historically been a highly stigmatized neighbourhood, commonly associated with organized crime, a deteriorated built environment and interlocking problems of environmental and social disadvantage. The chain of "neighbourhood effects" (Wilson 1987) impacting on residents' life chances has continued to persist in almost immutable forms through the centuries. Writing in the early 1990s, urban historians Giancarlo Alisio and Alfredo Buccaro summarized the profile of the area as follows:

> Over more than five centuries of existence, this area has not changed significantly in terms of its physical and functional characteristics, having always been centred on crime dynamics, prostitution and smuggling activities. The closed shape of the urban settlement determines the fact that nobody – except for local residents – goes there, if not for specific reasons; historical monuments, which can be found there, are unknown to the majority of people. (Alisio & Buccaro 1994: 29)

In the past, when mass tourism was even unthinkable in this area, the fact that the Spanish Quarters were allegedly less rich with monuments and buildings of high historic value, compared with other historical quarters in Naples, convinced mainstream urban planners and local politicians that the area would deserve only selective preservation of its historical built environment. In the mid-1980s, urban planners and architects joined mainstream political parties and local real-estate developers to create a growth coalition named "The Realm of the Possible", which proposed a drastic urban regeneration project for Naples' historic town. Demolitions of the most deteriorated buildings and the design of "modern" urban spaces were proposed for the Spanish Quarters. However, local environmentalist groups and intellectuals opposed the regeneration plan, which was never implemented. The approach to urban planning changed in the 1990s, with the culture of urban preservation becoming the priority in the city government's policy agenda. The preservation-based urban planning approach of the 1990s left aside previous distinctions between the different areas of the city's historic town in terms of the supposedly differential value of single parts of the historical built environment. This meant reconsidering the value of purportedly low-quality historical buildings in the Spanish Quarters and similar neighbourhoods.

An important role in the revaluing of the Spanish Quarters was played by the implementation of an EU-funded urban programme in the second half of the 1990s. The EU project put forth an integrated approach to urban renewal based on the combination of building restoration with the support to local economic activities (such as the traditional artisan shops and the textile workshops historically present in the area) and to residents coping with different social problems. When the urban programme ended, in the early 2000s, the municipality approved a pilot study to assess the feasibility of the reconversion of about a hundred *bassi* in the lower part of the Spanish Quarters (out of approximately a thousand *bassi* in the whole area) into artisan shops and craft workshops, seeking to offer to existing residents the possibility to stay in the area (Rossi 2009). For different reasons, the project never materialized but its objectives are illustrative of a conception of urban intervention that was centred on the idea of recreating local economies that have existed in the area historically. In this context, previous urban planning conceptions based on demolitions and urban social cleansing, which prevailed in the postwar decades up to the 1980s, lost much of their influence on public debates.

The sudden advent of platform-mediated mass tourism in the 2010s drastically altered the local regeneration options on the table for the area. In the second half of the 2010s, before the unprecedented popularity acquired by the giant mural and the related commemorative site dedicated to Maradona, the lower part of the Spanish Quarters saw the proliferation of restaurants and bars that attracted tourists and local consumers alike. The large majority of these restaurants and bars are locally owned, as corporate-owned chains are absent in the Spanish Quarters, unlike other touristic areas in Naples, such as the aforementioned sea promenade. However, despite being mostly locally owned, these business activities are nonetheless rife with contradictions. These activities tend to monopolize public space and the bars are noisy at night. Many longtime residents of the Spanish Quarters have left the area due to the noise and the unliveable conditions caused by the boom of restaurants and bars. Moreover, the employees of these establishments are hired with precarious contracts and their labour conditions are exploitative. And many suspect that local organized crime may be involved in these businesses. In this sense, the ambivalences of the urban economy that has developed in the Spanish Quarters around tourism are exemplificative of what Veronica Gago – studying the La Salada informal market in Buenos Aires – has termed "neoliberalism from below" (Gago 2017): an intricate juxtaposition of popular-economy formation with defining traits of neoliberal societies such as exploitation of labour and, in the context of the Spanish Quarters in Naples, gentrifying effects on the neighbourhood level.

After the break imposed by the pandemic, the retail bubble of restaurants and bars has inflated again, particularly following the creation of the commemorative site around the mural dedicated to Maradona after his death in 2020. The creation of this site has fuelled an informal urban economy based on counterfeit gadgets or hand-made products such as fake football shirts, prayer cards and statuettes (*The Guardian* 2020), which has added to the pre-existing retail bubble of bars and restaurants. The travel industry has invested in guided tours and excursions into iconic urban places, starting with Maradona's commemorative site in the Spanish Quarters, accompanied by culinary experiences of "authentic" local food. (Tripadvisor-2, n.d.).

At the same time, the popularity of Maradona's commemorative site contributes significantly to the shortage of affordable housing in the area, as a growing number of apartments are now offered to tourists as short-term rentals, making house prices unaffordable to local residents. Local real-estate agents mention the spatial proximity to Maradona's commemorative site as a positive asset in their advertisements of housing offers in the Spanish Quarters. Some of the neighbourhood shops historically present in the area (greengroceries, butcheries, fishmongers, convenience stores) still remain in the most touristic parts of the Spanish Quarters, but everyone thinks that these activities are bound to disappear, as their destiny is to be turned into bars, restaurants or souvenir shops sooner or later.

City administrators remain positive about the new phenomenon of mass tourism in Naples, despite the distortions created by its impact on local society and the persistent dysfunctions of the local economy, particularly in terms of jobs creation. Interviewed by a local newspaper, the new mayor of Naples, elected in 2021, Gaetano Manfredi, pointed out that "tourism in Naples is increasingly more experiential … with numbers of arrivals exceeding all expectations" (di Costanzo 2023). The city government, as well as the regional government, which in the Italian system has primary responsibilities for tourism policies, keep speaking about tourism mainly in terms of "opportunity". The wide array of environmental and social problems created by the excesses of tourism arrivals in Naples as well as in other places in the region are substantially ignored, as tourism is seen as a prosperous source of income generation in a struggling economy like that of Naples and its region.

CONCLUSION

The purpose of this chapter has been to dissect the more extra-economic ways in which a new wave of mass tourism has come to rely on the extraction of economic value from place-specific forms of life and associated "experiences" at a time of global techno-monopoly. In doing so, the chapter has drawn attention to what Giorgio Agamben has conceptualized as the ceremonial and liturgical dimensions of societal government. Demographically dense urban environments situated in the global periphery offer an especially fertile ground for the investigation of the aptly orchestrated ways in which place-specific life forms become commodified and monetized in contemporary techno-monopoly capitalism.

The international ascendancy of Naples, which has become a popular destination for mass tourism and an emerging laboratory for experience co-creation within the space of a few years, has been fostered by experiential events such as the Dolce & Gabbana fashion show as well as by the mobilization of popular icons, namely Hollywood celebrity Sophia Loren and football legend Diego Armando Maradona. The chapter has shown how these events and popular icons, both intimately connected to Naples-specific forms of life, have been used by the travel industry and real-estate business as mythical objects instrumental in the incorporation of the city into international tourism routes, as well as by the local government as a way to strengthen consensus.

The instrumentalization of events and popular icons as mythical objects functional to the extractive operations of technology corporations such as Airbnb has occurred within the political-symbolic framework of a reasserted attachment of the city to the forms of life of its subordinated classes and more disadvantaged historical districts. In particular, the mobilization of celebrities that are at the same time local and global icons, such as Loren and Maradona, has the function of resignifying forms of life that can be sold as lifestyles on the global marketplace. By awarding to both Loren and Maradona honorary citizenships, and through repeated liturgical acclamations, the local state has actively supported the construction of these icons for mass-tourism purposes, taking for granted the idea that there is no alternative to mass tourism in struggling economies of the European south like that of Naples. This densely populated city, rich in history and culture, embodies the ideal of the people-centred urbanism originally put forth by Jane Jacobs, which is embraced today by city-enthusiast economists and social scientists (from Richard Florida and Enrico Moretti to Richard Sennett).

However, the tourism boom is not expected to weaken the spiral of demographic decline that is expected to hit Naples' urban region in the coming decades, due to the persistence of structural economic weaknesses in this area. On the contrary, the increase of mass tourism can only aggravate the population decline, yet again demonstrating the contradictions that inescapably characterize the urban field and its valuation. In the age of techno-monopoly, for a southern city such as Naples being integrated into the global imaginary of mass consumption entails the risk of dissipating its historically defining characteristic as an urban place, namely population density (cf. Dorward *et al.* 2023), reducing this characteristic to an evocation of the past offered as a cultural commodity to the travel industry.

Along with the involvement of local authorities in the construction of their myths, what is characteristic of the acclamation of Sophia Loren and Diego Maradona is the fact that it is reproduced on an everyday basis in the historical districts of the city in a panoply of spontaneous forms enacted by local communities at the neighbourhood level. In the context of Naples, the almost mystical reverence for these popular icons has the effect of fuelling an urban economy that reproposes long-standing popular economic formations in this city: its legendary street-corner economy, or *economia del vicolo*, that attracted the attention of social scientists in the postwar decades (Allum 1973). At the same time, however, its more picturesque aspects aside, the tourism-driven economy has unprecedented and probably irreversible consequences on the city's social fabric in terms of gentrification of the retail sector and displacement of longtime urban dwellers.

Naples' pathway to becoming a mass-tourism city also offers useful lessons on the evolution of the so-called "experience economy" within the landscape of contemporary urbanism in the techno-monopoly age. The experience economy has migrated from the realm of theme parks and spectacular urban spaces, which attracted the attention of social scientists at the time of postmodern urbanism in the 1980s, the 1990s and the 2000s, such as Disneyland and Inner Harbor in Baltimore, to that of platform-driven experiential tourism in "real urban places" in the 2010s. The idea of the experience economy is due to management theorists who were the first to explore the marketization of human living and local forms of life in post-industrial economies, well before the advent of digital platforms, albeit in a mostly apologetic manner. What Chapter 1 of this book has termed the "tech boom 2.0", characterized by the advent of monopolist technology corporations, has expanded the economization of human living and place-specific forms of life. As a result, the experience economy is no longer a niche sector of the entertainment industry, but has come to permeate almost any aspect of the market economy, particularly at the urban level, at a time of global techno-monopoly.

CODA: THE VALUE OF THE URBAN FIELD

Urban environments have become primary sites in the creation and extraction of economic value in the age of techno-monopoly capitalism. We have suggested in the previous chapters that, given the osmosis between the dominant pattern of capitalist companies and urban environments, technology corporations and digital platforms have become significant constituents of the contemporary urban field. This has resulted in the technology-driven colonization of key aspects of urban life. Importantly, the contemporary condition has been made possible by the corporatized state that is closely implicated with the operations of today's techno-monopolists. In short, the control of the urban field and its human logistics – as a reservoir of entrepreneurship, labour, human capital and forms of life – is crucial for techno-monopoly capitalism.

This book has intended to offer a conceptually situated critique of the theorization of innovation-oriented urban economies in mainstream economics, particularly exemplified by the work of "superstar" economists such as Paul Romer, Richard Florida, Edward Glaeser and Enrico Moretti. Our critique has drawn attention to their elitist conceptions of agglomeration economies, human capital and economic growth, exposing how these conceptions have the effect of drawing a veil over the knowledge value of the urban labour force at large and, in doing so, of justifying social and spatial inequalities in contemporary societies.

At the same time, we have also engaged with ideas that are closer to our perspective, but from which we maintain a critical distance, namely the techno- or digital-feudalism and rentierism theses that have gained wide currency within the academic left and the public sphere in recent years, proposed by highly mediatized theorists such as Yanis Varoufakis and Mariana Mazzucato. Rather than the advent of an allegedly pre-capitalist, neo-feudalist era forged by the power of a new tech oligarchy, we in turn understand the contemporary age of techno-monopoly as an intensification of the capitalist logic of surplus value extraction in the context of post-Fordist cognitive capitalism. Despite their evident differences, it seems to us that what both the mainstream urban economists and the techno-feudal critics have in common is a kind of idealization of a lost "good capitalism" – identified with urban innovative entrepreneurs and the state-led entrepreneurial economy, respectively – whose potential in their view is today obfuscated by the power of Big Tech corporations.

For its part, this book has intended to repoliticize our understanding of today's techno-monopoly capitalism, showing how the contemporary economy is an intrinsically political construct in which the state and a multifaceted governmentality play a key role in forging an urban technological paradigm that economizes and transnationalizes urban development. The essence of the contemporary economy is hence political and constitutive of what we conceptualize as the urban field. In our opinion, appreciating that the contemporary economy is inherently political means recognizing that it can also be enacted in different ways, not as a profit-driven formation but as a collective endeavour (Merrifield 2014) aiming at redefining established modes of economic value creation.

To make conceptually visible some of the political processes of economic value creation and extraction, we have thought with and reworked the concept of the urban field, originally coined by Friedman and Miller (1965). In our conceptualization, the urban field is a historically conjunctural phenomenon that accommodates different entities together. The urban field does not refer to the city in an administrative or territorial/topographical sense. Rather, the urban field is a multifaceted, relational spatiality: its essence results from the juxtaposition of a set of heterogeneous elements such as digital data, labour, institutions and modes of regulation; the built environment; forms of governing; urban life; intellectual ideas regarding cities and their success and failure; investments; and the vast set of operations of capital. As such, the urban field not only brings together the digital, the material, the symbolic, the social and the discursive, but also provides different actors with a raft of potentials that can be mobilized in different ways.

The concept of the urban field, therefore, is an operational concept, which means that it is intended in a literal sense to throw light on the operations of capital and the governmental state in the economization and corporatization of urban processes. This concept enables us to study the essences of contemporary urban development, essences that exist beyond but also connect appearances of such developments. For instance, our analysis of startup companies underlines the importance of scrutinizing the fundamental, actually existing processes of market valuation of startups, rather than drawing attention to the mere appearance of their business activities in urban space.

The extraction of economic value from the urban field is a long-term feature of capitalist societies, particularly in relation to the relentless production and reproduction of land rent. In this book, we have expanded the notion of the urban field beyond the urban land question, elaborating on Hardt and Negri's idea that the increased role of ground rent is symptomatic of a deeper economic leverage of the urban field and its social relations in contemporary cognitive and affective capitalism (Hardt & Negri 2009). In doing so, we have suggested that, in order to understand the economic value creation and extraction in the contemporary context, one must focus on a set of phenomena that reverberate on the value of urban land in the age of techno-monopoly capitalism.

As such, our treatise has focused on the urban political economies that are customarily understood as being essentially bound to inter-spatial competition for particular types of firms, workers, human capital and consumers. Our analyses of labour, human capital, startups and place-specific forms of life hence seek to demonstrate the economic-political construction of the urban field as it unfolds today as a kind of expanded open-plan office, a living laboratory for social interaction, a community-making platform, or a test bed for technological innovation, entrepreneurial living and theatrical performance. In so doing, we have also discussed the ways in which contemporary techno-capitalism is not only characterized by but also based on the highly polarized urban space marked by deep inequalities. These inequalities are therefore not mere reflections of the technology-driven urban economies but also fundamental constituents of such a political-economic form.

The deepening polarization of the urban field that we observe today is built on the longer trajectory of the urban technological paradigm and related governmentalities. With the advent of a knowledge-based, technology-driven society during the post-Fordist transition of the 1980s and the 1990s, the governance of economic development has been premised on the assumption that wage inequalities are dependent on what labour economists define as "skill-biased technical change". According to this dominant conception, the ascendancy of information technology as the techno-economic paradigm of our society divides workers in terms of the skills they can offer to the production process and the earnings they consequently gain from their employment. This view consequently holds that workers' earnings in a market economy depend fundamentally on their productivity, which corresponds to the value they produce through their labour. Accordingly, workers' productivity is believed to depend on their capabilities and the practical skills that enable them to accomplish more or less difficult tasks.

As we have highlighted, this view bypasses the problem of value measurability in the context of the algorithmic management of capitalist economies. Moreover, this view ignores other factors behind the rise in wage inequalities in the last decades, such as policy choices adopted by national governments and other governmental entities in the first instance. Even so, despite the evident contradictions of the skill-biased technological change's conception and the widely debated wage inequalities problem in recent years, national and local governments continue to prioritize urban and national policy initiatives aimed at the attraction of high-skilled/high-paid workers and professionals at the city level. This has numerous repercussions for the urban field, as we discuss with the example of the affordable housing crisis.

In the constitution of the urban field at the time of techno-monopoly capitalism, the distinction between high-skill and low-skill jobs has enormous societal power. Its impact is also significant at a wider level, as it plays a productive role in the shaping of economic, education and immigration policies of nation-states across geographical contexts. We have also shown how the urban technological paradigm on cities that dictates to attract an elite of high-skilled professionals as a way to boost their economies ends up devaluing the majority of workers who are supposed to be low-skilled according to conventional parameters of labour-value measurement. This view is premised on the assumption that the influx of highly skilled professionals is crucial to a local economy and therefore also to local labour markets. Accordingly, the increase of highly paid knowledge workers is thought to be functional to the development of the consumption-based service economy.

In this book, we have sought to explore more deeply the trajectory of human capital theory and its political and intellectual reception from the postwar years up to now, as its influence has been decisive in the reshaping of contemporary capitalist societies along neoliberal lines, particularly at the urban level. Since the mid-1990s, the theory of human capital has become even more central to explanations of economic growth and technological change in mainstream economics, particularly within the framework of the so-called endogenous growth theory, also known as new growth theory. Our argument has been that the entire human capital approach to national economic development, which is typical today in the richer nation-states, is fundamentally premised on this distinction between skills, which generalizes an urban logic of social competition based on skill-based selectivity, as well as on the entrepreneurialization of human living.

Bob Jessop (2005) has suggested that, in the post-Fordist economy, "knowledge" is essentially a collectively generated resource, the generation of which depends on intellectual commons. In this context, Jessop goes on, the state is needed for the commodification of knowledge as a collective resource to intellectual property (to enable profit-making), as well as for protecting the intellectual commons in order to secure the competitive advantage for the economy as a whole. We have similarly highlighted the role of the state in the constitution of the urban field. We have underscored that the urban field is constantly constituted in the process of statification and the associated governmental practices. In this constitution, the state plays a central role as an imaginary, fictive or discursive object that links the multiplicity of governmental practices together and makes them appear as a given entity. We have sought to make visible the many roles of the corporatized state in the constitution of the urban field in the age of techno-monopoly and argued that our analysis discloses a ubiquitous process that we conceptualize as the strategic urbanization of the state. This wave of urbanization differs notably from the Fordist-Keynesian era but also marks a qualitative shift in the process of urban entrepreneurialism.

The strategic urbanization of the state does not signal the return of the late-Keynesian entrepreneurial state. Neither does it simply denote the process whereby cities functioning as complex and decentred business ecosystems internalize "entrepreneurial logics" (Peck 2014: 399; cf. Harvey 1989b). Compared with the neo-Keynesian entrepreneurial state, the strategic urbanization of the state points to a "hesitant state" when it comes to risk-taking in investment policy. At the same time, the state does not limit itself to the merely managerial and coordinating role envisaged by neo-Jacobsian theorizers of self-organized business ecosystems. Instead, the strategic urbanization of the state proceeds through the material and symbolic construction of visible, highly mediatized projects that would ideally result in a broad cultural change – tech-centred entrepreneurialization. It thus operates through indirect political technologies to generate the framework conditions for the tech-centred entrepreneurial life, and for the associated indirect realization of both private investments and economic value. In this capacity, the strategic urbanization of the state seeks to harness the full potential of human life to the expansion of its economic base at a time of techno-monopoly in which the power acquired by a handful of technology corporations has become unrivalled, not just in terms of market control but in wider cultural and societal senses. In so doing, the urbanization of the state and the corporatization of technology-based economies become two sides of the same coin.

The strategic urbanization of the state mobilizes urban imaginaries and governmentalities in particular to work towards the entrepreneurialization of society, and to carry out economic projects, agendas and planning projects that contribute to the rise of attractive tech-economic forms. In other words, in such a process the state is not only becoming more experimental in terms of bringing about a broad cultural change in the name of societal entrepreneurialization, but also in terms of generating economic activities that are infused with an urban mentality for the sake of national economy and competitiveness. We hence underscore that the strategic urbanization of the state should not be considered a non-statist and market-driven economic form that develops solely from the bottom-up activities of skilled startup heroes, their entrepreneurial mentalities and the actions of private venture capitalists, and that is "freed" from the conventionally regulatory practices of the state.

One interesting question at the moment of writing is whether the "polycrisis" that has followed the Covid-19 pandemic at economic, energetic and societal levels, coupled with the Russian invasion of Ukraine and the consequent turmoil in geopolitical relations, is resulting in a qualitative shift in today's tech-dominated capitalism. Reducing dependencies between states and efforts by national states to control global production and value chains is now constantly articulated as central geopolitical strategies in the middle of inter-state rivalries. A kind of geopolitical techno-nationalism is increasingly visible. In this new context, the role of the state in global circulation, and in global exchange, is constantly debated and articulated with notions such as technological, digital or strategic sovereignty (Edler *et al.* 2023), which, however, have almost entirely lost the progressive appeal of the postwar era as a tool for decolonization and emancipation from unequal exchange (Morozov 2023).

Rather than treating these developments – that Yeung (2023: 674) calls "Machiavellian infusion of geopolitical and national security imperatives into macro-regional and national economic processes" – as disruptions to the previous mode of global accumulation and circulation, it may be useful to examine these as constituting a qualitatively new era of capitalist globalization. In contemporary scholarship, these and other new tendencies in global capitalism have already been discussed as the emergence of new state capitalism in different forms: reluctant state capitalism (Palcic, Reeves & Whiteside 2023), uneven and combined state capitalism (Alami & Dixon 2023), financial state capitalism (Silverwood & Berry 2023) and the like.

Irrespective of the term, the central question for us is whether the more muscular role of the national state in the production process, in finance, in innovation, in the overall generation of economic value, and in social reproduction, transforms the nature of capitalism and the urban field as these currently unfold in the age of techno-monopoly. In other words, is the more assertive role of the state in economic activities – a state that in the meantime has become increasingly corporatized, as we have argued – affecting the contemporary urbanization of capital? Is a sort of renationalization of the urban field already underway, and what are the political repercussions of such development for urban societies? Does the new state capitalism signal new needs to foster national unity through mechanisms of redistribution also through urban spaces? What would the allegedly post-statist startup economy look like in the age of new state capitalism? These are potentially the types of questions that need to be addressed in the future.

Another important question touches upon the potential and the experience of the urban field as a space of contestation and political struggle. In a capitalist society, the extraction of economic value from urban spaces and urban living is beneficial primarily to dominant technology corporations and their elites, but this has also unintended implications for community-based and even post-capitalist projects of social experimentation and transformation. As David Harvey signalled in his writings of the 1980s on the urbanization of capital (Harvey 1987), the shift to urban entrepreneurialism in capitalist societies instigates different and potentially conflicting responses.

The urban shift in post-Fordist capitalist societies has put cities under stress, leading to heightened inter-city competition over increasingly scarce resources, but has also generated a variety of interstitial points of resistance and empowerment, as decentralization taken together with the cultural concern with qualities of place and space creates a climate in which the politics of community and place acquire new significance. The multiplication in recent years of new municipalist movements that challenge the dominance of the neoliberal agenda at the national level, the experimentation with community-based economies and the rise of different types of cooperative projects at a neighbourhood level are testament to this potential politics of the urban field in the current conjuncture (Beveridge & Koch 2023).

Finally, we have sought to demonstrate throughout the book that the economic value of the urban field is bound to ideas and hence intellectual power; that is, to the expert knowledge emanating from the academic field, particularly from mainstream approaches in disciplines such as economics and business management studies. As such, the academic field and the urban field are firmly connected to each other. The reworking of the urban field is therefore not possible without the operations of intellectual power and the related discursive formations. The performative and organizing power of the new urban economics and the corporate discourse in the technology sector have played a notable role in the political-economic constitution of the urban field in the age of techno-monopoly.

The power of these discursive apparatuses cannot be overemphasized here. Contemporary theorizations in urban and regional economics link performances in urban economic growth to the locational preferences of high-skill tech workers and professionals looking for socio-culturally or environmentally attractive urban environments. "Location, location, location", and "people move, jobs follow", are their mantras that have been carefully listened to by both local and national state authorities. As we have sought to demonstrate, these mantras effectively disclose some of the ways in which the interests of high-tech capital and the corporatist state are fused in the strategic urbanization of the state. Moreover, specific types of intellectual theories regarding human capital and business management have been absolutely central in the constitution of the urban field. Through our analysis of urban life and the commodification of popular culture in Naples, we have sought to make visible the power of these discursive constructions: the recent touristification of human living and place-specific forms of urban life, as well as the negative outcomes that this economization and the related urban regeneration brings about – a new housing shortage, displacement of urban dwellers, and the deep exploitation of living labour, to mention but a few.

Hardt and Negri consider the cultural dominance of location in contemporary business and economics discourse as illustrative of how "the metropolis" – or what we call here the urban field – has become "an enormous reservoir . . . of not only material but also and moreover immaterial factors" for the generation of economic value (Hardt & Negri 2009: 156). Changing the direction of this development needs to be premised on alternative knowledge and related discourse on the urban field. Herein remains one of the many challenges for a critical geographical political economy of the urban field.

REFERENCES

Agamben, G. (2011). *The Kingdom and the Glory: For a Theological Genealogy of Economy and Government*. Stanford, CA: Stanford University Press.
Ahlqvist, T. & S. Moisio (2014). "Neoliberalisation in a Nordic state: from cartel polity towards a corporate polity in Finland". *New Political Economy* 19(1): 21–55.
Alami, I. & A. Dixon (2023). "Uneven and combined state capitalism". *Environment and Planning A: Economy and Space* 55(1): 72–99.
Alisio, G. & A. Buccaro (1994). "Storia e disegno urbano nell'area di Montecalvario dal piano vicereale ai programmi di Ferdinando II ". In S. Bisogni (ed.), *Napoli: Montecalvario questione aperta*, 23–31. Naples: Clean.
Allum, P. (1973). *Politics and Society in Post-War Naples*. Cambridge: Cambridge University Press.
Amable, B. & S. Palombarini (2021). *The Last Neoliberal: Macron and the Origins of France's Political Crisis*. London: Verso.
Amin, A. & A. Malmberg (1992). "Competing structural and institutional influences on the geography of production in Europe". *Environment and Planning A: Economy and Space* 24(3): 401–16.
Anwar, M. & M. Graham (2020). "Hidden transcripts of the gig economy: labour agency and the new art of resistance among African gig workers". *Environment and Planning A: Economy and Space* 52(7): 1269–91.
Arantola, H. (2010). *Palveluiden Suomi*. Helsinki: Elinkeinoelämän valtuuskunta.
Arboleda, M. & T. Purcell (2021). "The turbulent circulation of rent: towards a political economy of property and ownership in supply chain capitalism". *Antipode* 53(6): 1599–618.
Arun, M. & M. Yap (2000). "Singapore: the development of an intelligent island and social dividends of information technology". *Urban Studies* 37(10): 1749–56.
Asheim, B., L. Coenen & J. Vang (2007). "Face-to-face, buzz, and knowledge bases: sociospatial implications for learning, innovation, and innovation policy". *Environment and Planning C: Politics and Space* 25(5): 655–70.
Aspers, P. (2006). "Contextual knowledge". *Current Sociology* 54(5): 745–63.
Autor, D. (2014). "Skills, education, and the rise of earnings inequality among the 'other 99 percent'". *Science* 344(6186): 843–51.
Aydalot, P. & D. Keeble (eds) (1988). *High Technology Industry and Innovative Environments: The European Experience*. London: Routledge.
Baran, P. (1963). "Review of *Capitalism and Freedom*". *Journal of Political Economy* 71(6): 591–94.
Baran, P. & P. Sweezy (1966). *Monopoly Capital: An Essay on the American Economic and Social Order*. New York: Monthly Review Press.

REFERENCES

Barber, B. (2013). *If Mayors Ruled the World*. New Haven, CT: Yale University Press.

Barbrook, R. & A. Cameron (1996). "The Californian ideology". *Science as Culture* 6(1): 44–72.

Barkan, J. (2013). *Corporate Sovereignty: Law and Government Under Capitalism*. Minneapolis, MN: Minnesota University Press.

Barns, S. (2020). *Platform Urbanism: Negotiating Platform Ecosystems in Connected Cities*. London: Palgrave Macmillan.

Barthes, R. (1973). *Mythologies*. New York: Farrar, Straus & Giroux.

Becker, G. (1964). *Human Capital: A Theoretical and Empirical Analysis with Special Reference to Education*. Chicago, IL: University of Chicago Press.

Bell, D. (1976). *The Coming of Post-Industrial Society: A Venture in Social Forecasting*. New York: Basic Books.

Beveridge, R. & P. Koch (2023). *How Cities Can Transform Democracy*. Cambridge: Polity.

Bhagat, A. & R. Phillips (2021). "The techfare state: the 'new' face of neoliberal state regulation". *Developing Economics*. https://developingeconomics.org/2021/06/15/the-techfare-state-the-new-face-of-neoliberal-state-regulation/

Billing, M. (2021). "Wolt acquisition leaves early investors with 200x payouts". *Sifted Magazine*, 10 November. https://sifted.eu/articles/wolt-doordash-investor-returns/

Blakely, E. & L. Small (1996). "Michael Porter: new gilder of ghettos". *Review of Black Political Economy* 24(2): 161–83.

Bok, R. (2019). "'By our metaphors you shall know us': the 'fix' of geographical political economy". *Progress in Human Geography* 43(6): 1087–108.

Bowles, S. & H. Gintis (1975). "The problem with human capital theory – a Marxian critique". *American Economic Review* 65(2): 74–82.

Bowles, S. & H. Gintis (1976). *Schooling in Capitalist America: Educational Reform and the Contradictions of Economic Life*. New York: Basic Books.

Boyle, M. (1999). "Growth machines and propaganda projects: a review of readings of the role of civic boosterism in the politics of local economic development". In A. Jonas & D. Wilson (eds), *The Urban Growth Machine: Critical Perspectives Two Decades Later*, 55–70. Albany, NY: SUNY Press.

Braithwaite, J. (2008). *Regulatory Capitalism: How it Works, Ideas for Making it Work Better*. Cheltenham: Edward Elgar.

Bremmer, I. (2008). "The return of state capitalism". *Survival* 50(3): 55–64.

Brenner, N. (1998). "Between fixity and motion: accumulation, territorial organization and the historical geography of spatial scales". *Environment and Planning D: Society and Space* 16(4): 459–81.

Brenner, N. (2004). *New State Spaces: Urban Governance and the Rescaling of Statehood*. Oxford: Oxford University Press.

Brenner, N. & C. Schmid (2014). "The 'urban age' in question". *International Journal of Urban and Regional Research* 38(3): 731–55.

Brenner, N. & N. Theodore (2002). "Cities and the geographies of 'actually existing neoliberalism'". *Antipode* 34: 349–79.

Brenner, R. (2012). "After boom, bubble and bust: where is the US economy going?". In M. Miller (ed.), *Worlds of Capitalism: Institutions, Economic Performance and Governance in the Era of Globalization*, 214–48. New York: Routledge.

Bröckling, U. (2015). *The Entrepreneurial Self: Fabricating a New Type of Subject*. London: Sage.

Brollo, B. & F. Celata (2023). "Temporary populations and sociospatial polarisation in the short-term city". *Urban Studies* 60(10): 1815–32.

Brown, W. (2003). "Neo-liberalism and the end of liberal democracy". *Theory & Event* 7(1): 37–59.

Bunnell, T. (2002). "Cities for nations? Examining the city–nation–state relation in Information Age Malaysia". *International Journal of Urban and Regional Research* 26(2): 284–98.

Buonincontri, P. *et al.* (2017). "Managing the experience co-creation process in tourism destinations: empirical findings from Naples". *Tourism Management* 62: 264–77.

Burnett, P. (2023). "Theodore W. Schultz (1902–1998)". In R. Cord (ed.), *The Palgrave Companion to Chicago Economics*, 401–20. Cham, CH: Palgrave Macmillan.

Calo, R. & A. Rosenblat (2017). "The taking economy: Uber, information, and power". *Columbia Law Review* 17(6): 1623–90.

Capps, K. (2019). "The hidden horror of Hudson Yards is how it was financed". *Bloomberg*, 12 April. https://www.bloomberg.com/news/articles/2019-04-12/the-visa-program-that-helped-pay-for-hudson-yards?utm_source=website&utm_medium=share&utm_campaign=copy

Carver, C., M. Scheier & J. Weintraub (1989). "Assessing coping strategies: a theoretically based approach". *Journal of Personality and Social Psychology* 56(2): 267–83.

Casilli, A. & J. Posada (2019). "The platformization of labor and society". In M. Graham & W. Dutton (eds), *Society and the Internet: How Networks of Information and Communication are Changing Our Lives*, 58–79. Oxford: Oxford University Press.

Castells, M. (1989). *The Informational City: Information Technology, Economic Restructuring and the Urban-Regional Process*. Oxford: Blackwell.

Castells, M. & P. Hall (1994). *Technopoles of the World: The Making of 21st Century Industrial Complexes*. New York: Routledge.

Center for an Urban Future (2012). *New York Tech City*. https://nycfuture.org/research/publications/new-tech-city

CERI/OECD (2001). *The Well-being of Nations: The Role of Human and Social Capital*. Paris: OECD Publications.

Cerny, P. (2003). "What next for the state?". In E. Kofman & G. Youngs (eds), *Globalization: Theory and Practice*. London: Continuum.

Chrisafis, A. (2022). "Emmanuel Macron 'proud' of supporting Uber's lobbying drive in France". *The Guardian*, 12 July. https://www.theguardian.com/news/2022/jul/12/emmanuel-macron-proud-of-supporting-ubers-lobbying-drive-in-france

Christophers, B. (2022). *Rentier Capitalism: Who Owns the Economy, and Who Pays for It?* London: Verso.

Cirolia, L. & J. Harber (2021). "Urban statecraft: the governance of transport infrastructures in African cities". *Urban Studies* 59(12): 2431–50.

Cision (2021). "DoorDash joins forces with Wolt". https://www.prnewswire.com/news-releases/doordash-joins-forces-with-wolt-301420417.html

Clark, P. (2017). "Why can't they build more homes where the jobs are?". Bloomberg, 23 June. https://www.bloomberg.com/news/articles/2017-06-23/why-can-t-they-build-more-homes-where-the-jobs-are

Coe, N. & H. Yeung (2015). *Global Production Networks: Theorizing Economic Development in an Interconnected World*. Oxford: Oxford University Press.

Cohen, B., E. Almirall & H. Chesbrough (2017). "The city as a lab: open innovation meets the collaborative economy". *California Management Review* 59(1): 5–13.

Cohen, B. & P. Muñoz (2015). "Toward a theory of purpose-driven urban entrepreneurship". *Organization & Environment* 28(3): 264–85.

Cohen, B. & P. Muñoz (2016). *The Emergence of the Urban Entrepreneur: How the Growth of Cities and the Sharing Economy Are Driving a New Breed of Innovators*. Westport, CT: Praeger.

Coldiron, K. (2022). "The world's most important product and the only two companies that can make it". *Forbes*, 15 December. https://www.forbes.com/sites/kevincoldiron/2022/12/15/the-worlds-most-important-product-and-the-only-two-companies-that-can-make-it/

Coletta, C., L. Heaphy & R. Kitchin (2019). "From the accidental to articulated smart city: the creation and work of 'Smart Dublin'". *European Urban and Regional Studies* 26(4): 349–64.

Cooke, P. & R. Huggins (2003). "High-technology clustering in Cambridge (UK)". In F. Sforzi & A. Amin (eds), *The Institutions of Local Development*, 51–74. Aldershot: Ashgate.

Cotton, J. (2000). "The Asian crisis and the perils of enterprise association: explaining the different outcomes in Singapore, Taiwan and Korea". In R. Robison *et al.* (eds), *Politics and Markets in the Wake of the Asian Crisis*. London: Routledge.

Cowen, D. & N. Smith (2009). "After geopolitics? From the geopolitical social to geoeconomics". *Antipode* 41: 22–48.

Crouch, C. (2009). "Privatised Keynesianism: an unacknowledged policy regime". *British Journal of Politics and International Relations* 11(3): 382–99.

Crouch, C. & P. Le Galès (2012). "Cities as national champions?". *Journal of European Public Policy* 19: 405–19.

Dandelar, V. (1966). "Transforming traditional agriculture: a critique of Professor Schultz". *Economic and Political Weekly* 1(1): 25–36.

Danyluk, M. (2018). "Capital's logistical fix: accumulation, globalization, and the survival of capitalism". *Environment and Planning D: Society and Space* 36(4): 630–47.

Daub, A. (2020). *What Tech Calls Thinking: An Inquiry into the Intellectual Bedrock of Silicon Valley*. New York: Farrar, Straus & Giroux.

Davies, H. *et al.* (2022). "Uber broke laws, duped police and secretly lobbied governments, leak reveals". *The Guardian*, 11 July. https://www.theguardian.com/news/2022/jul/10/uber-files-leak-reveals-global-lobbying-campaign

Dean, J. (2009). *Democracy and Other Neoliberal Fantasies: Communicative Capitalism and Left Politics*. Durham, NJ: Duke University Press.

Dean, J. (2020). "Communism or neo-feudalism?" *New Political Science* 42(1): 1–17.

Dean, M. (2017). "Political acclamation, social media and the public mood". *European Journal of Social Theory* 20(3): 417–34.

Dear, M. & S. Flusty (1998). "Postmodern urbanism". *Annals of the Association of American Geographers* 88(1): 50–72.

de Magistris, L. (2017). *La città ribelle. Il caso di Napoli*. Milan: Chiarelettere.

di Costanzo, A. (2023). "Napoli, il sindaco Manfredi: 'Sul turismo numeri superiori alle previsioni e ora i grandi eventi'". *La Repubblica*, Naples edition, 11 April. https://napoli.repubblica.it/cronaca/2023/04/11/news/manfredi_a_napoli_boom_di_turismo-395671569/

Dierwechter, Y. (2018). "The smart state as utopian space for urban politics". In K. Ward *et al.* (eds), *Routledge Handbook on Spaces of Urban Politics*, 47–57. London: Routledge.

Dorfman, N. (1983). "Route 128: the development of a regional high technology economy". *Research Policy* 12(6): 299–316.

Dorward, N. *et al.* (2023). "A spatial-demographic analysis of Africa's emerging urban geography". *Environment and Urbanization* 35(2): 310–27.

Dosi, G. (1982). "Technological paradigms and technological trajectories: a suggested interpretation of the determinants and directions of technical change". *Research Policy* 11(3): 147–62.

Dougherty, C. (2020). "Build Build Build Build Build Build Build Build Build Build Build Build Build". *New York Times*, 13 February. https://www.nytimes.com/2020/02/13/business/economy/housing-crisis-conor-dougherty-golden-gates.html

Dougherty, C. & E. Goldberg (2022). "What comes next for the most empty downtown in America". *New York Times*, 17 December. https://www.nytimes.com/2022/12/17/business/economy/california-san-francisco-empty-downtown.html

Drucker, J., C. Kayanan & H. Renski (2019). *Innovation Districts as a Strategy for Urban Economic Development: A Comparison of Four Cases*. https://scholarworks.umass.edu/ced_techrpts/192

Drucker, P. (1969). *The Age of Discontinuity: Guidelines to Our Changing Society*. London: Heineman.

Drucker, P. (1994). "The age of social transformation". *The Atlantic Monthly*, November issue: 53–80.

Duggan, G. (2001). "The greatest show on Earth: a look at contemporary fashion shows and their relationship to performance art". *Fashion Theory* 5(3): 243–70.

Durand, C. (2017). *Fictitious Capital: How Finance Is Appropriating Our Future*. London: Verso.

REFERENCES

Duranton, G. & D. Puga (2001). "Nursery cities: urban diversity, process innovation, and the life cycle of products". *American Economic Review* 91(5): 1454–77.

Ebner, N. & J. Peck (2022). "Fantasy island: Paul Romer and the multiplication of Hong Kong". *International Journal of Urban and Regional Research* 46(1): 26–49.

The Economist (2023). "Taiwan's dominance of the chip industry makes it more important". *The Economist*, 6 March. https://www.economist.com/special-report/2023/03/06/taiwans-dominance-of-the-chip-industry-makes-it-more-important

Edler, J. et al. (2023). "Technology sovereignty as an emerging frame for innovation policy. Defining rationales, ends and means". *Research Policy* 52(6): 104765.

Edwards J. (2015). "The CEO of Deliveroo delivers pizza on his bike on the weekends, and his customers have no idea who he is". *Business Insider UK*, 5 November. https://www.businessinsider.com/deliveroo-ceo-will-shu-delivers-pizza-on-the-weekends-2015-11?r=US&IR=T

Ehrenreich, B. (2002). *Nickel and Dimed: Undercover in Low-Wage America*. New York: Granta.

Eisinger, P. (1988). *The Rise of the Entrepreneurial State: State and Local Economic Development Policy in the United States*. Madison, WI: University of Wisconsin Press.

Esping-Andersen, G. (1990). *The Three Worlds of Welfare Capitalism*. Princeton, NJ: Princeton University Press.

Estevens, A. et al. (2023). "The role of the state in the touristification of Lisbon". *Cities* 137: 104275.

Ettlinger, N. (2022). *Algorithms and the Assault on Critical Thought: Digitalized Dilemmas of Automated Governance and Communitarian Practice*. Abingdon: Routledge.

Etzkowitz, H. (2008). *The Triple Helix: University–Industry–Government Innovation in Action*. New York: Routledge.

European Union (2023). *The Digital Strategy by the EU Commission*. https://digital–strategy.ec.europa.eu/en/policies/europes–digital–decade

Ferguson, C. (1988). "From the people who brought you voodoo economics". *Harvard Business Review* 66(3): 55–62.

Ferguson, J. & A. Gupta (2002). "Spatializing states: toward an ethnography of neoliberal governmentality". *American Ethnologist* 29: 981–1002.

Ferrari, F. & M. Graham (2021). "Fissures in algorithmic power: platforms, code, and contestation". *Cultural Studies* 35(4–5): 814–32.

Fields, D. (2022). "Automated landlord: digital technologies and post-crisis financial accumulation". *Environment and Planning A: Economy and Space* 54(1): 160–81.

Finnish Government (2023). *A Strong and Committed Finland – the Government's Vision*. https://valtioneuvosto.fi/en/governments/government-programme#/

Finnish National Broadcasting Company YLE (2022). *Woltin ja Doordashin yrityskauppa sai viimeisen sinetin – Suomeen lupailluista verotuloista merkittävä osa jäänee saamatta*. https://yle.fi/uutiset/3-12470748

Florida, R. (2012). *The Rise of the Creative Class Revisited*. New York: Basic Books.

Florida, R., P. Adler & C. Mellander (2017). "The city as innovation machine". *Regional Studies* 51(1): 86–96.

Florida, R. & K. King (2016). "Rise of the urban startup neighborhood: micro-clusters of venture capital and startup activity at the neighborhood level". Martin Prosperity Institute Working Paper.

Florida, R. & C. Mellander (2016). "Rise of the start-up city: the changing geography of the venture capital financed innovation". *California Management Review* 59(1): 14–38.

Fontana, G. (2023). "Projecting Europe's metro population growth from 2021–2100". Blog post, 29 March. https://www.visualcapitalist.com/cp/projecting-europes-metro-population-growth-2021-2100/

Fortune (2023). "Airbnb took in $4bn in rent in Italy. Now the country's Finance Police is seizing $835m of it because they allegedly didn't pay taxes". https://fortune.com/europe/2023/11/07/airbnb-4bn-rent-italy-finance-police-seizing-835m-taxes/

REFERENCES

Foucault, M. (1980). "Questions on geography". In C. Gordon (ed.), *Power/Knowledge: Selected Interviews and Other Writings, 1972–1977, by Michel Foucault*, 63–77. New York: Pantheon Books.

Foucault, M. (1991). "Governmentality". In G. Burchell, C. Gordon & P. Miller (eds), *The Foucault Effect: Studies in Governmentality*, 87–104. Chicago, IL: University of Chicago Press.

Foucault, M. (2008). *The Birth of Biopolitics: Lectures at the College de France, 1978–79*. Basingstoke: Palgrave Macmillan.

Fougner, T. (2006). "The state, international competitiveness and neoliberal globalization: is there a future beyond 'the competition state'?" *Review of International Studies* 32: 165–85.

Fourcade, M. & J. Gordon (2020). "Learning like a state: statecraft in the digital age". *Journal of Law and Political Economy* 1: 78–108.

Freemark, Y. (2020). "Upzoning Chicago: impacts of a zoning reform on property values and housing construction". *Urban Affairs Review* 56(3): 758–89.

Frey, W. (2022) "Big cities saw historic population losses while suburban growth declined during the pandemic". Brookings, 11 July. https://www.brookings.edu/articles/big-cities-saw-historic-population-losses-while-suburban-growth-declined-during-the-pandemic/

Friedman, M. (1955) "The role of government in education". In R. Solo (ed.), *Economics and the Public Interest*, 124–44. Binghamton, NY: Vail-Ballou Press.

Friedman, M. (1962). *Capitalism and Freedom*. Chicago, IL: University of Chicago Press.

Friedmann, J. & J. Miller (1965). "The urban field". *Journal of the American Institute of Planners* 31(4): 312–20.

Gabrys, J. (2016). *Program Earth: Environmental Sensing Technology and the Making of a Computational Planet*. Minneapolis, MN: Minnesota University Press.

Gago, V. (2017). *Neoliberalism from Below: Popular Pragmatics and Baroque Economies*. Durham, NC: Duke University Press.

Gebrial, D. (2022). "Racial platform capitalism: empire, migration and the making of Uber in London". *Environment and Planning A: Economy and Space*. https://doi.org/10.1177/0308518X221115439

Geschwindt, S. (2021). "Architects unveil Oslo Science City plans". *Build in Digital*, 16 December. https://buildindigital.com/architects-unveil-oslo-science-city-plans/

Glaeser, E. (1999). "Learning in cities". *Journal of Urban Economics* 46(2): 254–77.

Glaeser, E. (2011). *Triumph of the City: How Our Greatest Invention Makes Us Richer, Smarter, Greener, Healthier, and Happier*. New York: Penguin.

Glaeser, E. & J. Gottlieb (2009). "The wealth of cities: agglomeration economies and spatial equilibrium in the United States". *Journal of Economic Literature* 47(4): 983–1028.

Glaeser, E. et al. (1992). "Growth in cities". *Journal of Political Economy* 100(6): 126–52.

Glaeser, E. & A. Saiz (2004). "The rise of the skilled city". Brookings-Wharton Papers on Urban Affairs, 47–94.

Glaeser, E. & K. Tobio (2008). "The rise of the Sunbelt". *Southern Economic Journal* 74: 609–43.

Godechot, O. (2012). "Is finance responsible for the rise in wage inequality in France?". *Socio-Economic Review* 10(3): 447–70.

Godin, B. (2009). "National Innovation System: the system approach in historical perspective". *Science, Technology, & Human Values* 34(4): 476–501.

Goos, M. & A. Manning (2003). "McJobs and MacJobs: the growing polarisation of jobs in the UK". In R. Dickens, P. Gregg & J. Wadsworth (eds), *The Labour Market Under New Labour: The State of Working Britain 2003*, 70–85. Basingstoke: Palgrave Macmillan.

Gordon, R. (2016). *The Rise and Fall of American Growth: The U.S. Standard of Living since the Civil War*. Princeton, NJ: Princeton University Press.

Graham, P. (2010). "What we look for in founders". Blog post. http://www.paulgraham.com/founders.html

Greenfield, A. (2017). *Radical Technologies: The Design of Everyday Life*. London: Verso.

Grind, K. *et al.* (2023). "Elon Musk is planning a Texas utopia – his own town". *Wall Street Journal*, 9 March. https://www.wsj.com/articles/elon-musk-texas-town-52386513

The Guardian (2020). "The cult of Maradona – in pictures". *The Guardian*, 25 November. https://www.theguardian.com/football/gallery/2020/oct/30/the-cult-of-diego-maradona-in-pictures

Hall, S. (2022). "For feminist geographies of austerity". *Progress in Human Geography* 46: 299–318.

Hall, S. & D. Massey (2010). "Interpreting the crisis". *Soundings* 44: 57–71.

Hardt, M. & A. Negri (2000). *Empire*. Cambridge, MA: Harvard University Press.

Hardt, M. & A. Negri (2009). *Commonwealth*. Cambridge, MA: Harvard University Press.

Harrison, B. & B. Bluestone (1988). *The Great U-Turn: Corporate Restructuring and the Polarizing of America*. New York: Basic Books.

Harvey, D. (1979). "The urban process under capitalism: a framework for analysis". *International Journal of Urban and Regional Research* 2: 101–31.

Harvey, D. (1985a). *The Urbanization of Capital: Studies in the History and Theory of Capitalist Urbanization*. Baltimore, MD: Johns Hopkins University Press.

Harvey, D. (1985b). "The geopolitics of capitalism". In D. Gregory & J. Urry (eds), *Social Relations and Spatial Structures*, 128–63. London: Macmillan.

Harvey, D. (1987). "Flexible accumulation through urbanization: reflections on 'post-modernism in the American city'". *Antipode* 19(3): 260–86.

Harvey, D. (1989a). *The Condition of Postmodernity: An Enquiry into the Origins of Cultural Change*. Oxford: Blackwell.

Harvey, D. (1989b). "From managerialism to entrepreneurialism: the transformation in urban governance in late capitalism". *Geografiska Annaler B: Human Geography* 71(1): 3–17.

Harvey, D. (2005). *A Brief History of Neoliberalism*. Oxford: Oxford University Press.

Harvey, D. (2018). *A Companion to Marx's Capital: The Complete Edition*. London: Verso.

Haskel, J. & S. Westlake (2018). *Capitalism Without Capital: The Rise of the Intangible Economy*. Princeton, NJ: Princeton University Press.

Haskel, J. & S. Westlake (2022). *Restarting the Future: How to Fix the Intangible Economy*. Princeton, NJ: Princeton University Press.

Henderson, J. (1987). "Semiconductors, Scotland and the international division of labour". *Urban Studies* 24(5): 389–408.

Henshall, W. (2023). "E.U.'s AI regulation could be softened after pushback from biggest members". *Time*, 22 November. https://time.com/6338602/eu-ai-regulation-foundation-models/

Hernesniemi, H. (ed.) (2010). *Digitaalinen Suomi 2020. Älykäs Tie Menestykseen*. http://www.teknologiainfo.net/content/kirjat/pdf-iedostot/Sahko_elektroniikka_ja_tietoteollisuus/digitaalinen_suomi-ekirja.pdf?from=11376748755378896

Herrera, R. (2006). "The hidden face of endogenous growth theory: analytical and ideological perspectives in the era of neoliberal globalization". *Review of Radical Political Economics* 38(2): 243–57.

Hill, D. (1988). "Jane Jacobs' ideas on big, diverse cities: a review and commentary". *Journal of the American Planning Association* 54(3): 302–14.

Ho, E. (2017). "Smart subjects for a smart nation? Governing (smart)mentalities in Singapore". *Urban Studies* 54(13): 3101–18.

Ho-Dac, N. (2020). "The value of online user generated content in product development". *Journal of Business Research* 112: 136–46.

Hobart, E. (2020). "Italy's beloved 'fried pizza'". BBC Travel, 17 November. https://www.bbc.com/travel/article/20201116-italys-beloved-fried-pizza

Holgersen, S. (2015). "Economic crisis, (creative) destruction, and the current urban condition". *Antipode* 47(3): 689–707.

Horton, B. (2022). "Sweden's innovative wooden skyscraper can capture 9 million kilograms of CO2". Euronews.green, 28 September. https://www.euronews.com/green/2022/03/28/sweden-s-innovative-wooden-skyscraper-captures-as-much-carbon-as-10-000-forests

REFERENCES

Hughes, T. (1989). *American Genesis: A Century of Invention and Technology Enthusiasm, 1870–1970*. New York: Penguin.

Hung, H. & D. Thompson (2016). "Money supply, class power, and inflation: monetarism reassessed". *American Sociological Review* 81(3): 447–66.

Implementation Plan of the Government of Finland (2018). *Finland, a Land of Solutions*. Helsinki: The Government of Finland.

Jacobs, J. (1961). *The Death and Life of Great American Cities*. New York: Random House.

Jacobs, J. (1969). *The Economy of Cities*. New York: Random House.

Jacobs, J. (1984). *Cities and the Wealth of Nations*. New York: Random House.

Jaeggi, R. (2018). *Critique of Forms of Life*. Cambridge, MA: Harvard University Press.

Jenkins, S. (2015). "The trials and triumphs of the city: Edward Glaeser in conversation". *The Guardian*, 21 May. https://www.theguardian.com/cities/2015/may/21/what-are-cities-doing-so-right-and-so-wrong-the-experts-go-head-to-head

Jessen, M. & N. von Eggers (2020). "Governmentality and statification: towards a Foucauldian theory of the state". *Theory, Culture & Society* 37(1): 53–72.

Jessop, B. (1990). *State Theory: Putting the Capitalist State in Its Place*. Cambridge: Polity.

Jessop, B. (1992). "Fordism and post-Fordism: a critical reformulation". In M. Storper & A. Scott (eds), *Pathways to Industrialization and Regional Development*, 43–65. New York: Routledge.

Jessop, B. (1993). "Towards a Schumpeterian workfare state? Preliminary remarks on post-Fordist political economy". *Studies in Political Economy* 40(1): 7–39.

Jessop, B. (1997). "The entrepreneurial city: re-imaging localities, redesigning economic governance, or restructuring capital?". In N. Jewson & S. MacGregor (eds), *Realising Cities: New Spatial Divisions and Social Transformation*. London: Routledge.

Jessop, B. (2000). "The crisis of the national spatio-temporal fix and the tendential ecological dominance of globalizing capitalism". *International Journal of Urban and Regional Research* 24(2): 323–60.

Jessop, B. (2004). "Critical semiotic analysis and cultural political economy". *Critical Discourse Studies* 1(1): 1–16.

Jessop, B. (2005). "Cultural political economy, the knowledge-based economy and the state". In A. Barry & D. Slater (eds), *The Technological Economy*, 142–64. London: Routledge.

Jessop, B. (2007). *State Power: A Strategic-Relational Approach*. Cambridge: Polity.

Jessop, B. (2016). "The developmental state in an era of finance-dominated accumulation". In Y.-W. Chu (ed.), *The Asian Developmental State: Reexaminations and New Departures*. 27–55. London: Palgrave Macmillan.

Jessop, B. & N.-L. Sum (2006). *Beyond the Regulation Approach: Putting Capitalist Economies in Place*. Cheltenham: Edward Elgar.

Jonas, A. (1986). "Book review: Cities and the Wealth of Nations". *Progress in Human Geography* 10(1): 131–3.

Jonas, A. & D. Wilson (eds) (1999). *The Urban Growth Machine: Critical Perspectives Two Decades Later*. Albany, NY: SUNY Press.

Jones, M. (1997). "Spatial selectivity of the state? The regulationist enigma and local struggles over economic governance". *Environment and Planning A: Economy and Space* 29(5): 831–64.

Jones, P. (2021). *Work Without the Worker: Labour in the Age of Platform Capitalism*. London: Verso.

Jörnow, L. (2021). "Wolt joins DoorDash in €7bn deal". https://medium.com/eqtventures/wolt-joins-doordash-in-7bn-deal-6e3a942b9234

Katz, B. & J. Wagner (2014). *The Rise of Innovation Districts: A New Geography of Innovation in America*. Washington, DC: Brookings Institution Press.

Kayanan, C. (2021). "A critique of innovation districts: entrepreneurial living and the burden of shouldering urban development". *Environment and Planning A: Economy and Space* 54(1): 50–66.

Khanna, P. (2016). *Connectography: Mapping the Future of Global Civilization*. New York: Random House.
Koch, R. & S. Miles (2021). "Inviting the stranger in: intimacy, digital technology and new geographies of encounter". *Progress in Human Geography* 45(6): 1379–401.
Kornberger, M. (2010). *Brand Society: How Brands Transform Management and Lifestyle*. Cambridge: Cambridge University Press.
Kotkin, J. (2020). *The Coming of Neo-Feudalism: A Warning to the Global Middle Class*. New York: Encounter Books.
Krippner, G. (2012). *Capitalizing on Crisis: The Political Origins of the Rise of Finance*. Cambridge, MA: Harvard University Press.
Krivý, M. (2018). "Becoming-platform, the urban and the city". *Mediapolis Journal* 3(4). https://www.mediapolisjournal.com/2018/10/becoming-platform/
La Repubblica Napoli (2016). "Domenico Dolce: 'Stregato da Napoli'". https://video.repubblica.it/edizione/napoli/domenico-dolce-stregato-da-napoli/245439/245523
Laffey, M. & J. Weldes (2005). "Policing and global governance". In M. Barnett & R. Duvall (eds), *Power in Global Governance*, 59–79. Cambridge: Cambridge University Press.
Lapavitsas, C. (2013). *Profiting Without Producing: How Finance Exploits Us All*. London: Verso.
Lazzarato, M. (1996). "Immaterial labor". In P. Virno & M. Hardt (eds), *Radical Thought in Italy*, 133–50. Minneapolis, MN: University of Minnesota Press.
Lazzarato, M. (2004). "From capital-labour to capital-life". *ephemera* 4: 187–208.
Lazzarato, M. (2007). "Strategies of the political entrepreneur". *SubStance* 36(1): 86–97.
Lee, J. & S. Nellis (2022). "TSMC says it will have advanced ASML chipmaking tool in 2024". Reuters, 17 June. https://www.reuters.com/technology/tsmc-says-it-will-have-advanced-asml-chipmaking-tool-2024-2022-06-16/
Lefebvre, H. (2003). *The Urban Revolution*. Minneapolis, MN: University of Minnesota Press.
Leidner, R. (1993). *Fast Food, Fast Talk: Service Work and the Routinization of Everyday Life*. Berkeley, CA: University of California Press.
Leino, R. (2009). "IBM:n toimitusjohtaja Johan Sandell haluaa Suomen it-kuntokuurille: Tanska esikuvaksi". *Tekniikka & Talous* 9 April: 9.
Lemke, T. (2007). "An indigestible meal? Foucault, governmentality and state theory". *Distinktion: Journal of Social Theory* 8(2): 43–64.
Lepore, J. (2014). "The disruption machine. What the gospel of innovation gets wrong". *The New Yorker*, 16 June. https://www.newyorker.com/magazine/2014/06/23/the-disruption-machine
Levi Martin, J. (2003). "What is field theory?" *American Journal of Sociology* 109(1): 1–49.
Lieto, L. (2021). "Normative ecologies of planning: understanding norms in action". *Journal of Planning Education and Research*. https://doi.org/10.1177/0739456X211021150
Lofgren, M. (2016). *The Deep State: The Fall of the Constitution and the Rise of a Shadow Government*. New York: Penguin.
Longman, P. (2015). "Why the economic fates of America's cities diverged". *The Atlantic*, 28 November. http://www.theatlantic.com/business/archive/2015/11/cities-economic-fates-diverge/417372/
Lowry, W. (2022). "On the cusp of history: a small Texas city adapts to life with Elon Musk and SpaceX". *The National News*, 29 June. https://www.thenationalnews.com/world/2022/06/29/on-the-cusp-of-history-a-small-texas-city-adapts-to-life-with-elon-musk-and-spacex/
Lucas, R. (1988). "On the mechanics of economic development". *Journal of Monetary Economics* 22(1): 3–42.
Määttä, S. (2010). *Kaikki Yhden ja Yksi Kaikkien Puolesta. Valtion Konsernijohdon Vaativa Mutta Mahdollinen Tehtävä*. Helsinki: Sitran selvityksiä 21.
Macciocchi, M. (1973). *Letters from Inside the Italian Communist Party to Louis Althusser*. Atlantic Islands, NJ: Humanities Press.

MacKinnon, D. et al. (2022). "Reframing urban and regional 'development' for 'left behind' places". *Cambridge Journal of Regions, Economy and Society* 15(1): 39–56.

Mandel, E. (1975). *Late Capitalism*. London: New Left Books.

Marazzi, C. (2008). *Capital and Language: From the New Economy to the War Economy*. Los Angeles, CA: Semiotext(e).

Martin, B. (2013). "Tech boom 2.0: Lessons learned from the dot-com crash". *Wired*. https://www.wired.com/insights/2013/08/tech-boom-2-0-lessons-learned-from-the-dot-com-crash/

Marx, K. (1973) [1857–58]. *Grundrisse: Introduction to the Critique of Political Economy*. New York: Random House.

Marx, K. (2004) [1867]. *Capital: A Critique of Political Economy. Volume One*. New York: Penguin.

Marx, K. & F. Engels (1998) [1932]. *The German Ideology*. New York: Prometheus.

Massey D., P. Quintas & D. Wield (1992). *High-Tech Fantasies: Science Parks in Society, Science and Space*. London: Routledge.

Mathews, J. (1997). "A Silicon Valley of the East: Creating Taiwan's semiconductor industry". *California Management Review* 39(4): 26–54.

Matinen, M. (2020). "Maastapoistumisvero – mistä on kyse ja mistä ei?" https://vm.fi/-/maastapoistumisvero-mista-on-kyse-ja-mista-ei-

May, T. & B. Perry (2018). *Cities and the Knowledge Economy: Promise, Politics and Possibilities*. Abingdon: Routledge.

Mazzucato, M. (2013). *The Entrepreneurial State: Debunking Public vs Private Sectors Myths*. London: Anthem Press.

Mazzucato, M. (2018). *The Value of Everything: Making and Taking in the Global Economy*. London: Allen Lane.

Mazzucato, M. (2019). "Preventing digital feudalism". Social Europe. https://www.socialeurope.eu/preventing-digital-feudalism

McChesney, R. (2013). *Digital Disconnect: How Capitalism Is Turning the Internet Against Democracy*. New York: The New Press.

McCormack, D. (2012). "Governing economic futures through the war on inflation". *Environment and Planning A: Economy and Space* 44(7): 1536–53.

McElroy, E. (2020). "Digital nomads in siliconising Cluj: material and allegorical double dispossession". *Urban Studies* 57(15): 3078–94.

McNeill, D. (2015). "Global firms and smart technologies: IBM and the reduction of cities". *Transactions of the Institute of British Geographers* 40(4): 562–74.

McNeill, D. (2016). "Governing a city of unicorns: technology capital and the urban politics of San Francisco". *Urban Geography* 37(4): 494–513.

McNeill, D. (2017). "Start-ups and the entrepreneurial city". *City* 21(2): 232–9.

McNeill, D. (2021). "Urban geography 1: 'Big tech' and the reshaping of urban space". *Progress in Human Geography* 45(5): 1311–19.

Medina, E. (2011). *Cybernetic Revolutionaries: Technology and Politics in Allende's Chile*. Cambridge, MA: MIT Press.

Merrifield, A. (2014). "The entrepreneur's new clothes". *Geografiska Annaler: Series B, Human Geography* 96(4): 389–91.

Metz, C. (2023). "Mistral, French A.I. start-up, is valued at $2 billion in funding round". *New York Times*, 10 February. https://www.nytimes.com/2023/12/10/technology/mistral-ai-funding.html

Mezzadra, S. & B. Neilson (2019). *The Politics of Operations: Excavating Contemporary Capitalism*. Durham, NC: Duke University Press.

Miettinen, R. (2002). *National Innovation System: Scientific Concept or Political Rhetoric*. Helsinki: Edita.

Miller, C. (2022). *Chip War: The Fight for the World's Most Critical Technology*. New York: Scribner.

Mincer, J. (1958). "Investment in human capital and personal income distribution". *Journal of Political Economy* 66(4): 281–302.

Mishel, L., J. Schmitt & H. Shierholz (2014). "Wage inequality: a story of policy choices". *New Labor Forum* 23(3): 26–31.

Mitchell, C. (2023). "Silicon Zanzibar? Tourist islands want techies to stay". *African Business*, 11 January. https://african.business/2023/01/technology-information/silicon-zanzibar-tourist-islands-want-techies-to-stay

Mitchell, T. (1991). "The limits of the state: beyond statist approaches and their critics". *American Political Science Review* 85(1): 77–96.

Moisio, S. (2018a). *Geopolitics of the Knowledge-Based Economy*. Abingdon: Routledge.

Moisio, S. (2018b). "Urbanizing the nation-state? Notes on the geopolitical growth of cities and city-regions". *Urban Geography* 39(9): 1421–4.

Moisio, S. (2019). "Re-thinking geoeconomics: towards a political geography of economic geographies". *Geography Compass* 13: e12466.

Moisio, S. (2024). "Towards critical geoeconomics?". *Transactions of the Institute of British Geographers* 49: e12646.

Moisio, S. & A. Kangas (2016). "Reterritorializing the global knowledge economy: an analysis of geopolitical assemblages of higher education". *Global Networks* 16: 268–87.

Moisio, S. & A. Paasi (2013). "From geopolitical to geoeconomic? Changing political rationalities of state space". *Geopolitics* 18: 267–83.

Moisio, S. & U. Rossi (2020). "The start-up state: governing urbanised capitalism". *Environment and Planning A: Economy and Space* 52(3): 532–52.

Moisio, S. & U. Rossi (2023). "The value of the urban field in technology-driven knowledge economies: the role of the state". *Environment and Planning F*. https://doi.org/10.1177/26349825231154874

Moisio, S. & A. Tarvainen (2023). "Colonial geopolitics of the knowledge economy". Unpublished manuscript.

Montgomery, C. (2013). *Happy City: Transforming Our Lives Through Urban Design*. New York: Penguin.

Moretti, E. (2004). "Human capital externalities in cities". In V. Henderson & J. Thisse (eds), *Handbook of Regional and Urban Economics*, 2243–91. Amsterdam: North Holland-Elsevier.

Moretti, E. (2012). *The New Geography of Jobs*. Boston, MA: Mariner Books.

Morozov, E. (2013). *To Save Everything, Click Here: The Folly of Technological Solutionism*. New York: PublicAffairs.

Morozov, E. (2022). "Critique of techno-feudal reason". *New Left Review* 133/134: 89–126.

Morozov, E. (2023). "The lessons of Chile's struggle against Big Tech". *New Statesman*, 9 September. https://www.newstatesman.com/the-weekend-essay/2023/09/salvador-allende-fight-big-tech

Morris, K. (2019). "Amazon leases new Manhattan office space, less than a year after HQ2 pullout". *Wall Street Journal*, 6 December. https://www.wsj.com/articles/amazon-leases-new-manhattan-office-space-less-than-a-year-after-hq2-pullout-11575671243

Moulier Boutang, Y. (2011). *Cognitive Capitalism*. Cambridge: Polity.

Muhonen, T. (2022). "Olen oikeasti huolissani". sanoo VM:n kansliapäällikkö hallituksen valmistelemista uusista veroista. Helsingin Sanomat 25.10. https://www.hs.fi/politiikka/art-2000009156739.html

Mullins, B. & J. Bykowicz (2021). "Lobbyists for Silicon Valley giants like Facebook find glory days are over". *Wall Street Journal*, 17 June. https://www.wsj.com/articles/tech-industrys-glory-days-in-washington-are-over-11623936187

Napoleoni, C. (1998). "The enigma of value". *International Journal of Political Economy* 28(3): 35–51.

Negri, A. (1989). *The Politics of Subversion: A Manifesto for the Twenty-First Century*. Cambridge: Polity.

Negri, A. (2018). *From the Factory to the Metropolis: Essays Volume 2*. Cambridge: Polity.

Niemi, L. (2023). "Woltin emoyhtiön tappiot paisuivat 422 miljoonaan euroon viime vuonna". *Helsingin Sanomat* 20.9. https://www.hs.fi/talous/art-2000009868804.html

Nigro, R. (2018). "Workerism". *Krisis* 2: 171–4.

Noble, S. & S. Roberts (2019). "Technological elites, the meritocracy, and postracial myths in Silicon Valley". In R. Mukherjee, S. Banet-Weiser & H. Gray (eds), *Racism Postrace*, 113–29. Durham, NC: Duke University Press.

Offe, C. & V. Ronge (1982). "Theses on the theory of the state". In A. Giddens & D. Held (eds), *Classes, Power, and Conflict*, 249–56. Berkeley, CA: University of California Press.

Ohmae, K. (1993). "The rise of the 'region state'". *Foreign Affairs* 72: 78–87.

Ohmae, K. (1995). *The End of the Nation State: The Rise of Regional Economies*. New York: Simon & Schuster.

Ong, A. (2006). *Neoliberalism as Exception: Mutations in Citizenship and Sovereignty*. Durham, NC: Duke University Press.

O'Mara, M. (2020). *The Code: Silicon Valley and the Remaking of America*. New York: Penguin.

Paajanen, O.-P. (2023). "Wolt-kuski Emmanuel tekee jopa 90-tuntista työviikkoa, ja silti käteen jää vain vähän – 'Ennen tämä oli hyvä työ'". *Helsingin Sanomat*, 8 September. https://www.hs.fi/kotimaa/turku/art-2000009818190.html

Palcic, D., E. Reeves & H. Whiteside (2023). "Reluctant state capitalism: antipathy, accommodation and hybridity in Irish telecommunications". *Environment and Planning A: Economy and Space* 55(1): 100–21.

Parker, G., M. Van Alstyne & S. Choudary (2016). *Platform Revolution: How Networked Markets Are Transforming the Economy – and How to Make Them Work for You*. New York: Newton.

Pasquinelli, M. (2009). "Google's PageRank algorithm: a diagram of the cognitive capitalism and the rentier of the common intellect". In K. Becker & F. Stalder (eds), *Deep Search*, 152–62. London: Transaction Publishers.

Pasquinelli, M. & V. Joler (2021). "The Nooscope manifested: AI as instrument of knowledge extractivism". *AI & Society* 36: 1263–80.

Patomäki, H. (2007). *Uusliberalismi Suomessa: Lyhyt historia ja tulevaisuuden vaihtoehdot*. Helsinki: WSOY.

Pearson, C. & J. Schuetz (2022) "Where pro-housing groups are emerging". *Brookings*, 31 March. https://www.brookings.edu/articles/where-pro-housing-groups-are-emerging/

Peck, J. (2002). *Workfare States*. New York: Guilford Press.

Peck, J. (2010). *Constructions of Neoliberal Reason*. New York: Oxford University Press.

Peck, J. (2014). "Entrepreneurial urbanism between uncommon sense and dull compulsion". *Geografiska Annaler B: Human Geography* 96(4): 396–401.

Peck, J. (2016). "Economic rationality meets celebrity urbanology: exploring Edward Glaeser's city". *International Journal of Urban and Regional Research* 40(1): 1–30.

Perez, C. (2010). "Technological revolutions and techno-economic paradigms". *Cambridge Journal of Economics* 34(1): 185–202.

Pilling, D. (2023). "How to create a city". *Financial Times*, 18 January. https://www.ft.com/content/7a0419bf-e76f-4abb-8024-043ee24e4382

Pine II, J. & J. Gilmore (1998). "Welcome to the experience economy". *Harvard Business Review*, Jul–Aug: 97–105.

Pinto, M., Recano, L. & U. Rossi (2023). "New institutions and the politics of the interstices. Experimenting with a face-to-face democracy in Naples". *Urban Studies* 60(11): 2176–94.

Pitts, F. (2021). *Value*. Cambridge: Polity.

Polanyi, K. (2001). *The Great Transformation: The Political and Economic Origins of Our Time*. Boston, MA: Beacon Press.
Pollio, A. (2020). "Making the silicon cape of Africa: tales, theories and the narration of startup urbanism". *Urban Studies* 57(13): 2715–32.
Pollio, A. (2022). "Acceleration, development and technocapitalism at the Silicon Cape of Africa". *Economy and Society* 51(1): 46–70.
Pollio, A. & U. Rossi (2024). "Urban political economy". In R. Vogel (ed.), *Handbook of Urban Politics and Policy*. Cheltenham: Edward Elgar (in press).
Pollman, E. & J. Barry (2016). "Regulatory entrepreneurship". *Southern California Law Review* 90: 383–448.
Porter, M. (1995a). "The competitive advantage of the inner city". *Harvard Business Review*, May–Jun: 55–71.
Porter, M. (1995b). "The rise of the urban entrepreneur". *The State of Small Business* 17(7): 104–18.
Porter, M. (1997). "New strategies for inner city economic development". *Economic Development Quarterly* 11(1): 11–27.
Porter, M. (1998a). *The Competitive Advantage of Nations*. 2nd edn. Basingstoke: Macmillan.
Porter, M. (1998b). "Clusters and the new economics of competition". *Harvard Business Review* 76, Nov–Dec: 77–90.
Porter, M. (2008). *On Competition*. Cambridge, MA: Harvard Business Press.
Porter, M. & M. Kramer (2011). "Creating shared value". *Harvard Business Review*, Jan–Feb: 1–17.
Programme of Prime Minister Juha Sipilä's Government (2015). Helsinki: The Government of Finland.
Programme of Prime Minister Jyrki Katainen's Government (2011). Helsinki: The Government of Finland.
Programme of Prime Minister Sanna Marin's Government (2019). Inclusive and Competent Finland. https://julkaisut.valtioneuvosto.fi/handle/10024/161931
Pyyry, N. & H. Sirviö (2023). "Landscape of competition: education, economisation and young people's wellbeing". *Environment and Planning A: Economy and Space*. https://doi.org/10.1177/0308518X231197303
Quirk, J. & P. Friedman (2017). *Seasteading: How Floating Nations Will Restore the Environment, Enrich the Poor, Cure the Sick, and Liberate Humanity from Politicians*. New York: Free Press.
Rabe, S. (1999). *The Most Dangerous Area in the World. John F. Kennedy Confronts Communist Revolution in Latin America*. Chapel Hill, NC: University of North Carolina Press.
Raco, M. & R. Imrie (2000). "Governmentality and rights and responsibilities in urban policy". *Environment and Planning A: Economy and Space* 32(12): 2187–204.
Radaelli, M. (2016). "Sicily is our DNA". *Style Magazine*. https://luminosityitalia.com/pages/q-and-a-dolce-and-gabbana.html
Raeste, J.-P. (2023). "Miljardikone". *Helsingin Sanomat*, 27 May. https://www.hs.fi/talous/art-2000009571372.html
Rainisto, S. (2010). "Kuka sen tekee? … siis pelastaa Suomen julkisen talouden". *Talouselämä* 9/2010: 19–24.
Rani, U. & M. Furrer (2021). "Digital labour platforms and new forms of flexible work in developing countries: algorithmic management of work and workers". *Competition & Change* 25(2): 212–36.
Reich, R. (1992). *The Work of Nations: Preparing Ourselves for 21st Century Capitalism*. New York: Vintage.
Ries, E. (2011). *The Lean Startup: How Today's Entrepreneurs Use Continuous Innovation to Create Radically Successful Businesses*. New York: Crown Business.
Ritzer, G., P. Dean & N. Jurgenson (2012). "The coming of age of the prosumer". *American Behavioral Scientist* 56(4): 379–98.

Robinson, J. & K. Attuyer (2020). "Extracting value, London style: revisiting the role of the state in urban development". *International Journal of Urban and Regional Research* 45: 303–31.

Rodríguez-Pose, A. (2018). "The revenge of the places that don't matter (and what to do about it)". *Cambridge Journal of Regions, Economy and Society* 11(1): 189–209.

Rodríguez-Pose, A. & M. Storper (2020). "Housing, urban growth and inequalities: the limits to deregulation and upzoning in reducing economic and spatial inequality". *Urban Studies* 57(2): 223–48.

Roll, E. (2002). *A History of Economic Thought*. New York: Faber & Faber.

Romer, P. (1990). "Endogenous technological change". *Journal of Political Economy* 98: S71–S102.

Roper, S. & S. Grimes (2005). "Wireless valley, silicon wadi and digital island – Helsinki, Tel Aviv and Dublin and the ICT global production network". *Geoforum* 36(3): 297–313.

Rosenberg, D. (2002). *Cloning Silicon Valley: The Next Generation High-Tech Spots*. London: Reuters.

Rosenthal, S. & W. Strange (2004). "Evidence on the nature and sources of agglomeration economies". In V. Henderson & J. Thisse (eds), *Handbook of Regional and Urban Economics*, Vol. 4. 2119-71. Amsterdam: Elsevier.

Rossi, U. (2009). *Lo Spazio Conteso. Il Centro Storico di Napoli tra Coalizioni e Conflitti*. Naples: Guida.

Rossi, U. (2017). *Cities in Global Capitalism*. Cambridge: Polity.

Rossi, U. (2019). "The common-seekers: capturing and reclaiming value in the platform metropolis". *Environment and Planning C: Politics and Space* 37(8): 1418–33.

Rossi, U. (2020). "Fake friends: the illusionist revision of Western urbanology at the time of platform capitalism". *Urban Studies* 57(5): 1105–17.

Rossi, U. (2022). "The existential threat of urban social extractivism: urban revival and the extinction crisis in the European South". *Antipode* 54(3): 892–913.

Rossi, U. & A. Di Bella (2017). "Start-up urbanism: New York, Rio de Janeiro and the global urbanization of technology-based economies". *Environment and Planning A: Economy and Space* 49(5): 999–1018.

Rossi, U. & A. Vanolo (2013). "Regenerating what? The politics and geographies of actually existing regeneration". In: M. Leary & J. McCarty (eds), *The Routledge Companion to Urban Regeneration*, 159–67. London: Routledge.

Russell, B. (2019). "Beyond the local trap: new municipalism and the rise of the fearless cities". *Antipode* 51(3): 989–1010.

Sadowski, J. (2020). "The internet of landlords: digital platforms and new mechanisms of rentier capitalism". *Antipode* 52(2): 562–80.

Samans, R. *et al.* (2017). *The Global Human Capital Report: Preparing People for the Future of Work*. Geneva: World Economic Forum.

Savage, M. (2021). *The Return of Inequality*. Cambridge, MA: Harvard University Press.

Savage, N. (2022). "Strength in the life sciences sustains US advantage". *Nature*, 25 November. https://www.nature.com/articles/d41586-022-02885-4

Saxenian, A. (1990). "Regional networks and the resurgence of Silicon Valley". *California Management Review* 33(1): 89–112.

Scheiber, N. (2017). "How Uber uses psychological tricks to push its drivers' buttons". *New York Times*, 2 April. https://www.nytimes.com/interactive/2017/04/02/technology/uber-drivers-psychological-tricks.html

Schulman, B. (1991). *From Cotton Belt to Sunbelt: Federal Policy, Economic Development, and the Transformation of the South, 1938–1980*. New York: Oxford University Press.

Schultz, T. (1961). "Investment in human capital". *American Economic Review* 51(1): 1–17.

Schultz, T. (1964). *Transforming Traditional Agriculture*. New Haven, CT: Yale University Press.

Schultz, T. (1981). *Investing in People: The Economics of Population Quality*. Berkeley, CA: University of California Press.

Schumpeter, J. (2010). *Capitalism, Socialism and Democracy*. Abingdon: Routledge.

Scott, A. (1987). "The semiconductor industry in South-East Asia: organization, location and the international division of labour". *Regional Studies* 21(2): 143–59.

REFERENCES

Scott, A. (2014). "Beyond the creative city: cognitive-cultural capitalism and the new urbanism". *Regional Studies* 48(4): 565–78.

Scott, A. (2017). *The Constitution of the City*. Basingstoke: Palgrave Macmillan.

Sennett, R. (1998). *The Corrosion of Character: The Personal Consequences of Work in the New Capitalism*. New York: Norton.

Sennett, R. (2018a). "The open city". In T. Haas & H. Westlund (eds), *In the Post-Urban World: Emergent Transformation of Cities and Regions in the Innovative Global Economy*, 97–105. Abingdon: Routledge.

Sennett, R. (2018b). *Building and Dwelling: Ethics on the City*. New York: Farrar, Straus & Giroux.

Shapiro, A. (2017). "Between autonomy and control: strategies of arbitrage in the 'on-demand' economy". *New Media & Society* 20(8): 2954–71.

Sharif, N. (2006). "Emergence and development of the National Innovation Systems concept". *Research Policy* 35: 745–66.

Shaw, J. (2020). "Platform real estate: theory and practice of new urban real estate markets". *Urban Geography* 41(8): 1037–64.

Shearmur, R. (2007). "The new knowledge aristocracy: the creative class, mobility and urban growth". *Work Organisation, Labour & Globalisation* 1(1): 31–47.

Sheppard, E. (2002). "The spaces and times of globalization: place, scale, networks, and positionality". *Economic Geography* 78(3): 307–30.

Shiel, R. (2006). *Italian Neorealism: Rebuilding the Cinematic City*. New York: Columbia University Press.

Sigmund, P. (1983). "The rise and fall of the Chicago boys in Chile". *SAIS Review* 3(2): 41–58.

Sikkink, K. (1997). "Development ideas in Latin America: paradigm shift and the Economic Commission for Latin America". In F. Cooper & R. Packard (eds), *International Development and the Social Sciences: Essays in the History and Politics of Knowledge*, 228–56. Berkeley, CA: University of California Press.

Silverwood, J. & C. Berry (2023). "The distinctiveness of state capitalism in Britain: market-making, industrial policy and economic space". *Environment and Planning A: Economy and Space* 55(1): 122–42.

Slobodian, Q. (2023). *Crack-Up Capitalism: Market Radicals and the Dream of a World Without Democracy*. New York: Metropolitan.

Smith, A. (1977) [1776]. *An Inquiry into the Nature and Causes of the Wealth of Nations*. Chicago, IL: University of Chicago Press.

Smith, N. (2001). "Global social cleansing: postliberal revanchism and the export of zero tolerance". *Social Justice* 28(3(85)): 68–74.

Smith, P. (2012). "Triumph of the City by Edward Glaeser – review". *The Guardian*, 28 February. https://www.theguardian.com/books/2012/feb/28/triumph-city-edward-glaeser-review

Söderström O., T. Paasche & F. Klauser (2014). "Smart cities as corporate storytelling". *City* 18(3): 307–20.

Srnicek, N. (2017). *Platform Capitalism*. Cambridge: Polity.

Stein, S. (2019). *Capital City: Gentrification and the Real Estate State*. London: Verso.

Steinmetz, K. (2014). "San Francisco's new disruption". *Time*, 31 January. http://time.com/2852/disrupted/

Steinmetz, K. (2017). "Winning Amazon's new headquarters could come with hidden costs". *Time*, 18 October. http://time.com/4987883/amazon-hq2-headquarters-costs/

Stern, S. (2015) "Deliveroo and its ilk are serving up low wages, insecurity and social division". *The Guardian*, 17 December. https://www.theguardian.com/commentisfree/2015/dec/17/deliveroo-gig-economy-human-cost

Stiglitz, J. & B. Greenwald (2014). *Creating a Learning Society: A New Approach to Growth, Development, and Social Progress*. New York: Columbia University Press.

Stoller, M. (2019). *Goliath: The 100-Year War between Monopoly Power and Democracy*. New York: Simon & Schuster.

Stone, K. & R. Kuttner (2020). "The rise of neo-feudalism". *The American Prospect*, 8 April. https://prospect.org/economy/rise-of-neo-feudalism/

Storper, M. & A. Scott (2009). "Rethinking human capital, creativity and urban growth". *Journal of Economic Geography* 9(2): 147–67.

Storper, M. & A. Venables (2004). "Buzz: face-to-face contact and the urban economy". *Journal of Economic Geography* 4(4): 351–70.

Storper, M. & R. Walker (1989). *The Capitalist Imperative: Territory, Technology, and Industrial Growth*. Oxford: Basil Blackwell.

Strange, S. (2009). *The Retreat of the State: The Diffusion of Power in the World Economy*. Cambridge: Cambridge University Press.

Strange, S. (2016). *Casino Capitalism*. Manchester: Manchester University Press.

Streidfeld, D. (2023). "For tech companies, years of easy money yield to hard times". *New York Times*, 23 January. https://www.nytimes.com/2023/01/23/technology/tech-interest-rates-layoffs.html

Summers, L. (2016). "The age of secular stagnation: what it is and what to do about it". *Foreign Affairs* 95(2): 2–9.

Tarvainen, A. (2022). "The modern/colonial hell of innovation economy: future as a return to colonial mythologies". *Globalizations*. https://doi.org/10.1080/14747731.2022.2048460

Taylor, C. (2020). "Airbnb agrees deal to share data with local authorities in Europe". *The Irish Times*, 5 March. https://www.irishtimes.com/business/technology/airbnb-agrees-deal-to-share-data-with-local-authorities-in-europe-1.4194061

Tepper, J. (2018). *The Myth of Capitalism: Monopolies and the Death of Competition*. Malden, MA: Wiley-Blackwell.

Terhorst, P. & J. Van De Ven (1995). "The national urban growth coalition in the Netherlands". *Political Geography* 14(4): 343–61.

Thoburn N. (2003). *Deleuze, Marx and Politics*. London: Routledge.

Toews, R. (2023). "The geopolitics of AI chips will define the future of AI". *Forbes*, 7 May. https://www.forbes.com/sites/robtoews/2023/05/07/the-geopolitics-of-ai-chips-will-define-the-future-of-ai/

Tola, M. & U. Rossi (2019). "The common". In The Antipode Editorial Collective (ed.), *Keywords in Radical Geography: Antipode at 50*, 259–63. Malden, MA: Wiley.

Tondo, G. (2020). "Maradonaland: Naples plans statues and museum to honour 'Saint Diego'". *The Guardian*, 26 December. https://www.theguardian.com/world/2020/dec/25/maradonaland-naples-statues-museum-diego-maradona

Tooze, A. (2021). *Shutdown: How Covid Shook the World's Economy*. New York: Penguin.

Treiber, G. & T. Christiaens (2021). "Introduction: Italian theory and the problem of potentiality". *Italian Studies* 76(2): 121–27.

Tretter, E. & R. Heyman (2022). "Yimbism and the housing crisis in Canada and the United States: a critical reflection". *International Journal of Urban and Regional Research* 46(2): 287–95.

Tripadvisor–1. n.d. "Vascitour". Accessed 18 November 2023. https://www.tripadvisor.com/Attraction_Review-g187785-d12513473-Reviews-Vascitour-Naples_Province_of_Naples_Campania.html

Tripadvisor–2. n.d. "Murales Maradona 1990". Accessed 18 November 2023. https://www.tripadvisor.com/Attraction_Review-g187785-d13117992-Reviews-Murales_Maradona_1990-Naples_Province_of_Naples_Campania.html

Tsipursky, G. (2023). "The great reevaluation: how remote work and digital nomads are reshaping the future of work". *Forbes*, 22 March. https://www.forbes.com/sites/glebtsipursky/2023/03/22/are-remote-workers-becoming-digital-nomads/

Turkki, T. (2009). *Nykyaikaa Etsimässä. Suomen Digitaalinen Tulevaisuus*. Helsinki: Taloustieto.
Tuttitalia. n.d. "Popolazione Napoli 2001–2021". https://www.tuttitalia.it/campania/59-napoli/statistiche/popolazione-andamento-demografico/
United Nations Environment Programme & Yale Center for Ecosystems + Architecture (2023). Building Materials and the Climate: Constructing a New Future. https://wedocs.unep.org/20.500.11822/43293
van der Panne, G. (2004). "Agglomeration externalities: Marshall versus Jacobs". *Journal of Evolutionary Economics* 14: 593–604.
van Doorn, N. (2020). "A new institution on the block: on platform urbanism and Airbnb citizenship". *New Media & Society* 22(10): 1808–26.
van Horn, R. & P. Mirowski (2009). "The rise of the Chicago school of economics and the birth of neoliberalism". In P. Mirowski & D. Plehwe (eds), *The Road from Mont Pèlerin: The Making of the Neoliberal Thought Collective*, 139–78. Cambridge, MA: Harvard University Press.
Varoufakis, Y. (2023). *Technofeudalism: What Killed Capitalism*. London: Bodley Head.
Vercellone, C. (2010). "The crisis of the law of value and the becoming-rent of profit". In A. Fumagalli & S. Mezzadra (eds), *Crisis in the Global Economy*, 85–118. Los Angeles, CA: Semiotext(e).
Violante, G. (2008). "Skill-biased technical change". In L. Blume & S. Durlauf (eds), *New Palgrave Dictionary of Economics* (2nd edn). London: Palgrave Macmillan.
Virno, P. (1996). "Notes on the 'General Intellect'". In S. Makdisi, C. Casarino & R. Karl (eds), *Marxism Beyond Marxism*, 265–72. London: Routledge.
Virno, P. (2008). *Multitude Between Innovation and Negation*. Cambridge, MA: MIT Press.
Virno, P. & M. Hardt (eds) (1996). *Radical Thought in Italy: A Potential Politics*. Minneapolis, MN: University of Minnesota Press.
Wagner, J., B. Katz & T. Osha (2019). *The Evolution of Innovation Districts: The New Geography of Global Innovation*. New York: Global Institute on Innovation Districts.
Ward, K. & A. Jonas (2004). "Competitive city-regionalism as a politics of space: a critical reinterpretation of the new regionalism". *Environment and Planning A: Economy and Space* 36(12): 2119–39.
Wark, M. (2019). *Capital is Dead: Is This Something Worse?* London: Verso.
Warsh, D. (2007). *Knowledge and the Wealth of Nations: A Story of Economic Discovery*. New York: Norton.
Watts, M. (2004). "Resource curse? Governmentality, oil and power in the Niger Delta, Nigeria". *Geopolitics* 9(1): 50–80.
Weber, M. (1958). *The City*. New York: The Free Press.
Weber, R. (2002). "Extracting value from the city: neoliberalism and urban redevelopment". *Antipode* 34(3): 519–40.
Weiss, L. (2014). *America Inc.? Innovation and Enterprise in the National Security State*. Ithaca, NY: Cornell University Press.
Wetzstein, S. (2017). "The global urban housing affordability crisis". *Urban Studies* 54(14): 3159–77.
Wikipedia n.d. "Naples International Airport". Accessed 18 November 2023. https://en.wikipedia.org/wiki/Naples_International_Airport
Wilson, W. (1987). *The Truly Disadvantaged: The Inner City, the Underclass, and Public Policy*. Chicago, IL: The University of Chicago Press.
Wood, A. *et al.* (2019). "Good gig, bad gig: autonomy and algorithmic control in the global gig economy". *Work, Employment and Society* 33(1): 56–75.
Wu, X. *et al.* (2023). "The effect of algorithmic management and workers' coping behavior: an exploratory qualitative research of Chinese food-delivery platform". *Tourism Management* 96: 104716.
Xu, T. (2021). "DoorDash joins forces with Wolt". https://press.wolt.com/en-WW/204364-doordash-joins-forces-with-wolt

Yates, L. (2021). "How Airbnb and Uber use activist tactics that disguise their corporate lobbying as grassroots campaigns". *The Conversation*, 15 April. https://theconversation.com/how-airbnb-and-uber-use-activist-tactics-that-disguise-their-corporate-lobbying-as-grassroots-campaigns-15889

Yeung, H. (2022). *Interconnected Worlds: Global Electronics and Production Networks in East Asia*. Stanford, CA: Stanford University Press.

Yeung, H. (2023). "Troubling economic geography: new directions in the post-pandemic world". *Transactions of the Institute of British Geographers* 48(4): 672–80.

Young, I. (1990). *Justice and the Politics of Difference*. Princeton, NJ: Princeton University Press.

Zamora, D. & M. Behrent (eds) (2016). *Foucault and Neoliberalism*. Cambridge: Polity.

Zhang, L. (2023). *The Labor of Reinvention: Entrepreneurship in the New Chinese Digital Economy*. New York: Columbia University Press.

Zhou, Y. (2008). *The Inside Story of China's High-Tech Industry: Making Silicon Valley in Beijing*. Lanham, MA: Rowman & Littlefield.

Ziegler, J. (2005). *L'empire de la Honte*. Paris: Fayard.

Zipperer, B. *et al.* (2022). *National Survey of Gig Workers Paints a Picture of Poor Working Conditions, Low Pay*. Washington DC: Economic Policy Institute. https://www.epi.org/publication/gig-worker-survey/

Zuboff, S. (2019). *The Age of Surveillance Capitalism*. New York: PublicAffairs.

Zukin, S. (2010). *Naked City: The Death and Life of Authentic Urban Places*. New York: Oxford University Press.

Zukin, S. (2020). *The Innovation Complex: Cities, Tech, and the New Economy*. New York: Oxford University Press.

INDEX

Aalto University 119, 126
affordable housing 95, 97, 100, 146, 154
Agamben, Giorgio 131, 147
Airbnb 22, 26–7, 29, 97, 105, 130, 131, 133, 138–9, 147
Akon City 100
algorithms 1, 71, 72, 73, 116, 117
  algorithmic machinery 72; algorithmic management 22, 40, 68; algorithmic technology 13–14, 16, 18, 21–2, 69, 71, 73
Althusser, Louis 140
Amazon 22, 28, 74, 75, 77, 105, 114
Apple 28, 105
artificial intelligence 16, 23, 25, 29, 61
austerity 51, 54, 86, 132, 133, 136
  austerity government 47
autonomist theorists 62
  operaismo 62, 73

Bangalore 18
Barthes, Roland 131
Becker, Gary 83, 89
behaviour 21, 70, 73, 82, 86, 104, 112
  adaptive behaviour 72; behaviour surplus 70; behaviourist turn 83; corporate behaviour 28
Bell, Daniel 87
Bezos, Jeff 107
big data 21, 116
  data extractivism 22; data gathering 18, 70; data mining 21; data storage 65; datafication 112; dataist statecraft 48; open data 110
Big Tech 1, 52, 70, 112, 152
biometric sensors 21
Booking.com 29, 130
bootstrapping 115
Bowles, Samuel 84

Brenner, Neil 43
built environment 11, 26, 38, 39, 53, 91, 110, 125, 133, 141, 144, 152, 154
business 2, 6, 12, 17, 20, 24–6, 29, 38, 41
  business accelerators 19; business climate 18; business clusters 90, 93–4; business incubators 118; business management 92, 157; business model 27; business operations 113, 120; scalability of business 22, 107, 113

California 15, 18, 95, 96, 100
  Californian ideology 105; Californian ideology model of startups 106
Cambridge, UK 18
capital accumulation 14, 17, 25, 34–6, 39, 42, 43, 65, 66, 117–18, 124, 127, 156
capital appreciation 40
charter cities 6, 80, 98, 99, 100, 107, 110
Chicago School of Economics 79–86
  Chicago boys 86
China 16–17, 19, 51, 58, 98
circulation 1, 42, 65–6, 85, 156
Cisco 23
citizenship 86, 147
  citizen participation 23; platform-mediated citizenship 27
city entrepreneurialism 42
city life 89, 108, 135, 141
city networks 110
city of startups 108
city rankings 111
cloud computing 14, 21
  cloud capital 1; cloud rent 2
cognitive-affective capitalism 71
colonization 13, 107, 151
  colonial imaginary 107
commodification (of place) 7, 86, 129, 158

177

commons 112, 136, 137
    intellectual commons 154; urban commons 112, 136–7
community-based economies 157
competitiveness 42–4, 46, 50, 53, 93, 104, 119
    competitive advantage 93–4, 154; inter-city competition 157; inter-spatial competition 42, 44, 53, 92; national competitiveness 42, 47, 53, 93, 94, 102, 155
consultancy, consultants 37, 62, 113, 115
consumption (mass) 66, 73, 148
    consumer spending 91; consumers 21, 25, 61, 70–1, 119, 145, 153; consumption-based urban economy 24, 130, 154
construction sector 96–7
coping strategies 72
corporations 1, 2, 23, 38, 70, 74–6, 133
    corporate power 4, 24, 28; corporate rhetoric 67; corporatization 29–30, 43, 45, 53, 152, 155; tech corporations 1, 4, 22–6, 28–30, 36, 61, 67, 69, 71, 74–7, 102, 131, 147, 149, 151–2, 155, 157
couriers 67, 72, 119, 121–3
Covid-19 pandemic 19, 57, 66
creative city 25
creative class 3, 6, 58–9, 62, 94, 106
cultural industries 12

density (urban) 12, 20, 95, 96, 108, 110, 148
devaluation of capital 14
digital technologies 21, 22, 69, 103, 130
    digital island 18; digital nomads 89; digital platforms 1, 2, 7, 11, 21–6, 30, 40, 57, 66, 110, 112, 116, 125, 129, 132–4, 138, 149, 151; digitalization 5, 29, 33, 48, 50, 52, 54, 90, 106, 112; online retail services 22
diversity 89
    socio-ethnic diversity 12; urban diversity 89, 90
Dolce & Gabbana 134–9, 147
DoorDash 22, 105, 118–20, 122, 124–5
Drucker, Peter 45, 62–3, 76, 87

East Asia 17, 18, 80
eBay 22, 105
economic crises 14, 39, 40
    crisis of 2008–09 (or late 2000s great contraction, or 2008 economic downturn) 21, 22, 50, 91; global stagnation 43
economics 64, 79, 80, 82–3, 85, 86, 119, 151, 154, 157
    behavioural economics 83; development economics 85, 92; heterodox economics 3, 18, 60, 62; monetarist theory 81; neoclassical economics 64, 83; urban economics 2–3, 12, 30, 34, 37, 74, 90–1, 141, 157

economization 2, 4, 6, 7, 11, 30, 44, 101, 109, 122, 126, 129, 149, 152, 158
ecosystem 3, 6, 11, 20, 23, 29, 48, 91, 99, 103, 108, 109, 110–11, 118, 125–6
    business ecosystems 6, 74, 90, 101, 111, 155; ecosystem forum model 48
education 11, 23, 43, 46, 47–8, 54, 57, 59, 79, 81, 83–4, 88, 89, 91, 99, 101, 126, 154
    charter schools 81, 98; educational investments 84–5, 87
elites 36, 54, 59, 75, 85, 90, 102, 105, 132, 157
emerging markets 19
endogenous growth theory 80, 87–8, 90, 98, 154
entrepreneurship 12, 21, 46, 47, 48, 71, 89, 103, 106, 107, 111, 125, 128, 130
    entrepreneurial life 155; entrepreneurial subjectivity 127; high-risk entrepreneurship 106
environment 23, 57, 73, 133, 136, 144, 147, 157
    CO_2 emissions 96; environmental amenities 12; environmental crisis 96; environmentalist movements 96, 145
EQT Ventures 119
equity capital 47, 112
Europe 1, 15, 17, 29, 40–1, 51, 54, 58, 68, 87, 98, 119, 130, 133, 136
European Union 29, 51–2, 54, 81, 145
exchange value 39, 60, 91, 95
extractivist capitalism 65
experience economy 7, 65, 129–30, 132, 138, 149
    experience co-creation 147; experiential tourism 7, 129, 138–9, 140, 142, 148
externalities 3, 12, 77, 88, 90–1

Facebook 21, 22, 138
fictitious capital 7, 127
field (theory of) 35
financial capitalism 7, 39, 70, 127
financialization 43, 70, 92, 97, 123
Finland 7, 34, 46–51, 105, 118, 121–2, 124–6
firms 6, 15, 17, 21–4, 27, 29, 31, 41, 44, 52, 69, 75, 88, 90–1, 93–4, 98, 101, 103–4, 106, 107, 111, 112, 114–15, 117–18, 121–2, 124, 153
    complementary firms 90; firm creation 13, 15, 61; firm location and relocation 89; inter-firm competition 66; knowledge-intensive firms 94
fiscal policy 81
fixed capital 72
Florida, Richard 89, 94, 141, 148, 151
food delivery companies 114
Fordism and post-Fordism 11, 14, 41
    post-Fordist transition 2, 5, 28, 29, 153
Fortune 113

Foucault, Michel 3, 4, 5, 26, 35–6, 83, 84, 87
France 8, 27–30
free-market ideas 81
Friedman, Milton 81, 85, 98

Gago, Veronica 146
general intellect 62
geography 65, 80, 82, 96
  geographical political economy 34, 158; geographies of discontent 34; geography of labour demand 96; geography of state space 43; global geography of capital 43; new economic geography 92, 94
gentrification 74, 96, 132, 138, 148
geopolitics 16, 17, 30, 35, 51, 63, 156
gig economy 27
Gintis, Herbert 84
Glaeser, Edward 12, 18, 25, 75, 90, 95, 108, 151
global capitalism 3, 22, 75, 101, 156
Global North 7, 79, 132
Global South 79, 132
global tech city 74
Google 12, 13, 22, 28, 96, 105, 112
governance 6, 13–14, 27, 31, 45, 53, 76, 86, 98, 126, 127
  entrepreneurialization of governance 44; global governance 110; governance of economic development 54, 153
governmentality 3, 4, 13–14, 27, 30, 34, 43, 77, 82, 86, 97, 104
  authoritarian governmentality 26
graffiti 144

happy city 109
Hardt, Michael 3, 62, 71, 73, 74, 75, 120, 125, 153, 158
Harvey, David 39, 40, 66, 67, 91, 157
Homo economicus 84
Honduras 99
Hong Kong 17, 80, 98
housing bubble 90, 91
housing crisis 6, 18, 94–7, 154
housing as an investment asset 92
housing policy 97
housing project 139, 144
housing regulations 95, 96
housing shortage 18, 97, 129, 158
human capital 2, 3, 4, 6, 12, 18, 20, 31, 45, 71, 74, 77, 79–102, 103, 104, 107, 108, 113, 123, 126–8, 130, 151, 153–4, 157
  human capital density 20; human capital externalities 77, 90, 91; human capital orthodoxy 97; human capital policy 83; human capital stocks 91, 95; human resources 92, 94; investments in human capital 83, 92

IBM 23, 74
income 97, 100
  income generation 94, 147; income inequalities (or disparities) 6, 57, 59, 91
independent contractors 57, 58, 67, 121
industrial policy 4, 14
inequalities 3, 6, 24, 25, 59, 60, 64, 76, 77, 84, 91, 97, 151, 153–4
inflation 68, 81, 87
  prices-wages spiral 87
information and communications technologies (ICT) 5, 13, 15, 42, 76
  information flows 12; information spillovers 98; information society 17, 22; informational cities 11, 15, 19
infrastructure 11, 16, 21, 23, 38, 42, 51–2, 57, 65, 74, 77, 90, 91, 93, 100, 130, 133
inner city 94
  inner-city areas 19, 94; inner city's competitive advantages 94
innovation 89, 92, 103, 107, 117, 125, 153, 156
  digital innovation 113; disruptive innovation 106; incremental innovation 74; innovation complexes 117; innovation districts 20, 44, 80, 100, 125; innovation ecosystem 111, 118, 126; innovation gurus 110; innovation machine 30, 103–4, 107, 122, 128; innovation systems 45; milieux of innovation 15; open innovation 123
intangibles (assets, factors, investments) 26, 37, 39, 40, 48, 83
  intangible enclosures 38
intellectual property 154
intentional communities 21
internet, the 1, 13, 54, 108, 112
  internet-based service businesses 116; internet bubble of the 1990s 112; internet economy 20; Internet of Things 21, 25; internet startup companies 112
Instagram 21, 22, 138
Italy 6, 26, 28, 133, 134, 140

Jacobs, Jane 89, 90, 107, 110, 141, 142, 148
  Jacobs externalities 90; Jacobsian revival 89; neo-Jacobsian theorists 155
Japan 15, 16, 17, 120
Jessop, Bob 17, 20, 36, 154
jobs 9, 114, 133, 157
  expensive jobs 93; fun jobs 67; high-paying (high-skill) jobs 97, 114, 128; job creation 76, 94; job polarization 64; low-paying (low-skill) jobs 58, 76, 101, 128, 154

Keynesianism 11, 41, 53
  Keynesian state 42, 68; late Keynesianism 19, 20, 53, 109, 111, 155; private Keynesianism 91

179

knowledge economy 6, 59, 76, 92
   entrepreneurial knowledge 108; knowledge as an investment asset 6, 80, 88, 98, 101; knowledge capital 3, 93, 101; knowledge-creating institutions 12; knowledge labour 60; knowledge spillovers 74, 88, 98, 104; knowledge value 6, 62–3, 66, 71, 151; knowledge workers 3, 6, 60, 62–4, 79, 154

labour 60–73
   abstract labour 60; affective and cognitive labour 63; concrete labour 60; cost of 66, 67; dead labour 62; devaluation of 57, 66, 77; division of 41, 76, 123, 126; domestic labour 140; exploitation of 6, 24, 60, 61, 65, 66–9, 71, 76, 129, 130, 146, 158; high-skill labour 103, 128; immaterial labour 3, 62, 63; labour activists 67, 72; labour flexibility 68, 79; labour market 68, 76, 79, 99, 154; labour pooling 74, 104; labour power 39, 61, 66, 69, 71, 109; labour precariousness (or casualization) 58, 68; labour process 61, 66, 67, 68; labour saving machinery 68; labour theory of value, 60–1; labour time 62, 66, 71; labour-value measurement 79, 154; living labour 25, 38, 52, 62, 73, 121, 127, 129; low-skill labour 3; low wages 58, 66, 122; productivity of 77, 79
land 1 39, 83, 86
   landlords 2, 40, 130, 139, 141; land prices 91; land question 41, 153; land rent 11, 91, 120, 153; land use 42, 70, 96; land values 95; open land 38; uninhabited land 98, 107
Lazzarato, Maurizio 28, 63, 127
learning 79, 83, 92
   digitalized learning 105; learning by doing 88; learning regions 118; machine learning 21, 23, 61, 71
Lefebvre, Henri 4, 39, 91
leisure 11, 18, 23, 89, 109, 132
Lepore, Jill 106
libertarianism 29, 109–10, 116–17
   libertarian individualism 105; libertarian startup imaginaries 110, 117–18
location 42, 43, 50, 144, 158
   locational choice/preferences 74, 157; locational logic 20; location, location, location 157
logistics 38, 65
   human logistics 71, 72, 73, 151; logistical approach 65; logistics-led urban economy 66
local residents 21, 77, 96, 134, 139, 141, 144, 145, 146

inner-city residents 94; longtime residents 95, 97, 146; low-income residents 138
Loren, Sophia 131, 132, 134–9, 147, 148
Lucas, Robert 88–9, 90, 93, 98, 107
Lyft 22, 105

maintenance of the urban field 4, 30, 39, 131
makers and takers of economic value 65, 70, 127
management theory and theorists 37, 61, 64, 75, 79, 87, 92, 129, 131, 148, 157
Maradona, Diego 131, 132, 142–7
Marin, Sanna 46 125, 126
market competition 98
market incentives 88, 98
market power 1, 16, 25, 26, 69, 70, 88
market rationalities 43
market prices 64, 83, 87, 95, 96, 141
market regulation (and deregulation) 69, 88, 97
Marshall, Alfred 90, 103
Marx, Karl 60, 62, 66, 70
mass tourism 7, 128–4
   touristification 158; travel industry 140–1, 146–8
Mazzucato, Mariana 3, 62, 64–5, 69, 117, 126, 151
Meta 26, 28, 105
metabolism of cities 74
metropolis, the 71, 74, 75, 108, 120, 122, 158
microelectronics 16
   advanced microchips 16; global chip war 16; microprocessors 5, 13, 15, 17, 76; semiconductor industry 13–17
Microsoft 105
military-industrial complex 117
Mincer, Jacob 82–3, 89
mobile game developers 118
mobility 11, 23
   geographical mobility of financial capital 42; ideology of mobility 89
money 20, 42, 43, 115, 119
   cheap money 114; investment money 114, 120; monetary policy 15, 20; monetization 70, 129; money form 120, 121; money supply 81
Moretti, Enrico 12, 59, 75, 90–1, 94–6, 141, 148, 151
multiplier effect 3, 12, 59, 90
Musk, Elon 80, 99, 100, 107

Naples 129–9, 158
nation-state 5, 33, 35, 48, 50–4, 92, 101, 104, 110–11, 118, 125, 127, 154
   national competitiveness 42–3, 47; nationalization of urban development 30
Negri, Antonio 3, 62, 71, 73–5, 120, 125, 153, 158

neighbourhood characters 90
neighbourhood distinctiveness 90
neighbourhood effects 144
neighbourhood shops 146
neighbourliness without intimacy 141
neo-feudalism 1, 25, 151
   feudal lords 65; feudal-speak 2; techno-feudalism (or digital feudalism) 1, 2, 3, 6, 69, 70
neoliberalism 79, 83, 84, 85, 86, 87
   neoliberalism from below 132, 146; neoliberalization 34, 44, 46, 50; neoliberal narratives 117; neoliberal rationalities 43; neoliberal states 132; proto-neoliberalism 85
new growth theory *see* endogenous growth theory
new municipalism 136
New York 74, 75, 77, 91, 130, 141, 142

on-demand economy 67
online social networks *see* social media
open city 89, 139, 141, 142
operations of capital 5, 33, 37, 38, 42, 52, 53, 131, 142, 152
Oslo Science City 100

Palantir 117
PayPal 105
people-centred economy 109
Pinochet, Augusto 81, 85
place belonging/attachment 7, 111, 134, 147
place-specific forms of life 7, 31, 129, 130, 131, 139, 147, 149, 153
platform business 27, 61, 113
platform capitalism 5, 65, 67, 113
platform economy 6, 12, 23, 57, 64, 65, 66, 67, 68, 72, 113, 114, 121, 122, 125, 126
platform revolution 22, 61
platform society 22
Polanyi, Karl 68
policy choices 76, 154
policy discourse 24
policy practice 80, 86
populism, economic 25
polarization of the urban field 97, 103, 122, 127, 129, 153
   job polarization 64; wealth polarization 6, 59
Porter, Michael 90–4
postmodern city 132
post-statist cities 110
power of place 3
privatization 6, 23, 79, 86, 112
pro-housing development 95
pro-market think tanks 50
pro-real estate public policy 130

profit-making 1, 43, 71, 112, 154
   surplus profits 70
public housing 97
public-private partnerships 23

real estate/financial/technology complex 40
real-estate business 131, 140, 147
real-estate developers 130, 145
real-estate industry 39, 40, 111
real-estate speculation 91
Reich, Robert 121
rent control 95
rent extraction 65, 70, 71
rentierism 1, 69, 70, 151
rentiers 22, 65, 71
research and development 40, 48, 49, 61, 88
retail bubble 146
retail chains 58
Ricardo, David 60, 65, 70
right-to-the-city activists 138
risk-taking 47, 125, 155
   high-risk-taking venture capitalist 118; risk-taking economic subject 109; risk-taking entrepreneurship 106
Romer, Paul 80, 88–9, 93, 98, 99, 110, 151
Route 128 15–16

Salesforce 114
San Francisco 20, 21, 91, 96, 97, 100
scale economies 104
Schultz, Theodore 82–6, 89
science parks 11, 15, 19
secondary and tertiary circuits of capital 91
Sennett, Richard 141, 142, 148
service sector 58, 66, 77, 105
servile class 121
shareholder value 64, 120
sharing economy 22, 23, 65, 89, 97
Shenzhen 80, 91, 98
Shiel, Mark 135
Silicon Valley 15–19, 28–9, 91, 96, 101, 106, 110, 117
Silicon Zanzibar 99
Singapore 17, 80, 91
Slack 114
Slobodian, Quinn 75
Slush 119
skill-biased technological change 76, 77, 79, 153, 154
skill premium 76
smart cities 11, 13, 23, 24, 29
   smart city governance model 23; smart home 21; smart nation 18
Snailbrook 99, 100
social factory 73, 108
social media 14, 21, 22, 100, 131

181

social reproduction 43, 92, 109, 156
socio-spatial dialectic 111
special economic zones 80, 98, 111, 118
Starbase (city of) 100
startup cities 6, 80, 99, 100, 107, 110
startup economies 5, 47, 53, 103, 104, 108, 111–12, 116–17
startup ecosystems 6, 11, 23
startup ideology 105, 107
startup imaginaries 110
startup populace 109
state, the
  competition state 5, 14, 15, 17, 20, 43, 45, 68; digital service state 48, 50; digital state architecture 48; direct and indirect roles of the state 126; entrepreneurial state 3, 4, 18, 62, 117, 155; governmental state 2, 4, 31, 34, 130, 152; local state 4, 5, 23–4, 31, 33, 37, 39, 41–4, 48, 52, 118, 123, 148; startup state 2, 54, 101; state apparatuses 43, 52; state bureaucracy 105, 109, 111; state-capital interaction 14, 23; state capitalism 19, 29, 156; state intervention 4, 12, 13, 17, 18, 20, 34, 53, 110, 123; state regulative practices 111; state restructuring 111; state-sponsored investment 75; techfare state 52; tourist-experience state 134
Stein, Samuel 130
Sun Belt 18, 19, 95
supply of housing 18, 96
surplus value 6, 25, 60, 67, 69, 71, 113, 152
  absolute and relative 66

Taiwan 16, 17
talent 43, 59, 126
  clustering of talent 59; talent cities 80, 99; talented people 59, 99
taxation 26, 41, 125
  tax breaks 75, 97; tax cuts 79, 91, 111; tax deductions 91; tax revenue 24, 117, 124, 125; unpaid taxes 26
tech boom 2.0 14, 21, 22, 149
  tech giants 1, 30, 65, 75, 88, 105, 114; tech oligarchy 1, 151
techno-economic paradigm 76, 77, 153
techno-industrial complex 34, 46
techno-nationalism 156
  technological sovereignty 17, 29, 30
technocratic industrial systems 105
technological rents 70, 71
technological spillovers 12
technology capital 4, 7, 17, 48, 101
technology enthusiasm 108
technopoles 11, 15, 19, 109
Tesla 105
Thiel, Peter 117
TikTok 138

Tripadvisor 139, 146
triple helix 19, 73
Twitter 21, 100

Uber/Uberization 22, 27–9, 52, 105, 113
uneven geographical development 48
  unequal exchange 85, 156
unicorn startups 7, 113, 115, 118, 120, 124, 125
urban age 3, 4, 110
urban agglomeration 3, 89
urban authenticity 131, 132, 141
urban dwellers 128–9, 138–9, 148, 158
urban economy 127, 128, 146, 148
urban entrepreneur 94, 126
urban fabric 33, 37, 91, 108, 109, 111, 133, 137
urban growth machines 4, 12, 39
urban ideology 89
urban living 11, 12, 35, 44, 157
urban planning and planners 74, 137, 144, 145
urban policy 12, 90, 142
urban politics 33, 35
urban preservation 145
urban question 109
urban regeneration 129, 142, 145, 158
urban renewal 110, 145
urban revival 33, 90, 130, 131, 137, 138, 139, 142
urban symbols 129
urban technological paradigm 5, 11, 12, 13–15, 16, 17, 21, 30, 152, 153, 154
urban variety 89
urban way of life 141
urbanism 4, 101, 107, 131, 148
  anonymous urbanism 89; disaster urbanism 130; entrepreneurial urbanism 105; face-to-face urbanism 107; people-centred urbanism 141, 148; platform urbanism 6, 23, 40; postmodern urbanism 7, 132, 148; startup urbanism 44, 122
urbanization 34, 35, 40, 104, 120
  deurbanizing dynamics 134; planetary urbanization 4, 30; urbanization of corporate power 24; urbanization of knowledge and technology 12, 14, 31, 91; urbanization of venture capital 20
use value 60, 71, 92, 95
user-generated content 61

valuation 2, 7, 45, 64, 77, 103, 104, 111–16, 117, 119, 120, 121, 122, 123–7, 148, 152
  market valuation 104, 105, 113, 120, 121
value capture 25, 39, 69
value creation 7, 20, 25, 37, 42, 43, 60, 61, 62, 63, 63, 65, 70, 72, 75, 83, 101, 104, 111, 117, 130, 152, 153

value extraction 5, 6, 7, 11, 24, 26, 31, 34, 36, 38–9, 60, 64–6, 67, 69, 80, 105, 118, 129, 152
value professionals 113, 115
Varoufakis, Yannis 1–2, 151
venture capital 16, 21, 22, 40, 91, 106, 108, 110, 112, 115, 118, 119, 125, 156

wage inequalities 6, 59, 64, 76, 77, 153, 154
wealth 3, 97
  commonwealth 3, 112, 120; wealth generation 35, 75, 94, 110; wealth of cities 12; wealth polarization 6, 59
Weber, Max 35, 40
welfare state 41, 56, 52, 54, 87
  Keynesian social welfare 87; urban social welfare 59, 75
Wolt 118–23
workers 57–77
  casualized workers 67; critical infrastructure workers 57; essential workers (or key workers) 57–8; freelance workers 57, 67; frontline workers 58, 61, 66, 72, 73; gig workers 6, 57, 61, 67, 72; high-paid workers 77, 91, 97, 154; knowledge workers 3, 60, 62, 63, 64, 79, 154; manual workers 63; routine production workers 63; service workers 6, 57–60, 63, 64, 72, 77, 122; symbolic analysts 121; temporary workers 76; underpaid workers 61, 67; worker-bike complex 73; workers' agency 72; workplace 58, 109

Xu, Tony 119

YMBY 95
Young, Iris Marion 89

Zuboff, Shoshana 69, 70, 112
Zuckerberg, Mark 119
Zukin, Sharon 3, 12